THE HOPE FOR WHOLENESS

Katherine Zappone

The Hope for Wholeness

A Spirituality for Feminists

XXIII
TWENTY-THIRD PUBLICATIONS
Mystic, Connecticut 06355

Twenty-Third Publications
185 Willow Street
P.O. Box 180
Mystic, CT 06355
(203) 536-2611
800-321-0411

ISBN 0-89622-495-3
Library of Congress Catalog Card No. 91-65953

Dedication

To Ann Louise Gilligan

Whose imagination and friendship
has nurtured all that follows

Preface

There are several people who have taught me what it means to hope for wholeness. Their friendship and support fashion the heart of my own feminist spirituality, and sustained the writing effort. My family, especially my parents, Kathie and Bob Zappone, never tired of asking: "How is the book going?" Their fidelity to one another and to all of their children provides an exquisite example of mutuality in relationship.

Friends in Ireland and the United States have spent countless hours listening to me talk about a spirituality for feminists, offering me many helpful insights both in their words and deeds: Joni Crone, Barbara Fitzgerald, Joan Fitzgerald, Zola Golub, Rosemary Haughton, Betty Hegarty, Suzanne Hudson, Meriel Kilroy, Claire Lowery, Ann Morgan, Nóírín Ní Riain, Mary O'Callaghan, Aileen Ryan, Nancy Schwoyer, and Reesa Vaughter. I am particularly grateful to Mary Paula Walsh and Kay Conroy, leaders in the field of wholistic health. They have shown their support in countless ways, not the least of which was to sponsor a series of lectures that I gave at their center, Turning Point, in Dublin. Mary Condren, who read my entire manuscript, has inspired me for many years now by her formidable courage, compassionate intellect, and love for Ireland. Anne Kelly made several important suggestions for improving the quality of this work; her creativity has also contributed a great deal to feminist spirituality in Ireland. Gail Freyne's friendship and enthusiasm for my work has been a constant source of nourishment. Mary Daly's sensitivity, generosity, and amazing breadth and depth of vision provided a wellspring for this book. I also want to thank Chris McCarthy, Teresa Gallagher, Michelle Fields, and Joanna O'Connor from the Mercy Family Center (Dublin) whose courage and humor in the inner city taught me an enormous amount about friendship across social boundaries.

In 1986 "The Shanty Educational Project" was established in Ireland to offer educational opportunities to women who come from a background of poverty. The management committee of this project has not only successfully run courses in personal development, literacy, leadership training, etc. for over 200 participants a year, it has also provided me with a vibrant community of women exploring together the meaning of their spirituality. This is my "base community," and these women friends—through their honesty, integrity, and commitment—have fired much of what follows in these pages: Rose Cullen, Joan Foran, Ann Louise Gilligan, Carmel Habington, Julie Kiernan, Cora Marshall, Marie Moran, Sheila Norton, Brenda O'Malley-Farrell, Maura Roche, and Mary Sweeney.

Much gratitude also goes to colleagues in the theological arena. Professor Seán Freyne of Trinity College, Dublin, has been a rare combination of sponsor and friend. His keen mind and generous heart offered consistent sustenance and challenge. Thomas Groome of Boston College advised earlier work when the seeds of this book were one chapter in a doctoral thesis. Francine Cardman of the Weston School of Theology inspired my interest in the topic by her scholarship and skill in teaching. Students and colleagues at SUMORE, Seattle University, especially Gary Chamberlain and Loretta Jancoski, helped me to rework several of these ideas within a supportive community context.

During January 1990, I gave a series of lectures on feminist spirituality in four Australian cities. This was a tremendous experience for me; the vitality and creativity of the feminist spirituality movement in Australia has affected my work a great deal. I am grateful to all of the women and men who studied and celebrated with me, and to my sponsors of the trip: Alan Connors of the Aquinas Academy in Sydney, the Dominican Sisters of Adelaide, and Women and the Australian Church (W.A.T.A.C.), Pauline Smoothy and Greg Riley of the Catholic Education Office in Brisbane.

I am grateful to my publishers, Neil and Pat Kluepfel, for their personal and professional support. John van Bemmel, my editor, has carefully attended to all details. Seán O'Boyle of The Columba Press, Dublin, was very instrumental in initiating this publication. I am so delighted to have the artwork of an Irish theologian and feminist, Mary O'Reilly De Brún, on the cover of this book.

I have dedicated this book to Ann Louise Gilligan, as one way of thanking her for abundant friendship and affirmation throughout this project. But I also want to acknowledge her extraordinary ability to teach, both in the university and the local communities of Tallaght, Dublin, empowering women to believe in themselves so that this planet will survive.

Acknowledgments

Among the many works cited in this study (they are listed in the Notes starting on page 167), several deserve special acknowledgment. The author expresses gratitude for the following: Pp. 55–56: "The Gardener," Diane Mariechild, *The Inner Dance: A Guide to Spiritual and Psychological Unfolding* (Freedom CA: Crossing Press, 1987), p. 153. Pp. 60–61: Rosemary Radford Ruether, *Women-Church: The Theology and Practice of Feminist Liturgical Communities* (San Francisco: Harper & Row, 1985). Pp. 106–107: Carter Heywood, *The Redemption of God: A Theology of Mutual Relation* (Washington, D.C.: The University Press of America, 1982), p. 153. P. 109: Naomi Janowitz and Maggie Wenig, "Sabbath Prayers for Women," in Carol P. Christ and Judith Plaskow, *Womanspirit Rising: A Feminist Reader in Religion* (San Francisco: Harper & Row, 1979), p. 176. Pp. 134–136 Paula M. Smith, R.S.M., "Poor Women My Country" in *Listen: Journal of the Institute of Sisters of Mercy of Australia* (vol. 8, no. 2, 1989): 12. P. 140: Susan Griffin, "Forests (The Way We Stand)" in *Woman and Nature: The Roaring Inside Her* (San Francisco: Harper & Row, 1978), pp. 220–221. Pp. 153–154: Coralie Ling, "A Celebration of Women" in Elizabeth Wood Ellam, ed., *The Church Made Whole: National Conference on Women in the Uniting Church in Australia* (Melbourne: David Lovell Publishing, 1990), p. 73. Pp. 155–156: Janet Morley, "Psalm" in *All Desires Known: Prayers Uniting Faith and Feminism* (Wilton, CT: Morehouse-Barlow, 1988), p. 50. Pp. 156–157: Starhawk, "Meditation" (abridged) in *Truth or Dare: Encounters with Power, Authority and Mystery* (San Francisco: Harper & Row, 1987), pp. 101–103. P. 158: Diann Neu, "Blessing for the Journey" in *Women Church Celebrations: Feminist Liturgies for the Lenten Season* (Silver Spring, MD: WATERworks Press, 1989), p. 28.

Contents

Preface *vii*
Acknowledgments *ix*

Introduction **1**
Experience as a Theologian 3
Experience as an Educator 6
From Women to Feminists 8
Spirituality 10
Feminist Spirituality 12

—1—

A "Spirituality for Feminists": Origins *15*
The Origins of Feminist Spiritualities 16
Sacred Symbols/Sacred Stories 19
Women's Experience 20
A Consciousness of Interdependence 24
Sacred Symbols 27
Sacred Stories 34
Spiritualities of Women's Power 40
A Spirituality for Feminists 43

—2—

Woman's Self: Power Through Wholeness *45*
Woman's Relationship With Her Self: The Process 46
Woman's Relationship With Her Self: The Patterns 51
Patterns of Self-Integrity 52
Woman as Embodied Spirit 58

Patterns of Interrelatedness 62
Inseparability from All Other Beings 63
Equality with Others 64

—3—

Toward Mutuality With Others *67*

Not "A Little Less Than Angels" 68
What Makes a Relationship *Mutual?* 70
Love and Mutuality 71
Intimacy and Mutuality 75
Female Friendship 76
Female/Male Friendship 78
Friendship Across Social Divisions 79
Committed Relationships 80
Learning to Be Mutual 82
Motivation 82
The Habits of Mutuality 84

—4—

In the Presence of the Sacred *87*

The Absence of God 89
"So, What Is *Your* Image of God, Now?" 90
Naming Sacred Presence 92
Symbols of the Sacred 93
A History of Meaning 93
A Surplus of Meaning 94
Images and Metaphors 102
Images Shape Symbols of the Sacred 103
Metaphor: A Special Kind of Image 108
Concepts 110

—5—

Homemaking:
The Earth-Human Relationship **113**

The Demise of Woman and Nature 117
Philosophical Ingredients 118
Cosmology and Science: The Mechanistic Ingredients 120
The Economic Ingredients 121
Christian Symbols and the Genesis Myth:
The Religious Ingredients 123
Homemaking: The Spiritual Praxis of Feminists 128
The Nature of Culture 130
The Culture of Homemaking 134
Compassion: Where Philosophy Begins 136
Science for Life 138
The Economics of Sustainability 141
The Religious Ingredients for a Homemaking Culture 142

—6—

Embodying Hope for Wholeness:
Feminist Ritual **147**

What Is Feminist Ritual? 149
Feminist Ritual: Artistic, Creative, Imaginative 150
Feminist Ritual: Sensual 151
Feminist Ritual: Repetitive 152
What Is Feminist Ritual For? 159

Epilogue: Whispers of New Hope **163**

Notes **167**

Index **193**

Introduction

I am often asked, "What is feminist spirituality?" Many people display great interest in this newly emerging form of spirituality. In fact, there is an abundance of writing on issues related to this topic. A search is going on, as feminists attempt to describe how an awareness of woman's historical and contemporary inferior status affects the character and meaning of a person's spiritual journey.

As a result, several spiritualities have emerged from lifestyles guided by a consciousness that women have not been free for self-determination, and have been excluded from sharing power with men in the construction of a life-giving and livable earth. Feminists are fashioning spiritualities of women's power,[1] Jewish and Christian feminism,[2] the Wicca tradition,[3] Goddess religions,[4] "elemental feminism,"[5] and several other uncategorized forms. Although all these are rooted in the awareness of women's oppression and exclusion (especially how religious traditions contribute to this reality), such spiritualities are simply a starting point. These spiritualities are the result of the hard work of developing a vision and praxis[6] that hope for the wholeness of all reality.[7]

This "hope for wholeness" includes several components: that the broken selves of women (and men) may be healed through the process of self-determination; that separation due to racism, classism, poverty, sexism, and heterosexism[8] may be transformed into a freedom to seek mutual relationships; that polluting and exploiting of the natural world may be stopped through humanity's recognition that it is part of and not separate from nature; and that we may replace man-centered images of God with images of the deity that enable human responsibility for life on earth. All the diverse spiritualities of feminism share this hope for wholeness.

To discover such a fundamental commonality is possible only if one is able to converse with representatives of the different spiritualities. This calls for at least two things: recognizing the truth that exists in one's own tradition, and having the courage to have that truth confronted and enriched by the spiritual journeys of feminists in other traditions.

This book is about such a conversation. Furthermore, while I describe elements of various feminist spiritualities, I also want to propose a spirituality for feminists that surfaces when the pluralism of spiritual paths is hailed as necessary for the holiness of ourselves, God, and the earth. The weaving of such a model, or paradigm, comes from my own experience as a Christian feminist wherein I have discovered the need to call on several kinds of feminist spiritualities to interpret and celebrate a hope for wholeness. In practical terms, this means that I choose membership not only in Christian feminist spirituality groups, but also in circles of feminists who hold diverse traditions and radically different spiritual experiences from my own. This also means that my research and teaching take me into arenas beyond Christianity (even the feminist version) in order to understand myself, others, God, and the world.

The conversation is not always an easy one. Religious symbols and meanings that I deeply cherish are severely criticized; I often fear what is fundamentally different from mine. Yet I am motivated to continue when events such as "Women-Church" (Ohio, 1987)—though originating in the Catholic tradition—"invite the participation of faithful people of all traditions, all ethnic/racial backgrounds: Catholic, Protestant, Jewish, Goddess, Black, White, Hispanic, Asian, and Native American."[9] I am inspired by the diversity of women and men who gathered for an evening with Mary Daly at the Third International Interdisciplinary Congress on Women (Dublin, Ireland, 1987). My spiritual voyage is heartened by journals like *Woman of Power: A Magazine of Feminism, Spirituality, and Politics* (Boston) that "provide a multi-cultural and multi-racial regional and international network for all women involved in the many traditions of women's spirituality,"[10] or *Womanspirit: The Irish Journal of Feminist Spirituality* (Dublin) that aims "to be a country-wide resource to facilitate groups and individuals interested in feminist spirituality, in its most inclusive and holistic sense."[11]

I am encouraged to participate in the conversation engendered by events and networks of communication like these. Let me sketch the background that prompted this conversation and influences how I piece together a spirituality for feminists. This involves stating interests and convictions that are important to me as well as telling stories of my own spiritual journey. In this way I acknowledge—along with others—that "our own experience is the authoritative reference point for this spirituality."[12]

Experience as a Theologian

My parents are fond of telling me how they try to describe to their friends what I do. "She's a theologian," they say. The conversation usually comes to a halt at this stage. But once in a while a curious friend responds: "Yes, but what does she *do*?" The work of a theologian is not an easy thing to describe, except, of course, to other theologians. Even then it is often problematic, since a pluralism exists in theology as well as in spirituality. This means that theology itself is defined in a variety of ways.

I describe theology as a systematic study of the God-human-world relationship.[13] Theology investigates the nature and meaning of relationships among divinity, humanity, and the natural world. This includes an examination of each in itself—namely, the study of God's nature, the study of human nature, the study of the natural world—but *always* with an awareness that part of the essence of their natures is to be related to one another. This means that the being and activity of each radically affects the other.

The sources for such an inquiry include sacred texts, traditions, and contemporary experience. Being a theologian, then, means reflecting on these sources in order to make meaningful statements about God, humanity, and the world. I cannot end my description of theology here, however, because of the advent of political and liberation theologies. These theologies insist that we attend to at least three other issues: (1) the *purpose* of theological reflection (what is it for?); (2) the *place* of theology (where is it being done and who is doing it?); and (3) the *method* of theology (what steps are involved?).

A thorough analysis of each question is beyond the scope of the present work. However, it is important to state briefly my own responses to these questions, since they affect the intent and content of what follows.

1. *What is theology for?* Theology provides a picture of the way things ought to be. It imagines a world where God's will is done "on earth as it is in heaven." It depicts a process whereby creation can reach the fulfillment of God's promises for it. In this way theology offers a vision for the future of history. This is not to say that theology excludes reflection on "the last things" (eschatology); but its concept of the end-time and life after death is rooted in humanity's experience of and hope for history. This is the hope for wholeness, the salvation process that centers on all people and the natural world becoming whole in history. This hope, however, is not possible for many people unless the contemporary social and global structures of politics, education, economics, family, and religion radically change so that people are free to become themselves and to take responsibility for life on earth.

2. *Where is theology being done and who is doing it?* The liberation theologies (Latin American, Asian, black, feminist) point out that we must be attentive to the social status and the socio-historical context out of which the theologian fashions the hope for history. Why is this? Liberation theologies have demonstrated that both deeply affect the vision that is produced. Much of classical theology has been written by well-educated, economically resourceful, European, white males. There is nothing wrong with this in and of itself. But as less educated people, the economically resourceless, non-European, people of color, and fe-

males took up the theological task, it became apparent that their experience of history (especially the experience of being socially powerless[14]) radically challenged the theological vision of the socially powerful.

All of this leads me to recognize the importance of three things as I engage in the theological endeavor. First, my experience as a woman who is white, middle-class, highly educated, and a United States citizen affects my theological work. In all but one category—my gender—I come to this work as a socially powerful member of humanity. Even if I were to give away all that I possess and change my citizenship, my social history would *always* be part of me. Second, I recognize the need to place my experience of the world in dialogue with socially powerless members of humanity so that our visions might be correctives for each other. To imagine a world that nurtures all people is simply not possible if we exclude from our sources the past and present experiences of those who have suffered because of societal injustice. Third, I must consistently look for ways to initiate and facilitate such a dialogue. This brings me to the question of theological method.

3. *What steps are involved?* What is the process whereby we arrive at meaningful, truthful statements about God, humanity, and the world? I suppose Gustavo Gutierrez, more than any other theologian, has influenced the steps I take to prepare myself for theological articulation. In his earlier works, Gutierrez clearly outlines a praxis method for theology.[15] This includes two steps: (1) engagement in some form of activity that works for the freedom of those who experience injustice, and (2) critical reflection on that activity in light of the Scriptures and theological tradition. The theologian is one who acts for justice within a community context, and then tries to understand the truth and meaning of such activity in the context of her or his faith.

Gutierrez has somewhat modified this method over time.[16] Now he proposes that *silence* is the first step of the theological process. Silence is required in order to hear God's revelation being spoken through the voices of the poor. This is particularly true if the theologian does not experience the same form of injustice (in this case, poverty) as the group she or he works with. Through silence the theologian recognizes that the experience of those who suffer at the hands of the international economic order must be heard in order to imagine a world where no one is hungry. Then the theologian responds to what is heard through mutually agreed upon activity and critical reflection.

In adapting this proposal for feminist theology, I have discovered two things:[17] (1) As a theologian it is important to work with other women in the struggle against sexism; this is the activity out of which feminist theology is born. (2) It is not enough, though, to say simply that we must "work with other women." The theologian needs to be engaged in activity with women who experience other forms of injustice than she herself does. This may mean that if she is white she hears the experience of women of color. Or, if she is economically resourceful she hears the experience of women with little or no economic resources. In this way the theologian tries to hear truth for the world within various contexts of suffering. Each context provides another necessary piece for the future of a life-giving history for all.

In light of this, I propose that a step exists prior to the one of silence, which may be the most difficult one of all, namely, crossing the social boundaries that separate the theologian from those who experience deeper forms of injustice than she. We must *find* the world of the "other" before we can hear its voices. This takes courage, perserverance, patience, hope, and imagination. Why? Most people were not educated to move outside the social circles to which they belong. So, how do we find the other circles? What do we do when we get there? How shall we be a presence that does not "patronize"? We cannot answer these and other questions by ourselves, alone; they are only resolved through a process of mutual dialogue and shared activity. For me, this happens specifically in the educational arena.

Experience as an Educator

When describing the nature of education, educators are fond of pointing out that the English word comes from the Latin *ducere*, meaning "to lead," and the prefix *e*, meaning "out." Its etymology, then, suggests that education is an activity of "leading out." The word's history shapes my own understanding of it to a certain degree. I define education as the process of leading people into and out of themselves in order to take responsibility for the local and global community. Let us take a look at this definition in its two parts.

1. *"Education is the process of leading people into and out of themselves...."* This statement reflects my conviction that one of the primary goals of education is development of the self. Not only are people challenged to

learn about the communal knowledge of humanity that the various disciplines contain, but to use this heritage as a source to fashion the self they hope to become. The process enables them to reflect on themselves, and then, in turn, to find within the self an authoritative source to add a new word to humanity's search for truth. But what is the point of such activity? The totally self-actualized person? No; instead I suggest that education promotes such self-development (2)"*in order that people take responsibility for the local and global community.*" Education should enable people to move beyond themselves toward active participation in creating communities that nurture and sustain life in all its forms. This means that the educational process should consistently encourage people to discover the authority of their own experience, and to place that experience in dialogue with others' differing experiences of the one world.

This activity is the matrix for my theological reflection. The experiences I have as educator provide the grist for my God-talk. The first steps I take in theological method, then, are those of an educator. I look for the world of "the other" in order to hear the truth emerging from their self-development and action for community responsibility. In such settings I am being educated as much as I am educating. Although I may initiate the process, my own sense of self and what it means to take responsibility for the wider community are challenged once their word is spoken. This dynamic, dialectic exchange bestows to each participant new windows through which to see the way things ought to be.

In a context with the economically resourceful, my aims as educator shift slightly.[18] Yes, it is still important to invite women toward an awareness of societal restraints on their self-development because they are women: An essential piece of every woman's freedom includes her ability to participate in decisions that affect the local and global environment. I argue, however, that this is not enough. These women will not find justice for themselves (and cannot therefore *be* themselves) until they, too, look for the world of "the other woman." A justice that benefits only the economically resourceful or socially powerful will not radically change the system that promotes all women's contemporary oppression. The educator's task here, then, is to encourage women to cross the social boundaries for their *own* education as well as the education of the sisters they find.

What kind of education is this? First of all, it is a process that challenges women to trust one another. Such trust provides the only possibility of dismantling walls of separation that society builds between women of different racial, educational, and economic backgrounds. As trust grows, friendship across such divides enables each woman to disclose aspects of herself and her vision for the future. The knowledge thus created can then be placed in dialogue with visions from sources outside the group. Women then begin to generate a worldview of interdependence that is rooted in the real human experience of needing others for their own wholeness. They begin to imagine and work toward a local and global community that promotes this kind of wholeness for all.

Crossing social boundaries, then, educates the imagination in a particular way. It encourages the imagination to picture the neighborhood or world in a form that respects and benefits the history of diverse groups. Cross-cultural experience also enriches this activity. I have been living in Ireland for several years now. Rooting oneself in a culture that is "other" than the one of one's birth is a privileged experience.[19] It, too, provides a special set of eyeglasses that enable us to construct a common vision out of difference. The movement back and forth between cultures shapes the content of "wholeness" from a history of pluralism amid shared concerns.

These kinds of educational experiences influence not only my theology, but also help to form the model of spirituality that this book proposes. They direct the choice for a particular way of defining feminism, spirituality, and feminist spirituality. They furnish the discovery that a pluralism of spiritual sources is needed for feminists to "hope for wholeness," and they affect how conclusions are drawn from the conversation between representatives of the different feminist spiritualities. Here are some definitions to consider.

From Women to Feminists

I have deliberately chosen to write about a spirituality for feminists rather than a *women's* spirituality. Though the word "women" is often more palatable to the public, it is not specific enough. Needless to say, all women are not feminists (nor are all feminists women), and our focus centers on various spiritualities that come from a feminist experience of the world. In addition, I invite the public, particularly those interested in women's concerns for freedom, equality, and dignity to reconsider the term "feminism," especially if it is a word that triggers a negative reaction in them. Why does the word threaten so many? Why does it manipulate our imaginations to conjure a picture of abrasive, selfish, man-hating females?

A friend of mine is fond of describing "feminism" as a *bruised* word.[20] While it is a term that originated within a particular movement for freedom and justice, various connotations have been added that distort its original and evolving meaning. The distortion happens, I think, for the same reasons that women's lives have been distorted, bruised, and manipulated within a patriarchal culture.[21] A word that represents an incisive critique of the status quo is bound to be battered by those individuals and systems who benefit from the present structuring of power. This is not to deny that there may have been and continue to be pockets of women who are abrasive and want to dominate rather than relate equally to men. They do not, however, represent the increasing numbers of women and men who live as feminists in the hope of a humanized culture and a renewed earth.

Historian Joan Kelly points out that the historical movement of feminism is 400 years old.[22] In European society, even before the French Revolution, women began to advocate positions that we now term "feminist."[23] These positions led women then (as now) to strive for the same kinds of political, professional, educational, economic, and religious opportunities that men enjoy. Throughout this long history of struggle, though, women—and men in solidarity with women[24]—discovered that such activity engenders something far more substantial than "equal pay for equal work."

In light of this, I suggest that any definition of feminism should incorporate the following elements. Feminism is (1) a *consciousness* that patriarchal culture inhibits the full human development of all peoples—especially women, the economically resourceless, and people of color—and that it destructively exploits the natural world; (2) a *vision* of what life could be like so that more and more people are able to find meaning, work, a sense of dignity, and the possibility of self-determination; (3) a *set of activities* that challenge the present social structures of politics, education, family, religion, and the economy so that the vision becomes part of history; and (4) an *evolving culture* (produced by the consciousness, vision, and activities) that shifts the total pattern of human behavior toward sanctifying every individual and cleansing the earth.[25]

If we understand feminism in this broad sense (and I am arguing that such breadth is appropriate to its history), then the inclusive nature of the term comes to the fore. Although feminism originates in *women's* awareness and critical rejection of their oppressive experience in patriarchal society, its parameters expand to include concern for all of humanity and life in the natural world. At the heart of the feminist project, then, lies the collective imagination of a new world and a new way of being-in-the-world.

Spirituality

Like "feminism," the word "spirituality" connotes varied meanings and sparks diverse reactions within people. Many associate spirituality with mysticism, ascetic practices, a cloistered lifestyle, prayer, and "pious" devotions; these elements are perceived as having little significance in contemporary affairs. In fact, several of the activities named have constituted "spiritual life" during different periods of Christian history. But with the tremendous contemporary renewal of interest in spirituality by people who consider themselves religious as well as those who claim no loyalty to a religious heritage, the meaning of the term has expanded considerably. Such interest produces innumerable attempts to define the core of spirituality,[26] and points to the pluralism of spiritualities present in today's world.

One of the finest clarifications of the contemporary meaning of spirituality can be found in Sandra Schneiders's essay, "Theology and Spirituality: Strangers, Rivals or Partners?"[27] Schneiders distinguishes between spirituality as lived experience and spirituality as the academic discipline that studies that experience. In determining the content and nature of this "lived experience," she surveys the Christian history of the term's meaning. Schneiders reminds us that the adjective "spiritual" originates with Paul's use of it to describe objects (such as the Law or charisms) and people that were influenced by or deeply connected with the Holy Spirit of God. "Spiritual" persons, then, were ones who were particularly close to God's Spirit and exemplified this in their day-to-day living.

It was not until the twelfth century that the the word "spiritual" extended beyond its religious meaning to connote rationality. To be spiritual meant to possess an intellect; this was placed in direct contrast to non-rational life in creation. Though not the most popular understanding of the term, such a connotation influenced its future development. The seventeenth century marks the beginning of the "golden age" of spirituality; much of what it meant then stayed with us until the middle of the twentieth century. Spirituality centered on the "interior life" and the person's affective relationship with God. Christians sought "perfection," which often meant that they had to exceed the requirements of the ordinary Christian life (namely, the commandments and the practice of moral virtue), and included ascetical practices with the hope of preparing themselves for a mystical experience of God's spirit. Throughout the past three centuries, Christians debated whether or not mysticism was a possibility for all people or a special gift for the few. Against this backdrop, the pursuit of Christian perfection (or spirituality) was understood as a lifestyle that focused on interior growth toward union with God. It was not intended for the average Christian.

The latter half of the twentieth century breaks from this interiorized and elitist tradition of spirituality. Schneiders indicates four characteristics of contemporary spirituality: It is no longer exclusively a Roman Catholic, Christian, or even religious phenomenon; it is understood as a way toward personal integrity and transcendence; it is not a question of "perfection" but of "growth" toward a whole, human life and therefore open to everyone; and it no longer focuses solely on the "interior life" but on the process of integrating every aspect of being human.[28] In light of these characteristics she offers her own definition of spirituality as the "experience of integrating self-transcendence within the horizon of ultimacy."[29] This definition refers to two essential activities of spiritual experience: (1) integration of the self, which happens through (2) movement beyond the self (toward God or whatever is perceived to be the "horizon of ultimacy").

While I agree with Schneiders that contemporary authors (both religious and non-religious) concentrate on the process of self-transformation, I do not think that the language of "self-transcendence" adequately represents the reality it attempts to describe. Yes, the spiritual journey is about movement beyond the self—especially toward greater unity with the life-source—but this process takes place within the overall context of reality's interdependence. The primary source of the pivotal shift in spirituality's meaning for the twentieth century resides in the birth of a worldview of interdependence or relationality.[30] This means that we have moved beyond perceiving a dualistic split between the inner and the outer journey, the natural and the supernatural, matter and spirit, self and other, humanity and nature. Rather, the interdependence of reality means that every life form is *essentially* related to every other. So, the process of the self's becoming whole (the growth and integrity that Schneiders refers to) does not have to do with transcendence—since the self *is* essentially connected to God, others, and the natural world. It has to do with the self's becoming aware of its interconnectedness and then living in ways that nourish the relationships between self, others, God, and the world *that already exist*.

In its broadest sense, spirituality centers on our awareness and experience of relationality. It *is* the relational component of lived experience.[31] This component includes four distinct though interconnected dimensions: relations with self, others, God, and the natural world. A person's growth in one kind of relationship necessarily affects her or his development in another. For example, as relationship with self shifts, relationship with others will likewise take on new parameters and meaning. We see that the personal accounts of spiritual authors throughout the ages consistently concentrate on relationality; spiritual growth means becoming more aware of and looking for ways to fruitfully experience the various dimensions of relationships. Granted, the consciousness and interpretation of relational experience differs substantially when one lives within a dualistic worldview as compared with an interdependent one;[32] nevertheless, the focus has been and continues to be centered on relationship.

Feminist Spirituality

As already noted, contemporary feminist spiritualities root themselves within an awareness of women's historical exclusion and social oppression. Feminist spirituality, then, originates in the process of feminist consciousness-raising.[33] This activity produces an evolving cultural consciousness that necessarily affects feminists' perception and experience of relationality. At the heart of this new consciousness is the conviction that all beings are interconnected; each affects the other in the movement toward future life. When defining feminist spirituality, several authors refer to the interrelatedness of all reality.[34] They propose that a worldview of interdependence should guide our lived experience of relationships. This, in turn, may be the basic building block for a world beyond patriarchy, toward wholeness.

Feminist spirituality may be simply defined as *the praxis of imaging a whole world.* Such praxis depends on the lived experience of mutually supportive relations between self, others, God, and nature. This is a very difficult path to chart within present societal structures that encourage separation, domination, and exploitation between peoples, humanity, and the earth—even between the deity and human beings. Yet, women and men are doing just that and inviting others to hope for the future of history in a similar way.

—1—

A "Spirituality for Feminists": Origins

What I am about to describe is a process of origins. I begin with a story from somewhere in the middle.

> One day I left the university—ancient buildings, historic cobblestones, green grass and ebullient milieu—to walk to an "other" world, just little over a mile away. This was still an uncomfortable path, though I had traveled it many times before. It brought me to cement, thick pollution, and buildings that house the stories of those who never enter the university. Upon arrival I joined a group of women that I had been with for several months.

I had started the group to teach them about the ways in which women are oppressed by the social system. I wanted to guide them through a self- and social analysis so that they too could begin the journey of liberation. But this particular day I became the student and they the teachers. This was the day, after many months of building trust so that we could really share the secrets of our worlds with one another, when the women began to tell me how they felt about middle-class solutions for poverty and hunger. They described the anger and resentment they felt as they watched their neighbors and friends stand in line for hours to receive the "handouts" from recent E.E.C. (European Economic Community) policy. They described how, on the one hand this provided food only on the other hand, to take away human dignity. Why had no one consulted them about the roots of the problem? Why had no one asked them how to feed the body without destroying the spirit?

This was a turning point for me; I started to understand the meaning and truth of mutual relationship. From that day on we spent endless hours "hearing each other into speech," hoping against hope that our growing love for one another would save some from consistent depression, others from bodily violence, and still others from the belief that higher education ensures superiority over those who left school at thirteen.

The Origins of Feminist Spiritualities

The women's liberation movement challenged women (and men) toward a new way of being in the world. If women were to find freedom, then they had to *think* differently, *act* in ways that broke with past patterns of conditioning, and establish new kinds of *relationships*, especially with men. This unprecedented way of being has generated what is known today as feminist theory. The search for freedom in women's lifestyles inspired them to construct a theoretical framework that outlined how all people ought to think, act, and relate so that full liberation would be achieved.

An essential part of this process centered on women's awareness and experience of relationality, or spirituality. Through the liberation movement women began to live relationships in a distinctly different manner. They could no longer relate to a powerless self; they experienced themselves as agents of their own history and subjects (not objects) in the composition of social systems. Relationships with others shifted; they behaved as if they were equal to men and moved beyond patterns of inferior/superior relationships. Women with socially powerful backgrounds sought ways to establish mutual relationships with those of lower economic, educational, or ethnic status. And, eventually, women's relationships with the God of their fathers started to change. In *The Women's Bible* (originally published in 1895), Elizabeth Cady Stanton charged that the biblical God who supported women's inferior position within society was the creation of men who had never spoken with the real God.[1]

This revolution at the level of living relationships sparked a particular kind of theoretical response, one that addressed the question: How *ought* we to live in relation to self, others, God and the natural world? Because "new patterns of relationship are not fully clear,"[2] women recognized the need to reflect on the meaning of what was being experienced and to sketch an alternative conception of relationships, in order to bring about the freedom and wholeness of all people and the earth. Thus, in a more formal sense, "feminist spirituality" was born. As one of the architects of this theory has remarked: "The feminist movement, which began as a political, economic, and social struggle, is opening to a spiritual dimension."[3]

There are two contexts within which women explore the meaning of and create theory from these experiences of relationality. The first arena concentrates on sacred symbol systems and traditional sacred stories. *Feminist theology, feminist theaology,*[4] and *elemental feminist philosophy* all critique the suppression of the female in the deity and religious history. They argue that women's societal oppression is promoted by religions that exclude women's experience from the creation of sacred stories, symbols, and traditions. Therefore, sacred symbols—especially the symbol of "Father God"—must be critiqued or deconstructed if women are to discover social freedom and live a relationship with the deity that supports their own process of self-becoming. The female presence within sacred stories must be recovered or remembered. Feminist spiritualities that develop within this context propose different ways of reconstructing the symbol of the sacred, and they choose to remember different sacred stories. Yet they all agree that "the articulation of a new perception of the ultimate. . .will arise out of the discovery and recovery of women's experience."[5]

While these spiritualities also outline ways women ought to relate to self, others, and the world, the second context of the feminist spirituality movement directly focuses on these dimensions of relationality. *Spiritualities of women's power* critique the suppression of female power[6] both in the psyches of women and in the construction of the social order. Within this context women examine the psychological and sociological effects of patriarchy on the inner life and examine outer struggles of women to become themselves and take responsibility for creating a new order. Rooted in this critique they reconstruct a way of viewing reality that respects the sacredness of the female and the natural world. They develop meditations and rituals encouraging women to live relationships of wholeness with themselves, others, and the earth.

I suggested in the introduction that although we may root ourselves within a particular spiritual tradition, we should attend to the insights and practices that are contained within each kind of feminist spirituality. Both contexts, I think, provide key pieces to move beyond patriarchy and image a whole world. To explore this hypothesis it is necessary to examine representatives of each context more closely, note common concerns, and recognize radical differences. This provides the first step in weaving together a "spirituality for feminists."

As we consider the formal origins in more detail, though, it is important to remember that feminist spirituality begins informally in people's lives in very different ways. For some it originates at an intuitive level, of living relationships distinctively different from the patterns set by the conditioning process of patriarchy. For example, one woman records that "spirituality wasn't confined within the walls of churches. Early childhood was a time of unselfconscious identification with the natural world: I rarely felt separate from it."[7]

For others, myself included, awareness dawns through the conceptual study of the feminist critique of traditional religious symbols, which in turn encourages them to try on different ways of living in relationship. My journey from the university to the inner city was initially prompted by new ways of *conceiving* relationships with others. Convictions brought me to their door, but what made me stay was the eventual love of others who were not at all like me. That is why this is a story from the middle of the journey, while at the same time a story that marks the beginning. The origins of feminist spiritualities are still in process.

Sacred Symbols/Sacred Stories

In the early 1960s, feminists who were trained as theologians started to explore the sexist bias of traditional religion.[8] By the mid-1970s, several major publications indicated that a new kind of theological reflection was coming to birth, and they named it "feminist theology."[9] Jewish and Christian women were attempting to refashion sacred symbols and reinterpret stories of their religious heritage with a feminist consciousness. During the same period, another group of women reached behind patriarchal history to a time "When God Was a Woman,"[10] in order to recover stories of the "Goddess." Feminist thealogy insisted that the "God" of patriarchal religions could never adequately symbolize the female experience of the deity.[11] The 1970s held one more significant element: The creative intellect and personal journey of Mary Daly cultivated a spiritual philosophy that went "beyond God the Father,"[12] and eventually beyond "God."[13] Daly's works outlined one of the most incisive critiques of Jewish and Christian sacred symbols/sacred stories. They established the foundation for an "elemental feminist philosophy":[14] the creation of new language (symbols) rooted in the sacredness of woman and the earth, in order to birth the consciousness of a reality beyond patriarchy.

These analyses burgeoned in the 1980s, and the symbols and stories of feminist theology, thealogy and philosophy—rooted in women's altered experiences of relationality—encourage transformation in women's and men's spiritual journeys. For example, as women and men hear the stories of women prophets, preachers, apostles, missionaries, and deacons of early Christianity,[15] this challenges patterns of relationships in present Christian communities. The feminist spiritualities of the 1980s and 1990s, then, describe the conversion taking place in the lives of women and men as they confront the sacred symbols/stories of feminist reflection. The spiritualities also chart new paths, imaging new relationships among the deity, humanity, and the earth. Underneath the growth of these spiritualities, however, lie various assumptions, convictions, and beliefs about how to adequately interpret the meaning of changing experiences, and how to appropriately prescribe the future journey toward wholeness. Examining these will help us to understand both the differences and the common elements of feminist spiritualities within this context.

Women's Experience Traditional sacred symbols and stories have been fashioned from men's, not women's, experience of living in the world. In the past, women's experience was not considered revelatory of the truth about God, humanity, or the world. In order that religion affirm the truth and value of woman, its symbols and stories must change through an incorporation of women's experience. Even as feminists point this out, they know that it is still problematic. Mary Daly succinctly states why this is the case: "Women have been unable even to experience our own experience."[16]

Daly's poignant statement identifies the starting point of feminist religious reflection. Women recognize that their experience—namely, the activity of living—has been conditioned largely by the expectations of a patriarchal system. What does it mean to be a woman, a mother, a sister, a daughter, a wife? What is woman's role in culture, marriage, religion, politics? For a long time women lived the answers to these questions according to the social and cultural rules set in place by men. Breaking the rules—for example, to believe that she could be a *good* mother as a single woman—was simply unheard of and unacceptable. In this way she could not "experience her own experience."

This awareness, however, enables women to break open their experiences and start to sift through cultural expectations and what *they* really think and feel. Women begin to identify the "myth of the eternal feminine,"[17] namely, that women are passive, more proximate to nature than men, emotional, unable to lead in the public domain, etc. Women reject these myths and initiate the long haul of naming the meaning of their experiences for themselves. Membership in women's groups can assist this self-creative process. Within the safe space of women caring for other women, they hear common stories and respect different choices. A novel form of "women's experience" emerges that includes: (1) a *feminist* experience of being-in-the-world, namely, the liberative activity of recognizing and confronting women's social oppression; and (2) the *traditional* experiences associated with being woman (e.g., motherhood, nurturing relationships, the woman's menstrual cycle) reinterpreted with a feminist consciousness.[18] This signals women's "birth of themselves";[19] they are "experiencing their own experience."

It is this reality that provides a source for the transformation of religion and spirituality. As women name themselves and effect changes within the cultural order, they discover truths that require them to reconsider the religions that have shaped their spiritual journeys. They argue that women's experience has authority to determine the truthfulness and meaningfulness of how God has been and should be imaged, how the stories of religious people have been and should be told. For example, women know through their own experience that they are fully human and equal to men. This enables them to critique the suppression of female imagery for God authoritatively, and to challenge the superiority of the male within sacred history.

Is contemporary women's experience the sole criterion, though, for revising the tradition or re-imaging the spiritual journey toward wholeness? Whereas all feminists accept the authority of women's experience, they differ in judgment regarding its use. If we consider two major representatives of feminist theology, Rosemary Radford Ruether and Elisabeth Schüssler Fiorenza, we immediately see the difference. They both agree that feminist theology is fashioned through the dialogue between biblical religion and women's experience; they believe[20] that the symbols and stories of biblical religion are an essential source for promoting the wholeness of humanity and the earth. However, Schüssler Fiorenza reasons that women's experience of struggling for liberation provides the ultimate criterion for sifting out truth in the tradition. Any part of Scripture that is deemed sexist cannot be revelatory of God's truth for women and men today.[21] Ruether, on the other hand, insists that there exists a principle *within* Scripture, the prophetic tradition, that holds potential to critique the patriarchal ideologies of Scripture itself. The prophetic principle that challenges the status quo of ruling class privilege *and* contemporary women's experience are the authoritative sources for critique and reconstruction.[22]

Feminist thealogians also believe in the value of dialogue between present feminist consciousness and religious tradition. The ancient traditions of witchcraft and Goddess worship provide rich sources for their thealogical reflection. Unlike Ruether (and more closely resembling Schüssler Fiorenza), Starhawk, Naomi Goldenberg, and Carol Christ assert that the activity of living in the world as feminists furnishes the primary testing agent for judging the revelatory character of the traditions. Modern women's experience determines which dimensions of ancient traditions are recovered or rejected.[23] In addition, the imaging of the deity as female "confers a sense of reality and legitimacy on contemporary women's experience."[24] This is why they continue to look to the ancient past, yet discover its value only after it has been filtered through a feminist consciousness.

Mary Daly's advocacy of women's experience as *the* source of truth for a world beyond patriarchy differs substantially from any of the feminists already considered. Her own understanding and use of women's experience has changed as well throughout the past twenty years. In *The Church and the Second Sex*, Daly demonstrates that the experience women gained through the liberation movement necessitates a critique of the Christian tradition.[25] With the publication of *Beyond God the Father*, Daly's regard for and analysis of women's experience takes a significant leap. She unabashedly proposes that "the emergence of the communal vocational self-awareness of women is a *creative political ontophany*. It is a manifestation of the sacred (hierophany) precisely because it is an experience of participation in being...."[26] Because women's experience (of naming themselves and the world) is a source of divine revelation, it should be used to critique the Christian heritage in a radical way. She sees the value of dialoguing with the tradition, though she regards women's experience as the primary criterion for determining what to leave behind and what to bring forward.[27] Yet she also implies that the spiritual implications of radical feminism—without any concern for the tradition—may be all we need to create harmonious relations among ourselves, others, the world, and the source of Be-ing.[28] *Gyn/Ecology* and *Pure Lust* develop this conviction in a more explicit manner. Daly continues to converse with Christian symbols and stories, but only to repudiate their claims for meaning and truth. And, though she finds it useful to speak of the Goddess and analyze some of her sacred stories, Daly does not look to these ancient traditions to legitimize the use of radical feminist experience as *the* source of truth for imaging cosmic wholeness.

We see, then, that feminist spiritualities value and use women's experience in different ways to form symbols and stories that interpret the meaning of present relationships and sketch future patterns of relationality. But this generalized reality of "women's experience" is not the sole source of feminist spiritualities; the *particular experience* of each woman also contributes to the shaping of spiritualities and is the principal reason for the abundant diversity in feminist spirituality. Why have some women chosen to develop Jewish and Christian feminist spiritualities while others have constructed spiritual visions from ancient religious practices? Or why do some feminists speak of spirituality with no reference to sacred symbols and religious history? While it is true to say that this diversity arises from the different ways "women's experience" is used to analyze the traditional spiritual heritages critically, I think it is much more than that.

This "more than" has to do with the particular history of each woman on the spiritual path. Carol Christ suggests that "the reasons each of us has for continuing to work within inherited traditions or leaving them are complex and *not reducible* to intellectual, logical argument."[29] Women's personal stories contain "the reasons"; and these vary because of the communities they belong to, the time and place of their birth, their ethnic and economic backgrounds, their race and educational experience, their sexual orientation and psychological makeup. The reasons vary because of the time they have or have not spent in prison due to civil disobedience, the protest marches they have walked, their use of inclusive language, the rape victims they have held, the battered bodies they have seen. The reasons differ especially because of the forms and extent of their personal suffering due to patriarchal religious symbols and histories.

It is most important to be aware of this at the outset of the present analysis. First of all, it challenges us to respect insights emerging within a spirituality that is radically different from our own. Women who choose to create spirituality outside of the Jewish or Christian heritage may need to do that for their own personal survival: Their personal oppression within those frameworks may be so extensive that to stay within biblical religion is to choose death, not life. As a Christian feminist, I need to respect this. Likewise, members of the Goddess movement, witches, and elemental feminist philosophers are confronted with the reality that the feminist revision of Jewish and Christian symbols and stories is enabling countless women and men to image and act for freedom and wholeness. Belonging to Christian or Jewish feminist communities nurtures their passion and activity for justice and the earth's sustainability. Those outside of these traditions need to respect this.

Second, acknowledging the validity of different personal experiences provides the possibility for dialogue, and dialogue is an essential avenue for measuring the truth of our own experiences. Honest conversation with others not belonging to our primary communities offers a source of critique for personal experience that we cannot otherwise find. "Getting out of ourselves" helps us to confirm or question the convictions and beliefs shaped through the matrix of our personal histories. In this way, we not only discover truths that are distinctive but truths that are common. Both supply wellsprings for relationships which will bring about the future of history.

A Consciousness of Interdependence Perhaps the most critical discovery feminists make through an attentiveness to women's experience is the destructiveness of a dualistic worldview and the proposal for a consciousness of interdependence.[30] Rosemary Radford Ruether was one of the first feminist theologians to analyze the implications of a dualistic philosophy for women, other marginalized groups, and the nature world.[31] In dualism, very simply, reality is perceived as two separated levels—the supernatural (higher) level and the natural (lower) level. The primary separation has to do with the immense gulf between God (supernature) and humanity (nature). Humanity is created as *essentially separate* from God; a relationship is established only through God's initiation and offer of love. God is the beneficent ruler, requiring humanity to deny its natural will and act according to the "will of the Father."[32]

Other dualisms derive from the primary one. These are the separations between spirit and matter, humanity and nature, mind and body, spirituality and sexuality, man and woman. In each case, the first component of the dualism is perceived as part of or imaging the supernatural level of reality, and the second belongs to the natural level. Like the primary dualism, spirit, humanity, mind, spirituality, and man are perceived as essentially separate from and better than matter, nature, body, sexuality, and woman. The relationship between the two levels in each example is one of the higher level dominating and ruling the lower level. It also becomes quite clear in this schema that the male images the higher level ("When God becomes male, the male becomes God"[33]), and the female images the lower, less real level (making it very difficult for women to believe that they were truly made in God's image).[34] In dualism, then, we can see that maleness images the really real, the powerful, and the good; femaleness images inferior, less good reality.

This perception of the world becomes imbued in the social construction of reality—a dualistic and hierarchical mentality has not only informed Western theology (thus giving such a worldview divine sanction), but it has affected the creation and maintenance of social structures. Dualism encourages patterns of social dominance and oppression (between males and females, rich and poor, white and people of color) that continue to objectify and exploit varied peoples as well as nature. It provides philosophical and theological justification for economic, religious, and political activity that: (1) treats people as separate from one another in terms of race, gender, creed, and class; and (2) always identifies one side of the dualism as superior, the norm, closer to God, and therefore with the God-given right to rule the other side, beneficently or in an exploitative manner. It promotes activity that protects or exploits, not relationships that enable and empower self-determination, or respect and nurture nature.

Every form of feminist spirituality that we are considering rejects a dualistic paradigm of reality; this is a common conviction.[35] And, each kind insists that women's experience provides an eminently better way of perceiving connections between the various dimensions of reality.[36] As the introduction hinted, the feminist experience of living in the world convinces them of "the radical connectedness of all creation"[37] and the interdependence of the Life Source with the rest of reality. Starhawk describes it as a consciousness of immanence: "the awareness of the world and everything in it as alive, dynamic, interdependent, interacting, and infused with moving energies: a living being, a weaving dance."[38]

The perception of interdependence contains various components, and feminists differ in how they depict this developing consciousness. However, there are several shared principles that sketch a collective foundation for such a worldview. First, interdependence calls for a recognition of the inherent value of every living being. For humanity this means that no person is *essentially* superior to (holding more value than) any other person. As a way of expressing this, feminists struggle to be attentive to the truths contained in the experiences of various oppressed peoples.[39] Second, all human beings have individual identities and should be free to become themselves. Interdependent living requires that women and men have a strong sense of self in their relationships with others. The authors of *Sophia* speak of a "differentiated connectedness" and suggest that

> in this sense, interdependence is the opposite of fusion. This distinction is crucial for women because women have been all too often unable to distinguish their own identities from the identities of those they serve or nurture . . . we refer to a connection which becomes stronger the more we know that we are not identical to another being.[40]

The process of becoming an individual, however, happens through our relationships with others, God, and the natural world. Interdependence means that we perceive ourselves as *essentially related* to every other living being.[41] We are necessarily affected by the being and activity of the global community. We are part of, not separate from, the entire human race and the natural world in a very real sense. This is why feminists often say that until every woman is free, they are not free. This is why they argue that we must adopt a form of "reverence for life" as a basic attitude of feminist spirituality since "we are part of nature in an implacable way . . . we are . . . through and through, natural-historical beings, shapers of nature through culture and history."[42]

As I have already indicated, a consciousness of interdependence calls for a radical revisioning of the relation between the deity and nature (of which humanity is a part). Remembering that the primary dualism is the essential separation between supernature and nature, feminists are keenly interested in finding ways to imagine and express the interrelatedness of nature and the deity. They all insist that the "Father-God," the almighty one, absolutely other, and transcendentally supreme male must be rejected if models of hierarchical and dominating relations are to be eradicated in the world. What they propose in its stead is the subject of fundamental difference between those on the feminist spiritual journey, and we will explore this in the chapter on the Sacred. The chief point to stress here, however, is that feminist theologians, thealogians, and philosophers emphatically agree that wholeness and freedom for all will never happen if the deity is not imaged as an essential part of the natural life process.

Throughout the rest of the book we will examine specific ways in which the vision of interdependence arises from and attempts to express the feminist spiritual experience. Interdependence is *the* common thread of a spirituality for feminists. Anyone interested in this kind of spirituality knows that the root question has to do with the definition of reality. The way we define reality radically affects the creation of future stories. As many feminists have argued, they are trying to envision the world that they want to live in; one's worldview comes out of but also guides one's lifestyle. By the daily living of relationships that value, and are valued, by every form of life and each kind of person, we call for the rejection of a dualism that devalues the natural and justifies the brokenness of those who are not socially superior. A consciousness of interconnectedness bids us to revere what we are part of as the only way to promote full life for all on earth. If part of us is dying we cannot experience this fullness, this wholeness. Now we turn to a discussion of how sacred symbols and stories—ancient, biblical, and contemporary—encourage the fashioning of an interdependent reality.

Sacred Symbols "The importance of symbolism for spirituality cannot be overestimated."[43] Joann Conn's statement can be easily verified through a quick perusal of feminist writings on spirituality: Feminists consistently refer to the significance of symbolism. It is also confirmed in the lives of women and men who are no longer able to relate to a male God, or a God who absolutely transcends the natural order of life. What kind of phenomenon is this? What does it mean to say that traditional sacred symbols are losing credibility for contemporary women and men? Answering these questions is a complex task, yet one that is central to the expression of the feminist spiritual experience.

To begin, let's consider the meaning of symbol. Carol Christ makes use of the work of psychologist Carl Jung and anthropologist Clifford Geertz in her effort to uncover the essence of "symbol."[44] Jung maintains that people's deepest feelings and attitudes, situated in the unconscious, produce symbols. Symbols, in turn, are expressions of feelings and attitudes that give life its meaning and cohesiveness, especially in times of transition and difficulty. Religious symbols, according to Geertz, not only express deep-seated feelings but also "shape a cultural ethos, defining the deepest values of a society and the persons in it."[45] Drawing on the work of these two authors, Christ suggests that symbols originate in the inner psychic life of people and function to guide their lifestyles, both the personal values they choose and the political actions they take.[46] Although, according to Christ, women need to "develop a theory of symbol,"[47] she does not go beyond these initial musings even in her most recent work.

In developing a spirituality for feminists, I think that a clearer understanding of symbol is necessary and critical. An initial investigation of this should consider the following questions: (1) What is a symbol? (2) What makes a symbol sacred? (3) Why do sacred symbols need to change? (4) How are sacred symbols changing?

What is a symbol? As we have already seen, symbols are expressions of people's deepest feelings, yearnings, attitudes, and values. They often take the form of language—for example, the word "light" or "God"—but they also take physical forms such as rings or bread and wine. Whatever the form, symbols are imbued with meaning from our experiences of living in the world. Likewise, symbols offer meaning back to us. In this process, symbols participate in creating their meaning. A ring can refer to and encourage the depth of a relationship out of which choice for the ring came. Bread and wine were chosen by Jesus to capture the meaning of his life experience; Christians use them to connect with Jesus' life as a way of discovering coherent meaning in their own. Symbols not only come from human experience; they also affect the meaning of future experience.

Thus symbols, especially common ones,[48] tend to have a life of their own.[49] Though they originate from the particular experience of one person or a group of people, they also exist outside of the human psyche. This means at least three things. First, a symbol can pick up meaning from diverse human experiences. A country's flag may symbolize something very different for the present citizens than it did for the founders. The flag takes on an existence that is related to, yet outside of, the ones who created it. Contemporary natives of the country can reshape the meaning of the original symbol. Second, as Christ and others have indicated, symbols affect people's psyches and actions. Symbols are entities that direct the emotions and behavior of those who fashioned them, *and* those who did not. Third, the essence of common symbols changes when cultural values shift. Common symbols offer meaning because they represent and support values that are part of the cultural ethos of a people. They become meaningless and die if they do not illumine and deepen people's changing attitudes and values. The "life" of symbols is dependent on the relevance and power they contain for guiding future experience. With specific reference to religious symbols, Mary Daly suggests that they "fade and die when the cultural situation that gave rise to them and supported them ceases to give them plausibility."[50]

What makes a symbol sacred? Most of our authors speak about "religious" symbols. "Religious" indicates that these symbols hold meaning within a particular religion. They express fundamental attitudes and feelings about the relationship between the originator of life and the life that is created. This is their most distinguishing trait. Religious symbols also possess characteristics that are common to other symbols: They originate from human experience and subsist outside of it, they direct the inner and outer life of human activity, their meanings change because of altered cultural situations and novel human experience, and they can lose relevancy or become meaningless even for those who hold membership within religion.

Two other things are important to mention as we explore the significance and function of religious symbols in feminist spirituality. First of all, the Jewish and Christian religions have allowed only certain human experiences—namely, male—to shape the meaning of religious symbols. The symbols of Yahweh, God, covenant, exodus, Jesus, Mary, church, and eucharist have all been fashioned from the male experience of relationship with the source and sustainer of life. Female experience was deemed inappropriate or unworthy of fashioning the multi-dimensional meaning of religious symbols. Female experience of relatedness with the deity did not funnel into the construction of religious symbols. Second, religious symbols function as some of the most powerful symbols for directing the meaning and activity of human living. Because they are perceived as coming from human experience with ultimate authority (Yahweh or God the Father) they hold extraordinary authority in the lives of believers. To challenge the import or essence of religious symbols is often understood as confronting the power of God "himself."[51]

We have seen what makes a symbol "religious." But in developing a feminist spirituality, I prefer to use the adjective "sacred." "Sacred" connotes certain elements that can become obscured through using the word "religious." Sacred immediately focuses our attention on the holy, rather than on religion. A symbol is sacred if it represents the human experience of becoming whole. To be whole means to know, feel, and value an integrated self; and to know, feel, and value our connectedness or interdependence with the source of life, others, and the nature world. Sacred symbols capture the human experience of consciously feeling relatedness with the creative life-force and all reality. The symbols of Judaism and Christianity have not been influenced by the female experience of becoming whole. The symbols, therefore, do not represent the wholeness of the membership. Religious symbols are not sacred enough.

Why do sacred symbols need to change? Different strands throughout this chapter have indicated the inadequacy of sacred symbols. Now it is time to weave those threads together. Feminist theologians, thealogians, and philosophers demonstrate how the canonical traditions of the West suppress female symbolism for the deity. As women grow in this awareness, their analysis of the deficiency and oppressiveness of sacred symbols becomes more nuanced. Let me outline the core of their position.

Patriarchal symbol systems promote unequal power relations in our world. They encourage a dualistic worldview and the social patterns of dominance and oppression which this worldview supports. How does this happen? The exclusion of female experience from sacred symbols not only legitimates male rule of society (the outer lives of individuals), it also creates inner psychic conditions so that men (consciously or unconsciously) feel superior to women, and women (consciously or unconsciously) feel less valuable and more powerless in relation to men.

Traditional sacred symbols also encourage a feeling of powerlessness between humanity and God. Humanity's ability to participate in the world's redemptive process has been symbolized as ambiguous at best, but usually extinguished by the symbol of the all mighty, omnipotent God. As Dorothee Söelle astutely remarks: "Our own power is destroyed when God is imagined as the mighty or even omnipotent Father."[52] Finally, patriarchal symbols have not encouraged humanity's reverence of and care for the natural world. The unequal power between males and females, the deity and humanity replicates itself when spirit is imaged as separate from matter, or the soul is valued over the body. Most theological efforts to symbolize the deity as an essential part of the nature world have been branded with the heresy of pantheism. Nature has been imaged as separate from and less than God and humanity. Therefore it should be mastered and controlled rather than reverenced and respected as an interdependent element of our existence.

Feminism and feminist spirituality, however, produce a revolution in cultural consciousness. An entirely new ethos and worldview emerge from women's struggle for liberation in the world. A consciousness of interdependence severely critiques sacred symbols that value the male over the female, hierarchical and dominating relations between the deity and humanity, and humanity's devaluation and exploitation of nature. Traditional sacred symbols are being experienced as irrelevant, meaningless, and harmful by those who attempt to live interdependently. The authors of *Sophia* argue, "We must create and express a vision of connectedness in order to move beyond the unequal power relations that are tearing our world apart. Yet the symbol systems with which we understand reality are often essentially patriarchal."[53]

So feminists recognize the need to "take the shaping of the symbolic universe of meaning into their own hands."[54] Sacred symbols *must* represent humanity's experience of attempting to live equal relationships and of becoming whole within the self and with the rest of reality. They should express humanity's taking responsibility—in cooperation with the deity—for sustaining life on earth. Sacred symbols must capture these experiences in order to offer back to humanity the meaning and value of interdependence. Only in this way, feminists argue, will the cultural revolution continue so that creation does not destroy itself through the logical outcome of dominating and exploitive relations between the few and the many, humanity and its natural environment.

How are sacred symbols changing? The feminist experience of changing patriarchal sacred symbols is extremely complex. Though all feminists agree on the oppressive essence of traditional religious symbols, they take different paths in the process of symbol-building. Their starting point is similar, however, as are several of the activities they engage in to fashion symbols that both reflect and inspirit relationships of interdependence. Feminists initiate the journey through psychologically distancing themselves from the traditional symbols. For most women, this is an acutely painful experience. But the study of feminist religious writings, personal meditation, participation in rituals or liturgies that include their spiritual experiences, and praxis for the wholeness of themselves and others assist in the exorcism of sacred symbols that devalue themselves as women. Still, the distancing usually produces a deep experience of nothingness, emptiness, or impasse.[55] Only the reach for symbols that incorporate their experience, desire for, and activity of struggling for freedom and wholeness keeps the exorcism going. As Carol Christ says, "Symbol systems cannot simply be rejected, they must be replaced."[56]

The issue of replacement signals the feminist parting of ways. Feminist theologians believe that the core symbolism of Judaism and Christianity still holds potential for reflecting and pointing toward the reality of interdependence. They argue that the patriarchalization of sacred symbols does not capture the true meaning of the liberating essence of exodus or the gospel vision. They believe that the psyches of women and men will not always identify maleness or absolute omnipotence with God. For this to happen, however, feminist theological analysis must radically reconstruct sacred symbols.[57] Women and men must also form feminist communities that encourage inclusive liturgies and enable each person to participate in ritualizing their individual experiences of becoming whole. Ruether makes this point as she reflects on the need for "Women-Church":

> One needs communities of nurture to guide one through death to the old symbolic order of patriarchy to rebirth into a new community of being and living. One needs not only to engage in rational theoretical discourse about the journey; one also needs deep symbols and symbolic action to guide and interpret the actual experience of the journey from sexism to liberated humanity.[58]

Feminist thealogians and Mary Daly believe that the core symbolism of Judaism and Christianity *is* inherently patriarchal. Any liberating elements that can be recovered in the traditions of these religions are exceptions to rather than the essence of their sacred symbols. They believe that "God" will always be indistinguishable from maleness in the human psyche. Thealogians argue that patriarchal symbols should be replaced with the sacred symbols of ancient Goddess religions. "The Goddess" becomes the primary religious symbol and, because the "entire earth is conceptualized as being the 'body of the Goddess,'"[59] the earth is another important sacred symbol. Feminist theaology analyzes the meaning of the Goddess in ancient history and its meaning for women and men today. Theoretical analysis is only part of the journey. Again, rituals, meditations, feminist communities, and praxis are all necessary for the process of symbol-building.

Mary Daly does not look to ancient religions as a primary source for the construction of new symbols. Her project builds sacred symbols by creating new language that reflects her own personal growth in "biophilic consciousness." In conversation and community with many other feminist women, Daly believes that this new language will encourage women to think beyond patriarchal space and time, and act toward re-membering their broken selves and enabling the harmonious balance of earth, air, fire, and water.

I have pondered the feminist conceptual analyses of patriarchal sacred symbols for some time now. I have encouraged countless women and men in two strikingly different cultures to consider the diverse positions of feminists. I have participated in Christian feminist rituals, rituals facilitated by Starhawk, and rituals with Mary Daly where we celebrated the presence of earth, fire, air, and water in our own lives. I have guided and been guided by imaginative meditations that heal others and myself. These, and many other personal experiences convince me of the need for *both* the radical transformation *and* the creative replacement of patriarchal sacred symbols.

As a Christian feminist I have made a specific leap of faith: I believe that Christian symbols—if radically transformed with a feminist consciousness of interdependence—will enable people to live for themselves, each other, and the earth. And I have witnessed this taking place in the lives of many people. I do not believe, however, that these symbols hold the same power in every person's life. So, if I really am attempting to live interdependently—that is, valuing the connectedness and individual difference between all people—I must recognize and affirm others' efforts to replace *my* symbols (even the transformed species) with symbols that will challenge them.

At a theoretical yet still personal level, I want to point out that feminist thealogians and Mary Daly do not know with absolute certainty that radically reconstructed Jewish or Christian symbols will perpetuate a patriarchal culture, so they also make a leap of faith as they replace those symbols. But since patriarchal dualism is such a many-headed monster, I think that the diversity of feminist belief and symbol-building is exceedingly necessary. Constructing very different symbols out of the same fundamental worldview (one that emerges from similar ways of living relationship because of the liberation movement) may be the only way to transform the powerful patriarchal ethos. A spirituality for feminists challenges us to do our own symbol-building and to respect the symbols of other feminists. In this way we value the same journey while traveling different paths.

Sacred Stories Stories embrace meaning from the past activity of people; they are spun to pass that meaning on. Not unlike symbols, stories etch our attitudes, values, feelings, and desires. They also try to capture our truths. Stories weave these truths from the events that actually happen in our lives and from the meaning of those events as we experience them. As many scholars from diverse fields argue, the interpretation (or meaning) of stories cannot be separated from the historical events themselves. As soon as one starts to tell a story, one engages in the act of interpreting.

When I use the phrase "sacred stories," I am referring to the records of people's attempts to live and understand their relatedness to the deity, others, and the world. Sacred stories re-present these relationships through different forms: the biographical stories of a people; their hymns, psalms, and prayers; the myths of a people; and the artifacts of archeological findings. Each form carries the meaning and activity of how relationships were lived. People left records because they valued both the *ability* to relate and the *patterns* of relationships that were created. "Telling the story" through biography, prayer, myth, or art form indicated belief that their patterns of relationship were *true.* Therefore, they should inspire others to live in a similar way upon "hearing" the story.

Sacred stories supply sustenance for various feminist spiritualities. As feminists endeavor to image wholeness for themselves and the world, they search for clues in the stories of relationship from people of the past. Feminists choose stories that will nourish and guide their journey, stories that spark their ability to imagine ways of living interconnectedness. They select stories that value the female, the nature world, the deity who is with us—part of us—as we sustain our own lives and create new possibilities for life on earth.

It is obvious by now that feminists do not "listen" to the same sacred stories. They ask: (1) *Which* stories shall we remember so that we can imagine wholeness? and (2) *How* shall we imaginatively remember the stories? The first question concerns the personal and theoretical judgments that feminists make regarding religious traditions. Which religious stories, if any, inspire them to live with care for all that they are part of? The second question is an important methodological one: What method will they use to interpret the meaning and truth of ancient stories? How will they sift through the texts or artifacts to discover *all* the ways relationships were lived? If the stories are situated within a patriarchal culture, how will they find something that holds truth or value for an evolving feminist culture? What pieces of the stories liberate their imaginations; which tales paralyze?

Feminist theologians choose to remember the sacred stories of biblical religion. Although they acknowledge that these stories arise within the socio-political context of patriarchy and have been interpreted to support the continuation of a patriarchal ethos, theologians judge that feminist methods of interpretation surface elements within the stories that subvert patriarchal patterns of relation.[60] For example, Phyllis Trible identifies several female images for Yahweh in the Hebrew Scriptures.[61] Letty Russell interprets "shalom" as the activity and vision of living relationships that free people to become whole.[62] In Ruether's view, there exists God-language beyond patriarchy in the biblical tradition; she argues that the prophetic strand of the Hebrew and Christian Scriptures chastizes those who dominate others because of social power and prestige.[63] Elisabeth Schüssler Fiorenza imaginatively reconstructs Christian origins to break the silence of stories wherein women initiate and lead the early Christian communities. She persuasively reasons that the stories point toward communities guided by an egalitarian ethos and that Jesus called forth a "discipleship of equals."[64]

Feminist theologians also investigate the stories and/or writings of various Jewish and Christian women throughout the ages. Their task has been one of gathering and publishing stories that have not been heard,[65] as well as using a feminist method to interpret the lives and writings of better known women such as Julian of Norwich, Hildegard of Bingen, Catherine of Siena, and Teresa of Avila.[66] These are considered "sacred stories" and once again feminists cull the texts to find resourceful insights and/or behavior for feminist spirituality today.

Thealogians choose to remember the sacred stories of Goddess and Wicca religions. Most argue that the memory of biblical stories will only create future stories of patriarchal relationships. For example, Naomi Goldenberg insists that the feminist "retranslation of Jewish and Christian Scripture [is] a self-deceptive enterprise."[67] The all-pervasive sexism of the texts cannot be eradicated through any method of interpretation. Or, Carol Christ challenges theologians to remember that Yahweh was a "Holy Warrior"; he slaughtered people who would not abide by his ways.[68] While their reasons for rejecting biblical stories are many and diverse, all thealogians judge that these stories do not contain sufficient potency to encourage female power in the world, or to promote a consciousness of interconnectedness and love for the earth.

So, they have set about the task of reclaiming Goddess and Wicca history. Thealogians propose that these sacred stories are rooted in times before the evolution of patriarchy and can therefore enable us to image a way out of patriarchy. They draw on the work of anthropologists, archeologists, and historians who are establishing evidence of cultures where women and men were valued equally, there was little trace of war activity, and the Goddess (in various forms) was worshiped as supreme.[69] Though such evidence continues to increase, the myths, hymns, and prayers of Goddess religions only date back to 2400 B.C.E., which is *after* patriarchal culture arose. Thus there exists considerable debate between thealogians and theologians regarding the claim that these sacred stories do emerge within matri-centered cultures.[70]

Nevertheless, thealogians choose to remember stories of the Goddess:

This is the story we like to tell ourselves
    in the night
    when the fire seems nothing but dying embers winking
    out
    and the labor is too hard and goes on too long
    when we can't believe that we can make it
We like to tell ourselves
    that we remember the First Mother

* * * * *

When we are afraid, when it hurts too much
We like to tell ourselves
    stories of power

how we lost it
how we can reclaim it
We tell ourselves
the cries we hear may be those of labor
the pain we feel may yet be that of birth.[71]

Like other thealogians, Starhawk weaves together stories of the Goddess with her own experience of struggling for the world's freedom and wholeness. She gathers the sacred records of Wicca religion and interprets their meaning through the contemporary experience of feminist ritual and political activity for peace.[72] She does this with the hope—or wish—that the ancient sacred stories originate from times when the earth was considered sacred, the female was valued as the birth-giver, and relationships of mutuality existed between women and men. Her wish for such a history is not unlike Schüssler Fiorenza's insistence to imagine women at the *center* of early Christian history. Carol Christ has begun to use a similar imaginative method as she reclaims Goddess history for the contemporary feminist spirituality movement.[73] She asserts that, although written during patriarchal times, myths of and hymns to the Goddess do reflect a historical reality that is other than male dominance. In a similar way, Nelle Morton suggests that if images arise within women's psyche today (for example, that the deity is female), it is not unreasonable to believe that these images have an ancient history that lifts up the value and inherent worth of woman.[74]

But not all myths of the Goddess reflect a time when woman was free, the deity was imaged as immanent within humanity and the earth, and relations between women and men were equal and mutual. Thealogians analyze certain myths that reflect the transition from matrilineal to patriarchal times. Starhawk provides a poignant analysis as she calls us to remember three Mesopotamian myths that "echo the changes in the structures of power upon which society was based. . . . Together, they tell the story of the rise of power-over."[75] She insists that these stories are not sacred at all; they tell us about the dis-memberment of the world and the rupture of an interrelated reality. Still, we must remember these stories as well. For "without the story, we don't know what's wrong with us."[76]

Mary Daly offers a different analysis of one of the myths that Starhawk selects. Daly examines the Babylonian creation myth wherein the

Goddess Tiamut is literally dismembered by the God Marduk. This activity of destroying woman is what brings forth life on earth. Daly argues, in five brilliant yet harrowing chapters, that the Goddess murder has been re-enacted in the lives of real women under patriarchal rule through Indian suttee (widow-burning), Chinese footbinding, African genital mutilation, European witchburning, and American gynecology.[77] Such stories—again, far from sacred—should be remembered by women to motivate their leap beyond patriarchal consciousness (what Daly calls "metapatriarchal" consciousness), ideology, and religion. Like the thealogians, Daly chooses not to remember biblical stories as a source for feminist spirituality. She judges that these memories can only "destroy women's ancestral Memory,"[78] paralyze women's imaginations, and bind them to activity that breaks them apart.

Daly selects another set of sacred stories to remember, some of which have been told while many others still lie within the deep psyches of women. Daly asks: Can we create a language and philosophy of interconnectedness that supports the *real* becoming of women? Her answer is yes: The method centers on women reaching into their *own* memories, back to a self that is whole and interconnected with the rest of the cosmos. Daly proposes that women have their own stories of moments or events when patriarchy did not influence their wills, passions, emotions, or intellect. She challenges women to create these stories, to break the silence, and name reality as they have experienced it through writing, speech, and all forms of art. Why is this so essential? "The quest to re-member the qualitatively other, vivid, richly significant experiences of our past is especially urgent for women, for Realizing of such realities gives us the strength to exorcise patriarchal categories."[79] Daly believes that as women tell their own stories of wholeness, power, and freedom, metapatriarchal consciousness and relationships of interconnectedness will eventually break the necrophilia (death-centeredness) of our present world. She is convinced that women are the source of life beyond patriarchy; women hold the stories of biophilic (life-loving) consciousness within themselves. Women possess the potency to spin sacred stories that value the earth and all her creatures.

As an educator I am keenly aware of the powerful impact that sacred stories have on our lives. These stories shape our identity; they propose particular ways of engaging in relationships with God, others, and the world. We are taught a past that radically affects our present and future activity. Feminists have discovered that the Jewish and Christian sacred stories—the ways they have been written, interpreted, and preached by others—quell woman's inherent value and her equality with man. They respond by teaching themselves and others different versions of similar stories or different stories altogether. Learning these new sacred stories challenges feminists to change themselves and their relationships. They are also confronted with the task of changing social systems that patriarchal sacred stories continue to support.

A spirituality for feminists is sustained by listening to all the sacred stories of women's value, agency, and power. It is nourished by any past patterns of behavior that challenge dominating and oppressive relationships between people, and between humanity and the earth. It stands on all stories that teach us about our responsibility for life on earth. As a Christian feminist I have decided that my primary sacred stories come from the lives of Jesus and those who combine his vision with their own. Their struggles, hopes, and images of the future are the stories I listen to, with a feminist ear, over and over again. With other Christian feminists I continue to look for the ways Christians before me lived relationships of mutuality, equality, and stewardship. I believe that the survival of our world depends on surfacing and remembering these stories.

However, in journeying with other feminists, I have found that the sacred stories of Goddess religions affect my imagination in ways the Jesus story never will. Narratives of the Goddess, hymns to and images of her unequivocally symbolize the power and goodness of the female. A female symbol for the deity impacts the imagination in a very different way from the incarnate son of God. And as thealogians recover Goddess stories through the lens of their own feminist experiences, the story of the earth's sacredness and care for humanity provides a necessary corrective for the ways Christians have remembered: "Be fruitful and multiply, and fill the earth and subdue it . . . " (Genesis 1:28). Furthermore, sacred stories that point toward a time before patriarchy began contribute an important layer of realism to the imaging process. If we can image its beginning through remembering these stories, we hold more potential to image its end. Though we will explore each of these areas in greater detail, what I want to emphasize now is the sustenance that these stories hold for the spiritual journey of feminists who are Christian. Though Christians often resist listening to other sacred stories (a characteristic of monotheism, I suspect), a spirituality for feminists calls for it. So much has been lost in the androcentric texts of the Jesus story, we simply need other resources that contain a vision and lifestyle of interdependent living.

This means that though I strongly disagree with Daly's judgment of the death-centeredness of Christianity, I think her work is another essential piece in the passage toward wholeness. Daly represents many women who radically challenge other women to believe in themselves, to write their own stories, to know that they have the power to find wholeness amid the destructiveness of patriarchy. Although I believe that men with a feminist consciousness have sacred stories that are necessary for the salvation of our world, women need Daly's confronting challenge to tell their own stories, *first.* At this moment in history, it *is* time for men to listen to women. Men's stories will become more sacred if they really hear the surfacing of women's truths.

Obviously, the feminist telling of Jewish and Christian stories are valuable resources for feminists outside these traditions. Even though they may not be their primary stories, they contain clues for the ways people struggled against dominance, brokenness, and oppressiveness within a dualistic worldview and male-centered culture. For example, Christian feminist theologian Carter Heyward remembers Jesus as one who is healed by others as well as the one who heals.[80] Mutuality in relationship is what provides Jesus with the power to free *and be freed* by others. Here is the story of an authority figure who challenges the patterns of relation set by his patriarchal milieu. Remembering times when others resisted the influence of a destructive worldview similar to our own can inspire the process of subversion today, *especially* within the present religious systems.

Spiritualities of Women's Power

The feminist spirituality movement includes a tremendous variety of women whose primary focus encourages the growth of woman's power to heal themselves and all creatures of the earth.[81] Though several of them use Goddess, Wicca, Eastern, and Native American religions as resources for spiritual development, their central concern is to foster the creative, intuitive, healing, and relational activity of women. Most agree that the main force for cultural revolution emerges when women's personal power is nurtured to effect political change. But this is not just any kind of power: These feminists are talking about potency for effecting change that only comes when one "acknowledges that we are each part of a vast organism that is in trauma."[82] A common theme consistently surfaces throughout rich diversity in their writings: *We can only move beyond the ravaging of the planet and the oppression of peoples through a consciousness of interrelatedness.*[83]

The make-up of this awareness is similar to what we have looked at already in the other feminist spiritualities. Every form of life is intimately related to every other form. In fact, often drawing on modern physics and ecological theory, these spiritualities insist that matter and energy are not separate.[84] The natural elements of earth, air, fire, and water compose the essence of every being, humanity included. The air that we breathe is shared by all; what I breathe out you, the plants, and animals breathe in. Most authors speak of an original and sustaining energy distinguishable yet essentially connected with humanity and all of creation. This has different names: Mother-Earth, Goddess, the "life-force of the universe,"[85] the One. Women assert that such energy is immanent in life and that their experienced union with it enables them to act wisely for themselves and the rest of the universe.

A consciousness of interrelatedness provides the center from which a unique kind of personal and political power emanate. Feminists seek personal integration of mind, body, emotions, and spirit. They delve to the deepest parts of themselves—alone, with others, with nature—to break apart the patriarchal conditioning that they are powerless, unimaginative, and unable to heal themselves or the rest of life. They reach inside the self to find a new source of energy beyond patriarchy. The deep experience of personal integrity and interrelatedness with all reality motivates creative visioning, activity, and relationships that transform our world.[86] Most of these women invite men to consider a similar journey, though their main focus is work with women.[87] They believe that both the natural characteristics of woman (the menstrual cycle, the experience of giving birth, the ability to produce food with her own body) and the social history of women (the traditional roles of nurturer, care-taker, and mother) are the roots of a personal power that must enter the political arena in order that we all survive. So they look for ways to create and maintain such a resource.

What enables this power of interrelatedness? Or, as Diane Mariechild asks, "How do we re-establish our connections to the whole circle of life?"[88] The creativity of feminist spiritualities bursts forth in answers to these questions. They use numerous tools for their spiritual growth. Some center on the imaging process—how to tap images of wholeness and freedom that lie deep in the layers of the self. Feminists guide each other in fantasy; they try to understand the meaning of dreams. In her first book, *MotherWit*, Mariechild suggests several exercises for creative visualization to assist problem solving and healing the body of its own diseases.[89] Each of these exercises promotes psychic skills so that women can become stronger and wiser in everyday life. They tap subconscious or unconscious images to guide lifestyles of interdependence. "Imaging creates the possible."[90]

Meditation is another tool that develops inner wisdom for outer change. Feminists use both ancient and contemporary meditative techniques. Hallie Iglehart has developed several feminist meditative forms from her study of prepatriarchal history, Eastern religions, and living among the Tibetan people.[91] She documents the ways in which meditation has enabled herself and countless others to find deep personal integration. This sense of wholeness within the self is intensified further as she comes "in contact with the larger Self within me, the point of union with the life energy shared by all life forms."[92] Meditations, even the simplest forms, focus our attentiveness on the self, and beyond the self. They help us to know experientially what we hope for in vision and activity: All beings interconnect through the power of life. We must cooperate with this power in order to sustain and be sustained.

Sustenance and health for political work within the spiritual journey is also provided by feminist ritual. Spiritualities of women's power bestow a notable contribution in this regard.[93] They explore the meaning and function of ritual. They consistently encourage women to create symbolic expression of their inner journey and outer struggles. They offer practical advice for the design of individual and communal ritual. In a later chapter we will examine how the experience of ritual deepens the personal integrity of individuals, enables substantial bonding to take place within groups, and promotes reverence for the earth. For now, let me simply say that this is one of the most creative areas of these spiritualities. Ritual provides a place for feminists to share the power in themselves as they touch the One so that they can continue their work of supportive relation in the world.

A Spirituality for Feminists

What calls us to self-respect, mutuality with others, cooperation with the life force, and reverence for the earth? How ought we to live in relation? These questions prompt the praxis of imaging a whole world. They originate from both the experience of interdependent relationships and hope for societies that will bring them about. The hope for wholeness is a profound wish. We have seen how feminists shape symbols, remember stories, practice meditation, and create ritual to nourish this vision. It is the center of all feminist spiritualities; it is the wellspring of a spirituality for feminists.

Such a spirituality demands two things, and I have already hinted at them. A spirituality for feminists embodies growth in one's own spiritual path *and* conversation with all other spiritual journeys that envisage wholeness through interdependence. This conversation is essential if we are really trying to live according to what we imagine. A spirituality that hopes for wholeness—Jewish and Christian feminism, Goddess, Wicca, or women's power—cannot be nourished totally by itself. A consciousness of interrelatedness means that nothing becomes itself in isolation. We cannot create spiritual traditions that deny the holiness of others who do not belong. That is not to say that our conversation will be free of conflict. I have indicated major points of dispute that arise from the differences in feminist spiritualities, but if conflict happens in an atmosphere of mutual respect, we will see truth that is not visible from our own standpoint.

What sustains the conversation, though? I think that it must be the deep passion and compassion that only comes through mutual relationships across class, race, and ethnic divisions, and active care for peace and health of the earth. When we try to love those who should be separate from us or protest the contamination of the earth, an incredible strength wells up from deep inside the self. It is a power that enables the crossing of spiritual divisions. I have seen this happen time and again when feminists from varied backgrounds gather to support single mothers, embrace the airbase at Greenham Common, or set up community centers for the inner city. We find ourselves in the same place even though our sacred symbols, stories, and spiritual practices differ. Love for the "other"—one who is not like me at all—and reverence for the elements bring me to conversation with those who hold a similar love but different spiritual heritage. What we learn in shelters for the homeless, from those in jail because of civil disobedience, or from community organizing in disadvantaged areas is the same thing we can learn in a spirituality for feminists: *Individuality through relatedness creates the wholeness that we image.* We can now look at how a spirituality for feminists transforms the activity and experience of relationship with self, others, God, and the natural world.

— 2 —

Woman's Self:
Power Through Wholeness

During an interview with a journalist from an Irish newspaper, I was explaining why women gather without male presence in order to nurture their self-development. I spoke confidently about the psychological and physical space that women need with one another in order to surface fears, experiences of oppression, anger, hopes, and dreams. The presence of a man, even if he is sympathetic and open to feminism, can inhibit women's self-revelations because his gender images some of the oppression that they feel. This does not mean that mutuality with men is not part of the overall hope for wholeness. It does mean that real mutuality only happens when two selves, *each regarding the other as equal,* meet to see what can be done together. Through many years of experiences with women's groups, I knew that I was equal to the man who interviewed me. Our conversation was powerfully mutual.

Woman's Relationship With Her Self: The Process

I have described feminist spirituality as the praxis of imaging wholeness. What does this look like when we consider woman's relationship with her self? What kinds of changes take place within woman's self as she pursues the feminist spiritual path?[1] We can answer this question in terms of the *process* and *patterns* of self transformation. Women characterize the process with vivid phrases: "diving deep and surfacing" (Carol Christ); "spinning through the foreground to the background" (Mary Daly); going "beyond anger" (Carolyn Osiek); "the descent from the upper world to the land below" (Starhawk); "metanoia" (Rosemary Ruether and Elisabeth Schüssler Fiorenza); and participating in "the inner dance" (Diane Mariechild). These images depict a process that requires not only a deep consciousness of patriarchy's destructiveness, but also the willingess to search for personal power, namely, *the ability to effect change (for oneself, others, and the earth) that creates conditions for freedom and life.*

The quest for this kind of power (Starhawk calls it the "power-from-within"), is sometimes sketched in terms of psychic/spiritual stages that women travel through. Carol Christ offers one of the finest descriptions of this process in *Diving Deep and Surfacing*.[2] The search begins in *an experience of nothingness*. This is felt differently by different women. For some, it is an awareness that "being female means that *she* is not important, except in her relationship with boys or men."[3] For others, it is a deep-seated anxiety that they have not—or may not—find sufficient meaning in life. For most, however, it includes a consciousness that their be-ing has been defined by the social context of patriarchy. They have been shaped by sources of power outside the self. Once aware, women begin the process of emptying the conditioned self; they let go of "conventional sources of value" and search for something more.

This pursuit often leads to *an experience of awakening*, or enlightenment. Women slowly awaken to their own powers of be-ing and acting in the world. The ability to fashion the self resides within; women begin to experience inner value, authority, and responsibility. Awakening to the potential for self-determination does not happen in an individualistic spirit, though. Christ describes awakening as analogous to mystical experience. This means that woman's power to create her self happens as she experiences connections to what Christ calls the "powers of being." Women directly experience some form of union with the ultimate life power in their care for the earth, interpersonal relationships, and social justice activity. They touch the source of life and this, in turn, "leads to newfound *self*-awareness and *self*-confidence."[4] In other words, they do not lose the self in this union; rather, they come to a new powerful sense of self.

Woman's new self must speak. The process of self transformation continues through *new naming* of themselves and reality as they have experienced both. The creation of words, symbols and images—surfacing from self-determination in relation—redefines what it means to be woman and offers an interdependent view of reality. This is obviously an ongoing activity—But so is the movement through nothingness toward awakening. The process is not linear; it follows a spiral path. The spiritual quest for wholeness, within the self and as part of the larger order of be-ing, finds its home on the journey.

While Mary Daly does not outline specific stages of the self's journey, her works more than any other author's vigorously depict the process of woman's relationship with her Self.[5] In fact, Daly's key preoccupation (amid all theological and philosophical analyses) centers on the Self's dynamic process of be-coming. This portrait of "spinning through the foreground to the background" images both what the Self is (for Daly and other feminists) and what it ought to be-come. It is both descriptive and prescriptive of the spiritual journey.

In *Beyond God the Father* Daly does not use "foreground/background" language, but her agenda unabashedly focuses on the movement necessary for women to become themselves. She insists that woman's search for wholeness and self-determined be-ing is a "countercultural phenomenon."[6] This means that woman must move against or away from present culture (described by Daly as "patriarchal space/time") and into another space/place that is located on the boundary of patriarchal institutions. This can be woman's space where she is free to participate in her own revolution of becoming a valuable, whole, free, authoritative, and actual person. But as woman moves from one space to the other, she "requires existential courage to confront the experience of nothingness."[7] Woman must face the reality of her non-being or lack of value in patriarchal culture. The conscious experience of such alienation, encouraged and heightened by a feminist analysis of theology/ philosophy, propels woman to "create a counterworld to the counterfeit 'this world.'"[8]

Gyn/Ecology and *Pure Lust* name the counterworld as the "otherworld" or the deep "background" to the "foreground," which is patriarchy. The Self's journey to the Background, that is, the space and time where woman becomes an authentic Self, must include walking through the foreground with her "I's" wide open. For Daly, this means exposing the deadly symbols, myths, and rituals of patriarchal religion. It means exorcising all the internalized patriarchal values and virtues that tell woman that her worth is determined by men and that her greatest virtue is to sacrifice her self. In one of Daly's most poignant, searing sentences she asserts:

> Breaking through the foreground which is the Playboy's Playground means letting out the bunnies, the bitches, the beavers, the squirrels, the chicks, the pussycats, the cows, the nags, the foxy ladies, the old bats and biddies, so that they can at last begin naming themselves.[9]

Exorcism is followed by the ecstasy of "new naming." Woman experiences ecstasy as she begins to re-member her whole Self, and to participate in naming a world where her Self can live with integrity.

Though focused on woman's Self, Daly acknowledges that the journey cannot happen in isolation. In *Beyond God the Father* she speaks about this as the "two-edged courage to be."[10] Woman needs courage to become an individual, but she also needs it to live as part of the web of reality. Daly develops this theme in later works; in fact, it goes through a metamorphosis itself. Woman's Self becomes uniquely hers, but only through the power of participating in the life energy that flows through the natural elements and the be-coming of other self-identified women. Woman's Self experiences the life of wholeness as she acknowledges her elemental connection with the natural environment. Woman learns how to become Self as she ponders the reality of her relatedness to the earth.[11]

The process of Self development also requires the "fire of female friendship."[12] Woman needs other "Self-centering Selves" in order to exorcise all that binds her spirit and mind to the patriarchal state. Essential connection with other radical feminist sisters enables woman to continue the journey of choosing her Self. Daly discusses this in terms of an option for separatism. But how can she argue for interconnection and separation in the same work? Here, her definition of separatism is key: "separation from the State of Separation."[13] Separatism means that women intentionally disconnect themselves from those who embody and support patriarchal myths, systems, and symbols. They disassociate themselves from a culture that separates mind from body, spirit from matter, nature from humanity. Such activity is done for the purpose of real communication and radical connection with all that patriarchy separates. Friendship with those who deeply desire "becom(ing) in a healing environment, and to become the healing environment"[14] is a requisite for Self-integrity in the background. Ultimately, Daly hopes that women's Selves will transform that background into the foreground so that life survives.

Let's consider one more profile of the process, emerging from the context of Christian feminism, one that Carolyn Osiek calls "The Process of Awareness."[15] It includes six steps identified through her teaching of and being with women that trace the journey "toward claiming one's own identity as Christian woman in the face of a tradition and community that have not generally been receptive to that journey."[16] Osiek's description centers on the problem of self-integrity as one wishes to hold dual membership within the feminist movement and the Christian church. What happens to Christian woman's self within such a process?

Initially, she is *fearful* of feminism and *rejects* its confronting challenge. She senses that feminism will upset her self directly; a self that has been shaped by the requirements of a patriarchal society and church. Yet if she allows such intuition to grow within her she inevitably experiences a *turning point.* Whatever the specific circumstance, turning point experiences take place when she sees a blatant example of patriarchal culture affecting her life. This consciousness provokes dissonance within the self; she begins to question the very formation of her self. As the unsettlement continues, *anger* erupts. She is angry that people, the church, and society have oppressed her. She is angry that her self has been stunted and formed according to external authorities. But Osiek contends that "anger is no final resting place"[17] and so woman moves on to face its effects: *broken symbol systems* and *impasse.*

These stages of the journey highlight the direct connection between sacred symbols and woman's sense of self. In a helpful (though too brief) account, Osiek describes how an awareness of the patriarchalization of Christian sacred symbols (God, Jesus, Mary, the eucharist) affects woman's self. She feels denied, demeaned, silenced, and distorted—as woman. If God cannot be imaged with female language and metaphors, if women cannot mediate God's presence within the Christian community as it gathers for its central symbolic rite, and if Jesus' maleness obstructs woman's identification with the deity, these symbols *must* break apart if woman is to discover her own inherent value and experience the fullness of humanity within her self.

However, the disintegration of one's symbol system for the sake of the self's survival is exceedingly painful and confusing. Osiek proposes that this leads to a sense of *impasse;* a period where woman feels as if there is no way forward with her new-found awareness. She knows there is no turning back, but the path forward simply does not appear. What sacred symbols will enable her to become her self? Can Christian symbols change enough? Osiek insists that the alienation within impasse must be fully embraced in order for woman to experience *breakthrough.* To journey "through the break" means that woman—with others—slowly discovers how to refashion sacred symbols and images that will encourage the full becoming of her self.[18] Many Christian women are doing precisely this in the American Women-Church movement and the Irish networking of women's spirituality groups.[19]

What we've considered thus far are three depictions of woman's self-transformative process in the feminist spiritual journey. Though rooted in different contexts, they portray elements that are common to the process: moving through fear to courageously confront nothingness, awakening to the potential of self-determination, critiquing patriarchal symbols for self-survival, and creating self-integrity in and through relationship. For the process to happen at all, though, woman must be willing to "look within."[20] Diane Mariechild, Hallie Iglehart, and Starhawk accentuate the importance of this as they call woman to "the inner dance," the "wisdom within," and the "land below." For many women this is the hardest step of all to take. So much conditioning, so many sacred symbols tell them to look elsewhere. Yet the "look within" is key for generating power.

Once again, the sort of power that I and so many other feminists are referring to centers on the capacity to bring about change—but not just any kind of change. We mean changes in the self, in sacred symbol systems, in social structures, in worldviews, and in patterns of relationships that actively support the freedom of all people, and that unequivocally encourage the natural cycle of life to continue. How do feminists find this kind of power on the spiritual path? The simplest answer is this: They hope for wholeness. But what does that mean for woman's self?

Woman's Relationship With Her Self: The Patterns

The answer to the preceding question lies in women's patterns of being a self. These evolve throughout the transformation process and exhibit a deep sense of the "power-from-within." They identify ways in which women actually experience *power through wholeness*. In other words, the ability to effect change surfaces as women begin to experience wholeness within themselves—*self-integrity*[21]—and as they start to sense their *interrelatedness* to the whole web of life. I therefore propose to probe the patterns of woman's relationship with her self according to the categories of self-integrity and interrelatedness. I draw from the recorded experiences of feminists within different spiritual contexts, but I also draw upon the experience of crossing classes as an integral part of my own feminist journey. I do this for several reasons.

First of all, it is important to recognize that the following patterns come primarily from the experiences of white, middle-class, educated women. There is no pretense, then, that they reflect a "universal" feminist self. In fact, through my own experience of crossing economic classes, I know that women with less social power than myself do not discover personal power in the same way, nor as easily as I do. Their struggle for self-determination contains entirely different features.[22] So often their oppression is kept rigidly in place by the consistent depression in their lives. There is no apparent way out no matter which way they turn. But they too have a hope for wholeness, and this keeps them on the journey as they move in and out of societally-imposed despair. How remarkable it is to witness this: It deeply affects my own self-becoming in various ways. Perhaps the most significant way is this: Mutual friendship with those socially less powerful than I broadens my understanding and experience of self-integrity and radical relatedness in ways that would not otherwise be possible. I cannot know what power through wholeness means without them. This leads me to suggest that the feminist self's hope for wholeness must incorporate crossing social boundaries. It is an integral activity of the spiritual journey. This is a frightening thing to do for one who is socially powerful, for several things that we thought were necessary for freedom, life, and happiness will be lost. Yet as Christine Gudorf astutely reasons:

> Love in both individual and social relations involves the intention of mutuality and the probability of self-sacrifice to establish the interdependence of all which dictates that our ultimate self-interest demands sacrifice in the interest of the disadvantaged other.[23]

Patterns of Self-Integrity

The most basic requirement for an authentically integrated self is *knowledge of one's own inherent value.* Self-affirmation and a deep sense of immanent worth activate the discovery of one's unique individuality. Self-respect and self-love both enable and are the fruits of who I am, who I want to become, what my values are, and how I can live according to my goals and vision. Feminists from all spiritual traditions insist that woman's self-integrity stands firmly on her ability to love her self fiercely. In a vigorous and moving essay, Carter Heyward describes a self-respecting woman as one "who lives among us as someone proud, someone humble, a woman grounded and vulnerable, able to be touched. She owes no explanation, no defense, certainly no apology for her strong self-love."[24] Women's capacity to be themselves or, "to own our own souls once again,"[25] requires consistent acceptance of their ultimate goodness.

Most women do not embrace this pattern of be-ing easily. Starhawk argues that woman's inner psychic reality initially reflects the ways that power is culturally organized. Woman's "internal landscapes" have been sculpted to pass power over to external authority. The "I" does not know what to do; it must be instructed by someone who holds more authority or value. Under patriarchy, "the King" symbolizes the highest form of authority; woman's self internalizes the king image, resulting in her identity being shaped by obedience to outside authority.[26] Rooted in first-hand experiences of the American penal system, Starhawk offers an insightful analysis of how the "king within" operates to ensure the self's control by the social systems of power. Above all, the king as a model of authority "teaches us that our worth is not a given but must be earned and subordinated to the value of someone else whose status is higher than ours."[27]

Several psychological dynamics operate within woman's self as she internalizes society's definition of value. What she learns is to distrust her self, to doubt her knowledge of truth, and ultimately to deny her own inherent worth. Starhawk names this psychic structure as "the self-hater, the inner voice that judges and attacks."[28] The self-hater manifests itself in numerous ways. Starhawk suggests that it is controlled by the five faces of the internalized king. The king within governs woman's self by silencing her (the censor), by insisting that she denies her own need to serve others (the master of servants), by deeming her valuable if she obeys the rules (the judge), by fearing others (the conqueror), and by accepting rigid control of her activities (the orderer).[29] However, once woman becomes aware of the self-hater, she can start to exorcise its control over her identity. Thus begins the spiritual journey of healing the self by taking back the power that she gave away. As she does this, woman slowly moves toward knowledge of her own inner authority and immanent value.

For Christian women, the traditional ethic of self-sacrifice often blocks such conviction of inherent worth. Carter Heyward records her struggle in a poignant journal passage:

> I remember. I have not forgotten the fall, 1967. St. Luke's Hospital, Clark 8 Psychiatric unit. First-year seminarian: "confused." Seeking alone a vocation, I had come to New York City to work things out for myself. It was between "God" and me, and my confusion was simply the lot of a person seeking self-affirmation, yet attached fast to a narcissistic "God" who demands her self-negation.[30]

Comparable to Starhawk's notion of the king as "master of servants," the Christian God was (and is) often experienced by women as demanding self-denial and sacrifice of one's own needs for the sake of others. As Joann Conn pointed out in an important essay on Christian women's spirituality: "Women are led to believe that they are virtuous when actually they have not yet taken the necessary possession of their lives to have an authentic 'self' to give in self-donating love."[31] Like Heyward, Conn insists that the stunting of woman's self-development directly relates to her internalized God-images. Most feminists are convinced that woman's belief in her own intrinsic goodness has been obstructed by the predominance of male God language and the image of God as the One who requires self-negation for individual salvation. Following Valerie Saiving's lead, feminists also point out that the theological definitions of sin as pride and virtue as humility or self-effacement effectively encourage women to have no self of their own.[32] In spite of these obstacles, women have been creating conditions to change their lives. They deliberately engage in activities that free them to embrace the self. Again, this is an integral dimension of all feminist spiritualities. They hold in common several creative ways to develop a spirituality of self-love and self-integrity. Forming communities is one of the most important conditions for this kind of growth. Christian women sometimes call them base communities or their *women-church* group, witches call them covens, Mary Daly speaks of "be-friending," and some women simply name them their spirituality group. Women discover over and over again that membership within feminist communities provides the support needed to make important changes in the self. Communities are effective for self growth especially when each woman feels valued as an equal member. Creation of an unconditionally caring environment empowers women to risk self-determination. Needless to say, such an atmosphere is not instantaneous. Yet it is an image that draws women toward an intimacy that nurtures self-birth.

Transformation of sacred symbols is another component in the process of shaping self-integrity. Feminist theologians, thealogians, and elemental philosophers consistently demonstrate the negative effects on woman's ability to value her self because femaleness has been denigrated in sacred symbol systems. It is imperative, therefore, that women refashion sacred symbols out of their own experience of *valuing* be-ing woman in the world. This is happening within each context of feminist spirituality, its most radical manifestation being in contemporary Goddess spirituality. Here, women image the deity's power as an intimate part of the self. Starhawk asserts:

> We are ourselves, the living body of the sacred. This is what Witches mean when we say, 'Thou are Goddess,' and also what mavericks and heretics have always read into the biblical account of the creation of the world in the image of God.[33]

Thealogians and witches believe that the Sacred Life Spark is within woman's self.[34] They insist that imaging the Goddess in this way is central to restoring woman's immanent worth.

The practice of meditation also strengthens woman's knowledge of her inherent value. Meditation encourages woman to look within for insight, information, and images that will heal her self and the world. It requires woman to trust her self as an "expert" in the path toward wholeness. Hallie Iglehart explains: "We are learning to trust the depth of our inner wisdom and to integrate this guidance in our personal and political actions."[35] She recommends working with an "inner guide" as one of the most effective forms of meditation for enabling woman's self-love and self-reliance. In this exercise a woman imagines the most integrated and knowledgeable part of herself. This part takes on a human form, so that the "inner guide" is a personification of the woman's wisdom in herself. The "person" imaged may be female, male, or androgynous but should not be someone the woman knows in ordinary life. Iglehart gives explicit directions for woman's conversation with her "inner guide." The meditation results in woman discovering ways to resolve problems or make decisions through consulting her own wisdom.[36]

Meditation is an integral part of Diane Mariechild's "inner dance." Her book offers several exercises of "awe-robics" that encourage women to transform self-doubt, feelings of worthlessness, and lack of confidence into the courage to *be*. I have used the following meditation several times with many diverse groups, and am consistently amazed with the changes that it effects in my self and other women.

The Gardener

> Let your breath be slow and deep. Imagine that you are a great tree with roots extending deep into the center of the Earth. Let your breath move down into your roots and, at the same time, out through your highest branches. Breathe deeply into your root. Let

the energy from the Earth travel through your roots and up through your highest branches, out into the sky above you. Breathe deeply. Let the light of the sun touch your branches, travel down through your trunk, deep into your roots, and flow out into the Earth.

When you feel fully grounded, in touch with both the Earth and the sky, become aware that in your heart/mind there exists a garden. Its fruits spring from the energy of your thoughts. As your breath sinks deep within your body, let your mind travel deep within until you find yourself in this garden of the heart. Now is the time to weed the garden, to uproot from the garden any thoughts that are limiting, any emotional patterns that are negative, any actions that are incomplete. See yourself pulling up, weeding out, those thoughts of fear, separation, scarcity, and pain. As you carefully weed the garden, take time to bring to mind the ways in which these thoughts were strangling the beautiful plants in the garden. Weed the garden, aware that these weeds, these limiting thoughts, are no longer necessary. Throw the weeds onto the compost pile so that they can be used as fertilizer to help the new seeds to grow.

When you have uprooted all the weeds, imagine yourself spreading the compost over the garden. When the soil is ready, begin to plant new seed-thoughts, affirmations of courage, abundance and joy. Plant new seed thoughts of well-being for yourself and for all the Earth. As each new thought is planted, let its energy resonate like a mantra through your entire being.

Safe in the garden of the mind, let the new seeds take root. Affirm that they will feed all of life. Safe in the garden of the mind, allow the seeds to take root that they may be harvested for the good of all life.

Sometimes I guide a group of women in "The Gardener" meditation as the first part of a closing ritual for a workshop that has centered on ways to heal ourselves. So much of woman's fragmentation comes through the paralysis of self-doubt. Meditation and ritual assist her imagination to acquire habits of self-affirmation. Simply designed rituals provide a sacred atmosphere that empowers women to symbolically express the truth and value discovered within the self. After "The

Gardener" meditation, I invite women to come back to the group slowly, following their own self-rhythm. Some women need more time than others to complete the inner journey. Once everyone is present to the group, I ask them to reflect silently on three questions: (1) What weed do you want to let go of? What thoughts about your self inhibit your healing? (2) What do you want to affirm about your self? and (3) What do you want to affirm or appreciate in the person on your left? When a few minutes pass, each woman speaks in turn, voicing her ability to change her self, to love her self, and to value the woman beside her. The ritual ends with a reading or song that celebrates women.

Traditionally (or, what most women have been familiar with much of their lives), rituals were designed by men to mediate the deity's presence to a community. Men were the ones with the power to invoke the Godhead, to invite God's grace to be part of significant moments in the community's life. The kind of ritual that I have just described, and countless others like it that women are creating and participating in, not only challenge the exclusiveness of the tradition but also call forth woman's potential to ritualize. Feminist ritual—even when God is not explicitly addressed—invites woman to name or image the meaningfulness and truth of life. It encourages woman to know that *her* words, *her* symbols, *her* music, movement, and prayers are sacred. This profoundly affects woman's self. It flows forth from and confirms her immanent goodness. But it is also an essential component of the self-integration process. Rituals that *she* creates with others provide an opportunity to express the journey within and to integrate it with the sacred energy that moves throughout all of life.[37]

The preceding spiritual activities enable woman's love of self. Such love mends the personal brokenness that women suffer through cultural oppression. Searching for wholeness means that women must counteract social and religious messages of their inferiority and powerlessness. However, the process of self-becoming is always historical: It happens within a certain place, time, economic, and ethnic context. Therefore, whereas no woman finds the journey easy, a large number of women throughout the globe (those who are poor or women of color) face incredible obstacles. In suggesting that a spirituality for feminists calls women to cross social boundaries, why is this so important here?

First of all, in being with women who experience poverty, I come face to face with the near impossibility of their struggle for self love.

They are consistently perceived and treated as if they have no social power. This directly affects their sense of self; they meet tremendous resistance in any effort to assert themselves. Witnessing these experiences confronts the meaning of my own self-integrity. What can it possibly mean that I belong to feminist communities, practice meditation, design rituals, and refashion sacred symbols when so many women struggle for their daily bread? It does not mean that I stop such activities, for they sustain my own reach for wholeness. But it does challenge the *purpose* of my search for personal power, *how* it should be used, and for whose benefit.

Second, the virtue of hope consistently motivates movement toward self-integrity. Its possession is key for freedom to integrate a broken self. But how do we find such hope? This, perhaps, is one of the greatest gifts that women who experience poverty pass on to me. *Their* hope that life can be better, that women can stand proud, that themselves, their families, and local communities *will* survive in spite of every government cutback consistently inspires my own search for a similar reality. Their unending spirit and humor in the midst of multi-layered oppressions transforms romantic hope into a virtue with real and permanent power. And when they name the dimensions of such hope, as Alice Walker does in this passage, their self-integrity clears the path for every woman: "Womanist: Loves music. Loves dance. Loves the moon. Loves the Spirit. Loves love and food and roundness. Loves struggle. Loves the Folk. Loves herself. Regardless."[38]

Woman as Embodied Spirit Feminists discover that the self's power wells up inside woman as she accepts and nurtures the integration of body/spirit, emotions/intellect, intuition/logic, and sexuality/spirituality. The spiritual pilgrimage effects a pattern of be-ing wherein woman's self experiences its organic wholeness. Affirmation and celebration of each dimension of her self spurs an integrative mode of living. Her spirited body, thoughtful feelings, intuitive logic, and sexual soul empower passion for a self-determined life and responsibility for the earth's community.

Again, this pattern does not come easily for most women. The dualistic worldview that influences woman's social conditioning urges her to perceive that body is really separate from spirit, and that feelings, intuition, and sexuality should be divorced from the spiritual life. Perception of separation, however, is not the only dynamic that inhibits woman's self-integrity. Dualism impacts her self in two other significant ways. First, within a dualistic paradigm, the inherent goodness of the body, feelings, intuition, and sexuality are denied. Rosemary Ruether demonstrates how this affected traditional Christian spirituality.[39] A person seeks salvation by denying bodily needs and sexual desires. She remarks, "All that sustains physical life—sex, eating, reproduction, even sleep—comes to be seen as sustaining the realm of 'death,'"[40] and therefore obstructs the path toward eternal life. Anything that images nature—especially matter—must be disciplined (that is, negated) through ascetical practices. But this affects woman's self in an altogether different manner than man's self, which leads to our second point. Within dualism, woman's gender becomes identified with nature. She represents the natural order of existence; man symbolizes the supernatural. Not only should woman deny everything natural on the spiritual path, effectively this means that she has to distrust her very self.[41]

A spirituality for feminists rejects such disciplining of woman's self. Instead it puts forward spiritual practices that arise from and support an interdependent worldview. Ruether outlines the program: "Layer by layer we must strip off the false consciousness that alienates us from our bodies, from our roots in the earth, sky, and water."[42] Women affirm the inseparability of psyche/spirit from matter. This means that they intentionally deepen their awareness that "our bodies *are* ourselves." They attend to ways in which psychic/spiritual energy enables bodily healing. Examples include what Hallie Iglehart names "bodywork": laying on of hands, acupressure, massage, polarity therapy, and *shiatsu*.[43] They affirm the body and look for ways to meet its needs and desires in a balanced manner. Starhawk consistently reminds women of the need for pleasure, humor, laughter, fun, art, sex, food, and beauty. She insists that these activities free women to embody their spirits and so find power to change the world.[44]

Underlying all of these practices is woman's conviction that her body is holy; her body—her self—is immanently good. Though women were conditioned to despise their bodies, especially the natural cycles of menstruation, pregnancy, childbirth, and menopause, now they create rituals that celebrate the rites of passage through liturgies of the life cycle.[45] Rosemary Ruether records a "Menopause Liturgy":

Women gather in a circle. Women who have not yet reached menopause are given purple candles. Those who no longer menstruate are given yellow candles. The candles are lit, and each woman meditates on her candle while the meditation is read:

In woman is the great birthing and creating energy. This creating energy takes many forms. It is the power of ovaries to create eggs and womb to nurture the seeded egg into another human being. It is the creative energy to bring forth poetry, song, image. It is the creative energy to reflect on all reality, to mirror the world in the mind and bring forth rational discourse, and to teach others of the secrets of the workings of the world around us. It is the creative energy to create homes, communities, gatherings of people to accomplish tasks and to live together as friends. It is the creative energy to work the clay of the earth, the fibers of plants, and the wool of animals into useful vessels to carry things and many colored clothes to vest our bodies and the walls and floors of our homes. All of these are our many creative mother-energies. Today one among us lets go of one kind of birthing energy, the energy to create other human beings. As she relinquishes this one kind of birthing energy, she takes up all the more fully the other kinds of birthing energies, the energy to create poetry, art, song, vessels, textiles, knowledge, and communities of people who work and live together. As one kind of birthing energy ebbs away and is no more, she enters fully into her many other birthing energies. We pause for a moment of regret for the one birthing energy which is no more. *(All turn their candles upside down and pour out a drop of wax, and then turn them right side again).* We rejoice as she enters into her full powers in the many other birthing energies which are hers.

The menopausal woman extinguishes her purple candle and is handed a yellow candle which is lit by one of the other women with a yellow candle. The women with yellow candles say to her:

Welcome to the community of women who no longer ovulate and bleed and who create now with their minds and spirits.

The woman now has an opportunity to reflect on what this transition moment means in her life. She may speak of pleasures and regrets she had in her years as one who bled and could bear children, and what hopes she sees ahead of her as a creator of culture.

A cup of herbal tea is raised and is blessed with the words:

This is the healing tea which our mothers and their mothers before them drank to calm the distresses of the monthly cycle of egg and blood. This healing tea links all women—those who do not yet bleed, those who bleed, and those who no longer bleed—in one community of creators and caretakers of life in its many forms.

The cup of tea is passed and shared among all present.[46]

This ritual, as well as countless others that feminists create to lift up the holiness of woman's body, strengthen the integrative journey.

As women embrace the goodness of their bodies, it fosters the discovery that "we think with our feelings"[47] and that intuition is a key form of rationality. Emotion and intuition animate woman's embodied spirit; they enable her to sense the life energy flowing through her, connecting her with all creation. Meditative exercises nurture woman's intuitive ability to image self-healing, resolution of personal difficulties, and visions for a just world. They take her beyond logical speculation and tap the intuitive "muse." Feelings are acknowledged as clues for self-discovery. Spirituality groups provide a care-full atmosphere where women explore the meaning of emotions and attempt to integrate them with thoughts, judgments, decisions, and daily activities.

We are talking here about ways that woman empowers her self through integrity. She unearths her ability to make a difference in our world by accepting each part that makes her whole. One of the most potent forces within her is her sexuality. A spirituality for feminists cracks open traditional understandings of sexuality as genital love between woman and man. Starhawk speaks about the power of the "erotic" and contends that women must reclaim its goodness. Woman's eros not only motivates passion to become her self, but it also enables affirmation of her deep oneness with all being.[48] In a similar vein Beverly Harrison describes woman's sensuality as the ability to feel/know her deep relatedness with reality at every level.[49] Carter Heyward insists that sexuality not only has to do with profound personal love between heterosexuals and homosexuals; it encompasses every way in which people make love and justice in our world. She says:

> Our sexuality is our desire to participate in making love, making justice, in the world; our drive toward one another; our movement in love; our expression of our sense of being bonded together in life and death. Sexuality is expressed not only between lovers in personal relationship, but also in the work of an artist who loves her painting or her poetry, a father who loves his children, a revolutionary who loves her people.[50]

This is why sexuality is understood and celebrated as an intrinsic part of woman's embodied spirit.[51]

In being with women who are victims of family violence, I have come to see that affirmation of woman's body must not be an individualistic activity. My own personal struggle against dualistic social conditioning should have effects beyond myself. After witnessing the scars, the blood, the broken bones, and the medicinally drugged spirits, I am convinced that it is extremely urgent for women with social power to declare the sacredness of woman's body. Yes, it is important to begin with ourselves, to practice spiritual habits of living as "body-self" within the world. Yet we can no longer do this just with or for ourselves. As we practice meditation or create ritual to celebrate woman's body we must carry a deep consciousness that many women's natural cycles are thwarted through extreme physical abuse. As we acknowledge our erotic power we must remember the violence done to our sisters through rape, battering, and prostitution. And, when our own struggle for body-self integrity wanes, the willingness to go on can be instilled by the words of women who say no to their physical abuse. Once again, women unlike myself strengthen me with a virtue necessary for the spiritual journey. Their *will* to end bodily violence, even when it means leaving financial security, a home, neighbors, and friends, confronts my own inertia and utters without question, "my body *is* my very self."

Patterns of Interrelatedness

Woman's metamorphosis toward self-integrity does not take place in isolation. The preceding description of her self-transformation implicitly shows how wholeness within is dependent on relationships with others. A spirituality for feminists critiques the prevailing notion that the self is a separate, isolated object.[52] Woman integrates her self in and through relations with the "human and biological community."[53]

Inseparability from All Other Beings Each form of feminist spirituality encourages woman's conscious awareness that her self is essentially related to the community of life on earth. The "stuff" of woman's individuality evolves through creative integration of past and present relationships, always with hope that she will experience a deeper sense of oneness with all reality. She becomes her self, then, through relationships that are given (for example, family, ethnic, and religious community) and relationships of her own choosing. She discovers uniqueness within negotiations that are part and parcel of every relationship.[54] In addition, woman attends to the ways in which every life form affects and is affected by her own process of be-ing a self. Her ability to effect appropriate change (for self and world) deepens as her circles of relationship widen. Knowing that she is intimately part of the entire life community enables woman to care for and be cared for by it. Because of her "intuition that what is most deeply myself is more than ego, more than I,"[55] woman finds power to create conditions for freedom and life. In turn, an awareness of interrelatedness provides sustenance for her self-integrity.

Catherine Keller poses a question that several feminists ask: "How can we anchor this knowledge in consciousness and our consciousness in this knowledge?"[56] Or, how can we practice this pattern of be-ing a self so that we "experientially know . . . that neither our sisters and brothers nor the rest of nature is "the other"?[57] How can we dismantle the illusion of our separateness? Women discover the truth of inseparability through their praxis. They acknowledge the need to *act* out of a perception of interrelatedness so that such perception deepens. The feminist spiritual journey incorporates many forms of praxis in this regard: Women act to end classism and global poverty, especially the "feminization of poverty";[58] women challenge the racism within themselves and the social systems;[59] women confront the terror of nuclearism through peaceful protest;[60] women care for the earth and her creatures with ecological wisdom;[61] and women resist the divisions of sexual orientation.[62] Obviously, not all women engage in all of these activities. But this portrait indicates the feminist conviction that woman's self is one part of the life web. She is motivated to confront societal systemic forms of separation because they oppress—and sometimes destroy—so much life of which she is a part. Her own wholeness, her own integrity is radically connected with the quality of life on earth.

This is a difficult conviction to carry, especially if one is not poor, is not illiterate, or does not have a colorful body-spirit. The illusion of separation from others and the environment tends to harden according to the social power one possesses. Economic security, education, ethnic power, and social upward mobility tempt the belief that "I can make it on my own." Those of us who share some or all of the preceding categories do not automatically experience how the lifestyles or be-ing of others affects our own. We are "protected" by our privileges. My sisters in the inner city, though, save me from this deception. They have extraordinary clarity about the interdependence of be-ing. They know that self-survival is intimately connected with the patterns of selves who live outside their community. They open my eyes by their own perspicuity.

Many women find that meditation complements the praxis of crossing social boundaries and active care for the environment. It, too, increases their sense of oneness which in turn motivates self-development by laboring for the quality of the whole. Meditations are designed and practiced to "transform any feelings of separation we may hold"[63] so that woman's self experiences power through wholeness.

Equality with Others The wisdom of inseparability effects integrity within woman's self only if she experientially knows that she is equal to others. Otherwise, woman loses her ability for self-determination amid efforts to experience union with all. This is why the authors of *Sophia* argue:

> Religions traditionally oppressive of women and some theologians and philosophers who may be inactive in the concrete struggle for human liberation are still comfortable using a language of connectedness. Until women and people of color are fully accepted as equals within their own species, it will be difficult or even

> inappropriate for them to take as their first priority human oneness with all species or with the planet itself.[64]

Lifestyles of interrelatedness cannot sidestep the equality requirement. This is why those who are other than women and people of color cannot insist on "human" liberation and unity if they are not willing to treat all with equal regard. For woman, however, this means that consciousness of innate equality is the *sine qua non* for emergence of the self's uniqueness within relationship. Without it she tends to denigrate—therefore, fuse and lose rather than interconnect—her self if she feels inferior. This can often happen with men. As my opening story indicates, woman's relationship with man can be mutual only if each knows the equality that exists between them. Then the possibility of self-integrity through relationship emerges for both. Neither becomes fused in the other's identity as some form of partnership is explored.

—3—

Toward Mutuality With Others

Even a cursory glance at the classic works of Western spirituality uncovers a perennial interest in the self's relationship with others. Within the Jewish and Christian traditions, this relationship was usually characterized as "love of neighbor" and constituted a central ingredient in the spiritual pilgrimage. One's salvation was, to a certain extent, dependent on adhering to the second great commandment, "love your neighbor as your self." Loving God "with your whole heart" was not complete without the self's attentiveness to the neighbor.

A spirituality for feminists also highlights the significance of the self-other relation. As mentioned in the introduction, the praxis of imaging a whole world is dependent on mutually supportive relations between ourselves and others. Movement toward wholeness requires a particular kind of relationship—best characterized as *mutuality*—with a multiplicity of others. We have already seen that wholeness for woman's self centers on developing integrity within the complex web of her relationships. Now, however, it is time to sketch in finer detail the nature and variety of relation between persons that is needed for the health of ourselves and the earth.

Not "A Little Less Than Angels"

In choosing "mutuality" as an appropriate symbol to typify human relationship, I opt for a word that not only appears consistently in the literature of feminist spirituality, but also represents a reality that directly opposes the hierarchical relations found within dualism. One dictionary defines "hierarchy" this way:

1. Each of three divisions of angels; the angels.
2. Priestly government; organized priesthood in successive grades.
3. Organization with grades or classes ranked one above the other.[1]

As we recall, dualism images an essential separateness between God and humanity, between the individual self and others. It views *super*nature as superior to the natural realm, and sets up a "hierarchy of being" that identifies the value of each form of being in relation to the others. So, we have the classic ladder of God, angels, man, animals, plants, and so on. And, within the category of "man," human beings are valued according to gender, race, ethnicity, economic class, and other sociocultural categories. The hierarchical relation between the deity and humanity models how persons should be in relation to one another. Social systems guided by philosophical dualism organize human beings "with grades or classes ranked one above the other."

Within this overall schema, the spiritual path toward salvation or wholeness[2] requires "love of neighbor" in order to experience the rewards of ultimate union with God. However, such love can still happen in a hierarchical fashion. It does not necessarily challenge the "superior" and "inferior" status of individuals. In fact, "love of neighbor" for those who hold superior social positions (in terms of gender, race, economic class) effectively means that they should protect, care, and provide for those who are socially inferior. Likewise, the subordinate members of society are to cooperate with, receive from and respect (or obey) the privileged.[3] This kind of love relationship secures the separation of peoples, effectively maintaining the distance within social divisions.[4]

Dualism also sketches a real separation between history and eternal life. The "life hereafter" claims eminent value over "life here and now." Again, though humanity may possess some potential to effect change toward goodness and justice within history, this is viewed as a requirement for ultimate happiness, which only God can effect for each individual. The self's behavior toward another essentially saves neither the self nor the other. One's relationship with others does not really affect his or her experience of wholeness. That is between the self and God; it is God who provides freedom, transformation, and healing if we have observed God's conditions for it. Our love of neighbor in history makes possible the self's salvation *after* history.

All of this dramatically shifts within the worldview of interdependence proposed by feminists. We were not created separate from one another or God. The One who gives birth to humanity and the life of the earth does not dominate and judge creation from afar. The deity's intimate relationship with nature (inclusive of humanity) provides guidance and sustenance for the future of life within the natural cycle. Every living being holds its own intrinsic value. While varied complexities of life exist, the most complex forms are not independent of the life of simpler ones. Likewise, the vitality of humanity's natural environment is affected by our choices and lifestyles. Such interrelatedness requires a "give and take" between different kinds of being if life for all is to proceed.

And what about human beings' relationships with one another? Wholeness or health for the self cannot be experienced in isolation from others. A spirituality for feminists rejects an individualistic image of salvation. This means that it does indeed recognize "love of neighbor" as an indispensable activity for self-integrity. However, an interdependent consciousness radically shifts not only the meaning of such love but its character and fruits as well. Love for an other within an interrelated order points to a particular way of living. It originates in an awareness that what we do and who we are affect and are affected by the character and activity of the rest of the human community. This awareness both surfaces from and encourages a distinctive genre of self-other relationship. Whether the "other" is an acquaintaince, colleague, friend, lover, partner, sister, brother, mother, father; or whether the "other" is one who differs radically from the self's own sociocultural make-up, a mutually supportive relationship is necessary for genuine self-integrity.

The character of this relationship, then, does not leave the self or the "other" essentially unchanged. Openness to change is a requirement for mutual relationship. This means that we are willing to have our "superior" or "inferior" social status challenged. Men will need to let go of notions and feelings of preeminence in relation to women; it will be imperative for women to transform a diminished sense of self in relation to men. Persons who experience poverty or lack literacy skills cannot efface their selves in the presence of the economically secure and literate. Those who possess abundant material resources and the power of knowledge must confront the ways in which these social privileges promote an elitist self image. For any of this to happen, the self has to risk passage through social divisions. Then it is possible to discover knowledge of our true inherent worth without exaggeration or diminishment.

The crossing also puts us in touch with power that exists nowhere else. We enable one another to participate in the healing of history. Freedom for transformation holds value "here and now." Even though we may experience a different kind of wholeness after death, "love of neighbor" in radical mutual fashion makes an authentic healing of self and other possible now. A spirituality for feminists acknowledges the deity's initiation of and effective participation in this process, but the self's salvation is also somehow connected with the health of the human community. If we really are interdependent and one part of the whole, the brokenness of one or millions of others affects us in a fundamental way. If we really are one part of the whole, the healing of others is necessary for the health of self. The pursuit of mutual relationships is an indispensable step toward salvation understood in this manner.

What Makes a Relationship *Mutual?*

Webster's New World Dictionary defines "mutual" as something "done, felt, etc. by each of two or more for or toward the other or others" and something "shared in common; joint." So, two people could have mutual feelings of affection or mutual feelings of animosity toward each other. This definition barely resembles the multiple dimensions of meaning that the word acquires as women search for self-determination within an interdependent world. Let me gather those various pieces of meaning to sketch an image of the self-other relation in a spirituality for feminists.

Love and Mutuality

I have already hinted that the self's relationships with others have something to do with "love." Not only do we carry an awareness of "being an integral and inseparable part of the human . . . community,"[5] but we also realize that only *mutual love* can both nurture the self-integration process and heal the other. This is a love where self and other know and feel that each needs to receive as well as give for the wholeness of both. We are able to enter this kind of relationship because of the sensuality of our embodied selves. It is through our body-spirits that we are able to *feel* the intrinsic connection present between self and every other. Only as feelings deepen does our knowledge of interdependence increase. As our senses open, the societally-imposed separations break down and the self becomes free both to care for and be cared for by others.

Such love and care-fullness contain several features. Of prime importance is the *recognition of equal value* between the two people. My worth is equal to your worth; I value my self as much as I value your self. And yet how difficult this is to do. So much of the conditioning process encourages us to perceive ourselves as either better than or inferior to the person we are with. Though there are countless examples of this, I remember so clearly the day that I offered a lift to one of the women that I had been working with in Jobstown, West Tallaght. Patricia is a woman with extraordinary enthusiasm and is determined to make life better for herself and others despite a background of economic insecurity and learning disability. As we were driving down Dame Street toward Trinity College, she suddenly turned to me and asked, "What do you *do*, anyway?"

I told her that I lecture in Trinity. Immediately she started to look out the car window at the people walking on the footpath. When I asked her what she was doing, Patricia replied, "I'm looking to see if any of my friends are watching me drive through town with such an important person!" What a bittersweet moment that was for me. I felt proud to be with her; she felt privileged to be with me. And yet, the challenge of *equal* regard for the other lingered.[6]

For those of us with a certain amount of social power, "what needs to change is not just our words but our emotional need to prove ourselves superior."[7] This becomes possible as acceptance of and security with our own selves deepen. Self-love not only enables integration, its stillness of inherent satisfaction allows respect for the other to surface. Reverence for the other includes honoring our differences as well as our common features. While this solicits recognition that we are "different but equal," it does not mean that we determine the difference of the other. So often the preceding slogan simply masks the self's desire to specify the nature and role of the other.[8] Such a motive is strongly rooted in the self's assumption of superiority over the other, and the societal context usually encourages certain selves to assume more worth than other selves. Because society has this kind of impact on one's psyche, self-love must include a critical assessment of how the social order assigns value if it is to be the base of mutual love.

Equal regard and respect for the other also requires acknowledgment of differences in people's natural abilities. Some people are born with more intelligence, creativity, physical ability, artistic talent, etc., than others. Again, it is self-love that enables one to heed and applaud the gifts and talents of the other. Yet we consistently need to guard against the ways in which competitiveness within the present social order encourages comparison in relationship. Mutuality emerges only as we celebrate the other *without* denigrating our self. A former student of mine was once acknowledging the intellectual creativity of a friend and colleague, yet his remarks finished with: "I feel so *inadequate* in relation to her." By academic standards this young man is a very promising theologian; such a comparison, however, not only stunts his own creativity but also hinders the fruits of mutual relationship for both of them.

The pursuit of mutual respect amid difference in ability incorporates more than this kind of interpersonal challenge. The self's readiness to equally value every "other" is dependent on an awareness of how natural ability is often hidden or underdeveloped because of oppressive conditions. A woman whose formal education terminated at the age of fourteen may not appear immediately "intelligent." Here, respect for the other means an active attentiveness to the unique features that intelligence takes within the life of someone who had to quit school in order to support her family. So we see that respect for the other does not happen automatically; it is a process that usually requires considerable self-growth, especially development of a critical consciousness regarding social value. We may often need to challenge what society values in order to experience a profound honoring of the other. This, in turn, occasions a mode of self-growth that is simply not possible outside the context of mutual love.

Reciprocity is the central dynamic of such love. Several factors comprise reciprocal activity and feeling in a relationship that is mutual. The starting point is each person's willingness to be an active agent in the relationship. This means that neither person perceives the other as doing all the giving or all the taking. Instead, each one recognizes her or his ability to contribute toward as well as to receive from the goodness and bounty of the other. Though "reciprocal" is often taken to mean that one acquires virtually the same amount that one provides, the quantity factor loses its significance in mutual relationship. In fact, the benefits of such activity usually evaporate concern for "return in kind or degree" from the other, as each discovers unique ways of supporting the other.

This indicates a conversion of sorts taking place through the power (effectiveness) of mutual love. Because we receive so much through giving, it transforms our notion of what we had hoped to receive. This seems to be as true for intimate relationships as it is for relations between those of differing social backgrounds. I am quite struck by how often people say to me, "I gained so much more than I gave" when speaking of their involvement with people who lack social privilege. What is going on underneath such a statement? First of all, the act of "passing on our selves" to those outside our social circle challenges our perception of what these people possess within themselves. Why are we so surprised to prosper in the act of giving? Usually it has something to do with our preconceptions of what people who differ from us are like. The insightful, feeling-filled moment of our own gain enables sight of the other's dignity and wealth. Further, it also confronts an appraisal that it is better to give than to receive. As Elisabeth Moltmann-Wendel argues, "In the [mutual] relationship receptivity is again taken seriously as a basis of human experience."[9] Genuine mutuality requires willingness to allow the other a significant, equal agency within the relationship. This does not always happen during the initial encounter; an authentic reciprocal dynamic often takes time and faithful commitment.

Reciprocity in love likewise alters images of the nature and value of our own contributions to the other. Secure knowledge of the other's receptive presence enables us to risk self-gifts that we have not previously imaged. Reciprocity sets up a safe environment. Men can look for qualities other than courage, assertiveness, rationality, and leadership to give to women. Women can explore their abilities to administer, project budgets, take the intiative, and confront conflict within their relationships with men. Both women and men can alter their way of being with one another, sometimes needing an enormous amount of support and other times offering a solid sanctuary for the fragility of the other. Our gifts diversify and mature as they are unconditionally received by another. There exists one condition, though, for this kind of "give and take," and it is the willingess of both to be *vulnerable.* As Carter Heyward writes in her straightforward manner:

> Vulnerability . . . is the willingness and ability to be seen as well as to see, to be touched as well as to touch. Vulnerability is the giving up of control, the turning of oneself over to the common life, not to be absorbed, stepped on, or negated, but rather to experience ourselves as co-creators of the world we want and believe in.[10]

Vulnerability means that we let go of protective mechanisms that close us to the possiblity of being deeply influenced by the other. We allow others virtually to change our lives. At the base of this behavior is both the conviction and experience that we are essentially linked with one another; we *cannot* make it on our own.

The identified features that comprise mutual relationship come from the contemporary experience of feminists who live toward such a world. Yet they also claim that the vision and practice of mutual relations existed prior to their search for it in the twentieth century. Diverse spiritual traditions converge in their common concern for mutuality. For example, Elisabeth Moltmann-Wendel writes that "the stories about Jesus seem to be a still undisclosed source for 'mutuality,'"[11] and that the women disciples with Jesus exemplify "the dialogue of feelings, actions, remaining a person, recognizing the autonomy of the other person,"[12] necessary for mutual relationship. In a more radical fashion, Heyward puts forth an image of Jesus as one who loved with profound mutuality. Jesus himself did not contain all the power of God's redemption for the world; *with others* Jesus discovered the ability to heal and preach God's vision of justice. What are the consequences of such a story? "For we have here an image of a Jesus who needed friends, a Jesus who lived into the immediate and intimate dimensions of relation. *This image can reflect our own possibility.*"[13]

From the thealogical tradition, Starhawk and others speak about a time when hierarchical relation between individuals was not the predominant model for social interaction and change. Before the dualistic, mechanistic consciousness of patriarchy—encouraging relationships whereby individuals yielded "power-over" others—certain cultures and religious traditions supported cooperative relationships that were based on "power-from-within."[14] Because these cultures (Goddess-centered from paleolithic times, Native Americans, tribal peoples in Africa, Asia, and Polynesia) viewed the interrelatedness and inherent value of every being, each person carried the potential to affect the life of others; each person had the power of agency.

In a similar vein, Riane Eisler analyzes recent archaeological studies of early civilizations such as Catal Huyuk, in Turkey, the Balkans, and the Minoan civilization of Crete.[15] Here she discovers intimations of what she calls a "partnership" model of society; women and men cooperating with one another to create and nurture life. This provides a marked contrast to a "dominator" model of social relations similar to Starhawk's notion of "power-over," whereby a minority controls the majority, enforced through the potential of physical threat and warfare. Both Starhawk and Eisler are convinced that individuals, especially women, must view themselves as inherently valuable and worthwhile in order to discover the "power-from-within" that will affect and be affected by others in creating peaceful, just relations among individuals and within society. A history of mutuality and partnership should prove beneficial in such an attempt.

Intimacy and Mutuality

A spirituality for feminists prescribes mutual love as the ideal genre of human relationship. The ability to care for and be cared for by others through a reciprocal, equal sharing of our selves is a cardinal dimension of living toward wholeness. Other kinds of relationships develop within this generic form that provide immense sustenance in the spiritual journey. The word "intimacy," I think, aptly characterizes the core of such relationships. Heyward defines intimacy as "a fundamental bonding between persons' innermost senses of identity."[16] This may or may not include genital sexuality. Amid mutual care, people often move to a depth of relationship that sparks self-growth for both in a most unique way. While most of us would take this for granted, feminists are probing the experience and meaning of intimacy *within* a consciousness of interdependence, and beyond the patriarchal structuring of relations.[17] How can we be genuinely intimate—truly bonded with the core of another—without losing our selves or without subjugating the other? How can our closeness to another be a relation that frees instead of binds our self? Are the benefits of intimacy confined to the two selves or do they spill over into the lives of many others? Is it possible, even desirable, for women to be intimate with one another?

Female Friendship Feminist theorists have long recognized the ways in which patriarchy divided women and encouraged them to distrust each other. Within the liberation movement, "women discovered that the patriarchal conditioning that they had received, which taught them not to value other women, to see other women as competition for men's attention, and later men's protection, was destructive of their deepest selves."[18] And so, women began to bond with one another, intuiting that solidarity was an essential piece of fighting their "reduction to low caste."[19] Such bonding they named "sisterhood," and found that it was "powerful." But, as Janice Raymond insists, it is not enough simply to oppose patriarchy; women must also create a new world, a new culture to put in its place. She astutely queries: "How do women live in the world as men have defined it while creating the world as women imagine it could be?"[20] Though the answer includes several elements, it must contain the nurturing of *female friendship*.

This does not necessarily mean that women's mutual friendship with men cannot also be a source for a new culture to emerge. What it does mean—and I believe that women must state this baldly, *without* reservation—is that female friendship provides an invaluable wellspring, first, for woman's self and second, for the future of history. As Mary Hunt and others have pointed out, women's friendship with one another has usually been at the heart of their most effective political and social activity to change the world.[21] I have seen this time and time again in my own work both in Ireland and the United States. Women's intimacy with one another empowers not only the struggle against nuclearism, homelessness, global poverty, and racism, their deep care for each other consistently endows the imagination with a unique vision of peace, prosperity, and justice.

What, then, is female friendship all about? As with any friendship, it originates in the person's possession of a "self." To bond or connect with another—inclusive of feelings of attraction for and the desire to be present to—women must first love, admire, and be present to their own selves. Otherwise, the bond can slip easily into bondage or woman's self can be subsumed into the self of another. Janice Raymond puts it this way: "Female friendship begins with the companionship of the Self. Aristotle maintained that 'the friend is another self.' Until the Self is another friend, however, women can easily lose their Selves in the company of others."[22]

The starting point of female friendship is woman's affirmation of her self. This frees her, then, to be truly present, without fear, and with openness to discover the beautiful self of another woman. In her unique metaphorical fashion Daly describes this dynamic as "the moving presence of each Self [that] calls forth the living presence of other journeying/enspiriting Selves."[23]

This movement challenges what Raymond calls "hetero-reality." It critiques the patriarchal notion that woman was made from and for man; female friendship means that women choose to be for women. As I often point out in lectures and workshops, to be for women is not to be *against* men; it is simply to be *for* women. The need to make such a statement arises from the uncomfortableness that both women and men experience as they intuit that women for other women is indeed a countercultural activity. Hunt clearly outlines what is happening here: "Women's friendships deny the need for men to be central to every human exchange."[24] Instead, women can be "primary to each other."[25] Women can choose to put other women first, they can and do covenant with one another, promising reciprocal fidelity, honor, and affection that no one else can take away. Though this is experienced and lived differently by lesbian and heterosexual women, all women can choose another or several other female friends to be central to their lives. Whether the intimacy includes a sexual relationship or not, women's friendships affirm the beauty, delightfulness, utter uniqueness, and power of woman. And if the intimacy happens in mutual fashion, such beauty and power is bound to be released beyond the two women friends.

Female/Male Friendship Having witnessed the personal growth of hundreds of women as they participate in and contribute toward a feminist vision of reality, I think it safe to say that feminism shifts the patterns of women's friendships with men. As women come to their own distinctive power (see Chapter 2), this necessarily causes ripples (or waves) in their intimate relationships with men. Perhaps the major changes result from woman's desire for "a room of her own" or the psychic (sometimes physical) space to explore her own potential that is other than partner, wife, mother, or lover. This sparks a paradoxical dynamic of distance *within* the bond of friendship. From a distance the woman considers her social conditioning, her place within family and society, who she is in her self, and choice for a lifestyle that may or may not include a profession. Often women feel/know that such distance is imperative in order to break relational patterns of female focus on the male.

Needless to say, this holds immediate repercussions for the male friend. Social roles may become blurred as a woman seeks the reciprocity of space for self, especially if this has not before been part of the friendship. From the center of intimacy, she requires support and encouragement to be woman as she defines it for her self. This may mean that the man relinquishes preconceived expectations so that real respect for the other is operative. In a similar fashion, she too should provide the care-filled milieu that enables his free exploration of self. Conflict, pain, and misunderstanding are bound to be part of such a process. Because the interpersonal exchange takes place within a society of patriarchal rules, a genuinely mutual intimacy between woman and man is not straightforward by any means. Yet the experience of intimacy itself offers the vigor to keep moving toward it.

As patterns of female/male friendship shift, several people name "complementarity" as the new ideal. This term is used, I think, to suggest that interdependence should be part of women's friendships with men. However, it also carries connotations that women possess certain qualities that men need but do not have, and vice versa. It implies that the agenda for the friendship is set: Men bring the manly qualities, women bring the womanly qualities, and true human wholeness is achieved through such a bond. Man completes woman; woman completes man. Not only are these notions heterosexist and disparaging of the single lifestyle—and therefore unacceptable in a spirituality for feminists—they inhibit the free self-development of women and men. For these reasons "mutuality," not complementarity, best depicts the ideal of women's intimacy with men.[26] And mutual friendship between women and men is another essential component of a free and peaceful culture.

Friendship Across Social Divisions Over the years I have learned that nourishment for the spiritual journey often exists in worlds or cultures that are not my own. Several feminists claim that "building alliances across barriers" (Starhawk) or "building coalitions with those who are different" (authors of *Women's Spirit Bonding*) are indispensable activities within feminist spirituality. Starhawk writes: "To reconnect across the lines of our common differences of race, gender, class, religion, sexual orientation, physical condition, or appearance is the creative act that founds a new world."[27]

While I wholeheartedly agree with these convictions, I want to push them further by suggesting that *friendship* across social divisions must be part of our reconnections. Why? The "creative act that founds a new world" is an ongoing, complex process; above all this new world must have a sustainable place for everyone. We need an abundant amount of hope for such a "long haul." We need an extraordinary quantity of faith, courage, and patience to sustain the reconnections so vital to a world that does not sever the interdependent relations of people. To cross social divisions we have to move beyond the fear of difference and unfamiliar ground; we must learn to cope with conflicts that necessarily arise between people who have been conditioned to be separate from one another. Only the affection, intimacy, and loyalty of mutual friendship will invite us through the complexity and difficulty.

I am not proposing that we make friends with all those who are not like us; this is naïve as well as impossible. Yet, even the experience of one or two fundamental bondings between socially dissimilar selves dissolves like nothing else the conditioned need for hierarchical relations. While diverse praxis is imperative, there is no replacement for loving our way into the new world. Intimacy opens the doors of unequal cultures. It eases the conversion of "'going out of our minds' to enter the world of the other."[28] Once I am there, my socially powerful imagination receives another way of visioning the future of history. The empathy of friendship persistently seeps into and redirects my creativity. Our closeness provides courage to learn one another's language and culture.

It is true that this kind of intimacy is particularly scary. As Starhawk rightly remarks, those with privilege will feel guilty, those with suffering will feel anger.[29] Both these emotional/insightful states can paralyze or embitter us; we correctly fear the possibility of getting stuck on the journey. Birthing a new world, however, necessarily includes coming to terms with various forms of guilt and anger. We *will* have to move with both, shedding inappropriate forms while choosing creative action that frees us of appropriate guilt and is inspired by righteous anger. Friends can help us here. Faithfulness across divides keeps us going in the right direction. These friendships sustain the movement and offer a rare source of wisdom for correct discernment. Not all of this is a struggle, however. Festivity, utter delight, and pure refreshment of celebration spills out of as well as solidifies intimacy. The party "rules" of another culture may be different from our own, but making mutual merriment provides memories powerful enough to ameliorate socially imposed disrespect, unequal regard, and lack of reciprocity.

Committed Relationships Sometimes intimate friendships become committed relationships. Mutuality takes on additional dimensions within partnership. Commitment calls for a particular kind of give and take. In *Personal Commitments*, Margaret Farley offers a fine, highly nuanced analysis of the meaning and obligations of commitment. She helps us with two important questions.

1. *What is commitment?* Farley writes:

> Commitment, then, entails a new relation in the *present*—a relation of binding and being-bound, giving and being-claimed. But commitment points to the *future*. The whole reason for the present relation as "obligating" is to try to influence the future, to try to determine ourselves to do the actions we intend and promise.[30]

Commitment means that we promise to love the other in the future. We rightfully expect the other's future love. We intend reciprocal faithfulness to our promise. Commitment creates a context wherein the mutuality of intimate friendship is assured to continue. This necessarily affects the meaning of our relationship in the present. The joy of self-discovery, the absolute delight in another's beauty reach profound depths in the present promise of permanency. A sustained commitment claims presence and perserverance amid the most difficult conflicts and misunderstandings. Commitment assures the other and strengthens our self to love forever.[31]

2. *Does commitment limit our freedom?* This touches a previously raised question: How can our closeness to another be a relation that frees instead of binds our self? As Farley insists, the commitment to love "is the yielding of a claim, the giving of my word, to the one I love."[32] We do bind ourselves; the other has a right to expect the love we've promised. But, does such a permanent bond limit our freedom? Are we free to make *every* choice possible for self-growth? A simple "no" does not answer these questions. Farley outlines three significant points:[33] (1) Some commitments that we make do limit future choices. Life partnerships close off several other options. (2) Committed relationships, however, free us to actualize the possible in our lives. "When we are faced with mutually exclusive alternatives . . . we shall do nothing at all if we cannot commit ourselves to one and let the others go. Commitment limits self-process, but it is also what makes it possible."[34] While we do restrict our choices, self-growth—including the freedom to be whole and integrated—is indeed nurtured within the intentional milieu of lifelong mutual intimacy. And, paradoxically, commitment binds us to keep on freely choosing the other. (3) Once we have limited ourselves to the committed relationship, our journey toward wholeness takes on directions and dimensions that we could not have imaged outside of it. The ways in which the other insists that we be our best selves, receives our risks, demands our active presence, and hopes for ever deeper vulnerability evoke previously unimagined forms of healing. The consistent mutuality of supportive presence, especially during the most troubled times, contains the potential to call forth our most authentic selves.[35]

Mutuality within partnership also confronts the socially conditioned patterns of genital sexual relationships. Beverly Harrison makes the claim that

> ...we have very little sex which enhances our self-respect and sense of well-being, and simultaneously deepens our relations to each other. The truth is that we cannot have one without the other—deeper self-respect and deeper intimacy. We have little of either in this society.[36]

If sexuality within committed love is to be mutual, it must be both self-affirming and other-sustaining. This will not come to pass if one lover is the active agent and the other is the passive recipient. Both lovers must give as well as receive tenderness, attentiveness, and sexual pleasure. Committed love challenges each partner to perceive the other as equally active and receptive in sexual intimacy. This need not happen simultaneously; the timing is for each couple to care-fully discover for themselves. No doubt this will not be automatic, and it will probably change over time. At the heart of sexual intimacy, however, is the desire to wholly express and nurture the mutuality of committed relationship. Commitment, as described above, requires the same kind of vulnerability, openness, risk-taking, and trust at the level of genital sexuality as it does within every other dimension of the partnership.

Learning to Be Mutual

A spirituality for feminists affirms mutual relationship as the most appropriate way of living interdependence. Reciprocal respect and care for every other establishes the possibility of living from our own center while creating a life-supportive environment for others. As already indicated, this pattern is *not* the current formula for relationship in today's world.

Motivation

What, then, motivates us toward this way of being with an other (all others)? All feminists share the hope for wholeness, as described in Chapter 1. While this hope originates from diverse sources, it generates a common conviction that interpersonal patterns of hierarchical relations must be done away with if a new cultural order is to emerge. The practice of mutuality between individuals provides a powerful source to transform social systems that violate and enslave selves, especially socially powerless ones. The experience of mutual relationships nourishes our imaginations with insight toward a world of peace, justice, and freedom. Likewise, the experience sustains our hope for wholeness; we know that wholeness *is* possible as we move in and out of mutuality. Interpersonal healing *does* take place; visions for an interdependent world *are* imaged.

So we see that motivation for mutuality comes from feminists' common hope and present experience. Something else, though, inspires many feminists toward this way of being. Arising out of and inviting the human experience of mutual relationship is a new image of the divine-human covenant. The deity's relation with humanity has often been a model for relations between human persons. Certainly this is true within the Jewish and Christian traditions. Margaret Farley reminds us, however, that the model has been one "of a transcendent God in relation to a submissive people. Historically these patterns, then, have tended to be ones of superiority and subordination, command and obedience, initiative and response . . ."[37] There exists little mutuality in such a relationship. In Starhawk's words, it is a relation of "power-over."

Feminist theology rejects this as the prototypical relationship. Theologians re-image the divine-human relation with mutuality as a central characteristic. Farley offers an example of this in her re-interpretation of the Jewish and Christian covenant tradition. She contends that humanity's friendship with God is the essence of the covenant. "Since friendship requires a responding mutual love" humanity's intimacy with God cannot be forced.[38] Humanity is an active partner; we choose friendship with God through creatively discerning ways to be faithful to God's vision in history, and God receives these choices within Godself. Farley also intimates that God seeks some form of equality with humanity. "So far does the covenant story go in pointing to the goal of mutuality that it tells even of God's not fearing to 'empty' Godself, to make possible a kind of equality with the persons God creates."[39] Jesus brings the power of God's life to humanity.

Several feminist theologians view Jesus' life as a vivid portrayal of God's mutuality with humanity and God's call for humanity's mutual love of one another. Carter Heyward develops the thesis that Jesus' ability to heal and redeem depended on his mutual intimacy with the Creator *and* openness to the healing intimacy of others.[40] Elisabeth Schüssler Fiorenza and others observe that the Sophia-God of Jesus especially loves the socially powerless.[41] Jesus' own friendship with social outcasts challenges the powerful to live some form of equality with "the least." Rosemary Ruether describes the ways Jesus broke the societally-set hierarchical patterns of relation. It is this kind of activity that redeems, heals, and liberates humanity.[42] Jesus' vision and praxis invites others to do the same.

The Habits of Mutuality

Mutual love does not come easily for most people. Compelling visions and hopes still must be translated into direct action. We have to practice mutuality if we are to learn how to be mutual. We need to acquire certain habits—things that we do often, eventually with some kind of ease—to sustain a lifestyle of mutual relationships. A spirituality for feminists will include the following habits, to be practiced regularly:

1. Self-love
2. Taking our selves and one another seriously
3. Being present to our selves and others
4. Seeing the sacred in our selves and others
5. Acknowledging and respecting differences
6. Facing conflict
7. Participating in supportive communities.

We have already seen that self-love is the starting point of mutual love. The practice of presence—with serious intent—negates society's tendency to absent so many from the center of our care and concern. To see the sacred in our selves and others is to declare the inherent goodness and equal worthiness of all. Feminist theology takes seriously the *imago Dei* tradition. Feminist thealogy declares that we are the living body of the sacred; the Goddess is within. Mary Daly writes of the divine spark in each woman's Self. Perceiving sacredness as part of humanity is one spiritual habit that leads to another. As Janet Kalven states, "Seeing God/dess in the other, seeing the other as sacred, is the theological basis for respecting differences."[43] Valuing and receiving others as they are in themselves means to receive, love, and celebrate the difference. This no doubt generates conflict. Our participation in supportive communities provides safe space to face the conflicts and mend the brokenness that they cause. These communities—whether they be our homes, spirituality groups, covens, or women-church centers—are stabilized through our own search for wholeness within mutual love. They are built by and sustain this pursuit.[44]

Interdependent "love of neighbor" sunders our illusion of separateness. We cannot be healed by ourselves. The healing happens now, even as we anticipate future wholeness. Mutual relationships empower imagination of a new world, even as we live in the present one. Friendship animates politics; we cannot transform the world alone. In a spirituality for feminists, God can't do it alone either.

— 4 —

In the Presence of the Sacred

Nelle Morton (1905-1987) concludes her creatively evocative collection of essays, *The Journey Is Home*, with these sage words: "Maybe 'journey' is not so much a journey ahead, or a journey into space, but a journey into presence. The farthest place on earth is the journey into the presence of the nearest person to you."[1] The meaning of Morton's words is not readily apparent. True to her unique metaphorical style, she paints an image of "presence" that shatters our familiar notions of it and offers something new in its stead. In mining that "newness" Morton helps me to see in a sparkling way an implicit, though central, element of my prior reflections: A spirituality for feminists alters one's experience of presence.

As we have already seen, a consciousness of interdependence calls feminists to be present to themselves, others, and the earth in ways strikingly different from contemporary cultural norms. Presence to self empowers integrity. This in turn requires the mutual presence of others and a reverent sense of the earth. Such presence is often far from us, though, as we struggle to live against and through the patriarchal tide of dualism. Central obstacles for each form of presence have been religious symbols that encourage separation, distance, and subordination in humanity's relationship with the sacred. As feminists distance themselves from these symbols, they create a space within which they can sense the sacred anew. Yet this is a pain-filled process; it requires passage through the "dark night of the soul," an experience of the sharp absence of the God of their fathers. Many women have described to me their profound sense of loss and a corresponding inability to pray. Their courage to search for the presence of the Sacred amid such deep absence, however, is the wellspring of feminist sacred symbols and metaphoric imagery.

Both the transformation and replacement of patriarchal sacred symbols is rooted in this kind of "women's experience." Earlier, however, I noted that it is not sufficient to speak of a generalized notion of "women's experience" as we try to understand why some feminists reinterpret "God" and others leave it behind.[2] As Judith Plaskow and Carol Christ point out: "The experience of being a woman is inseparable from being the kind of woman one is."[3] So we must recognize that the particularity of each woman's experience contributes different facets to feminist imagery. A woman's ethnicity, race, culture, religious heritage, sexual orientation, and class interact with her gender;[4] the *whole* experience affects how sacred symbols function in *her* life and what they mean to *her*. Therefore, it is not possible to say with absolute certainty that any one sacred symbol is better than all others for all people.[5]

The content of "women's experience," however, is even more complex than this. The feminist shifting of sacred symbols and imagery is anchored in women's experience of self-integrity and interdependence. As women "hope for wholeness," all their patterns of relationship change; the shift in one affects a transformation in the others. When it comes to "God," we have seen how the search for self-integrity encourages women to re-image the divine within themselves. Or, growth in mutuality with others calls for a way of visualizing humanity's mutual interdependence with the Sacred. Now it is time to explore in much greater detail the ways in which women's experience of self-integrity and interdependence moves them through absence and empowers new forms of presence to the Sacred. Sometimes this presence is indistinguishable from other experiences of relationship, and sometimes it is not. "Naming the Sacred"[6] for most feminists, however, surfaces from within the experience of being present to something that moves within and beyond them, whether that "beyond" is a personal being or a life force that moves in and through every piece of spirited matter.

The Absence of God

There are several reasons why feminists can no longer pray to the God of their fathers. Earliest criticism analyzed the impact of male God-imagery on the psyches of women and the structures of society.[7] Though the biblical tradition contains some female imagery for God, the plethora of male images and their consistent appearance in official worship and doctrine legitimate male rule in society and promote female psychological inferiority.[8] The use of "God the Father" as the central—if not exclusive—image for the Christian God not only deifies the male on earth, but must also answer to the charge of idolatry. To use one image at the expense of all others (including traditional and contemporary imagery) suggests that God is *literally* a father.[9] Judaism is also subject to the accusation of idolatry if it continues to exclude female God-language.[10] We see, then, that the androcentrism of God-imagery impoverishes the Sacred and damages women.

As feminists continued exploring the reasons for their journey away from God,[11] several stated that God's power was unacceptable to them.[12] In her analysis of the different meanings of "power," Starhawk finds that "the God of patriarchal religions has been the ultimate source and repository of power-over."[13] God's power enables "him" to rule through domination.[14] The conception of God as Omnipotent One denies the power of humanity in the world and sustains the "power-over" behavior of many dominant groups. These ideas are bolstered by the imperialistic imagery of "God the King." As Gerda Lerner, Starhawk, and others have shown through analyses of history, archaeology, and myth, the Hebrew and Christian "King imagery" for God roots itself in Near Eastern mythology and the political history of kingship.[15]

Similar to the earthly king, God the King images a Being wherein all power for creation, sustenance, and protection is centralized. Feminists claim that such an image does not support human responsibility for the world. The King does not share his power. Likewise, the foundational biblical symbol "Kingdom of God" is problematic as the central way in which God's relationship with the world has been imaged.[16]

There is still another dimension of King imagery that feminists reject. Divine kingship means that God, like the kings on earth, may need military reinforcement to protect "his" kingdom. As Starhawk aptly demonstrates, the rise of historical kingship meant that "the war leader was now the permanent holder of political power . . . . Kings made war for glory and for profit—and war consolidated the power of kings."[17] King-imagery for God legitimates and sustains the power of the military. This is totally unacceptable in an age threatened with nuclear holocaust.[18] Furthermore, some feminists oppose a God who makes war in order to liberate "his" chosen people. Carol Christ designates the liberator of the exodus tradition as "Yahweh the Holy Warrior."[19] She argues that "the image of Yahweh as liberator of the oppressed in the exodus and as concerned for social justice in the prophets cannot be extricated from the image of Yahweh as warrior."[20]

God's absence was keenly felt, then, because feminists could no longer believe in the maleness, dominating power, kingship, and militancy of the divine. Paradoxically, they can also no longer accept the concept of an "absent God"; a God whose total Otherness and transcendence means that "he" is essentially separate from them, and that the gap between God and the world is infinite. The transcendence of God, as conceptualized by a theology and philosophy of dualism, means that God can never be an integral part of our history and an intimate presence in the nature-world's cycle of life and death. Mary Daly, Rosemary Ruether, Starhawk, Sallie McFague, Carol Christ, Carter Heyward, and many others have led feminists away from this kind of absent God. Indeed, their repudiation of a dualistic notion of transcendence has been and continues to be a central component of the feminist critique.

"So, What Is *Your* Image of God, Now?"

As an educator, I am keenly aware of the dramatic impact that this feminist critique can have on women's and men's relationship with God.

For many, it both confirms their own suspicions and prompts them to ask deeper questions. As it challenges and accompanies their religious *reflection,* it radically disrupts their *relation* with God. They, too, begin to confront the absence of God in their lives. Like the mystics, they enter a confusing and empty period wherein every trace of the Sacred appears to vanish.

This is the juncture where several people find themselves today. This is why I am often asked: "So, what is *your* image of God, now?" Though the questioner's intensity tempts an immediate response, I usually hesitate. There are several images that express my experience of being in the presence of the Sacred, but I am convinced that each woman and man must wander through her or his own feeling of absence *first,* in order to appropriate new imagery.[21] There are no shortcuts.

Yet, *how* does one do this? What sparks our imagination to sense a transformed Sacred amidst the emptiness? As an educator, these are central concerns for me. The question, "So, what is *your* image of God, now?," provides an insightful clue. There exists an integral connection, I think, between *image* and *presence.* When we are really present to someone or something, we are in a much better position to image that experience. Time spent with a friend where there are no preoccupations provides the raw material for an exquisite image of the relationship, whether it be through poetry, letter-writing, art, or song. Deep, centered presence to someone or something enables the eruption of our own imagery. At the same time—and this is particularly key for the role of imagery in spirituality—other people's images often guide us to the presence we seek. Other people's images often help us to name our own.

The passage through absence, then, opens as our senses—sight, touch, hearing, smell, and taste—intuit relatedness with the creative life-force and all reality. When do we experience moments of self-integrity and interdependence? Which images best capture the meaning of those moments? These questions comprise the spiritual discipline of feminist discernment that we must do for ourselves. Only when we have entered this process of "sensibility" can the sacred imagery of others beacon us toward a more intimate encounter.[22] So, if I tell someone what my imagery is, it may prove interesting but meaningless if their own senses have not opened. On the other hand, the images of others are a critical resource for unveiling Sacred presence in places and moments we may not otherwise look for.

Women within varied spiritual traditions imagine and intuit their way toward the Sacred. A spirituality for feminists is nurtured by this abundance of imagery, metaphors, and symbols. In making our own journey, I think it is essential to hear the imagery coming from those who share our spiritual heritage and from those who do not. Once again I propose that the hope for wholeness must incorporate truth discovered through sharing differences as well as similarities. This is not to say that we must all agree with one another. Rather, it is to propose that a consciousness of interdependence requires our affirmation of relationship within diversity. How can we experience the presence of the Other if we cannot converse with those who are other than ourselves? A central test of our hope for wholeness lies in our willingness to allow the imagery of others to evoke a form of Sacred presence that we cannot find within our own sphere. For example, as a Christian feminist, prayers addressed to "Goddess" may assist my encounter with a face of the Sacred that has been veiled by the Christian tradition. At the same time we must delve into our own histories and present experience, keeping in mind Nelle Morton's prophetic question:

> If we take our tradition (Jewish, Christian, Buddhist, Islamic, humanist, or what have you) with dead seriousness and remain faithful to it, will it push us beyond itself or draw us inward, separating us further from one another?[23]

Naming Sacred Presence

The feminist transformation of sacred symbols demonstrates both a *process* of interpreting sacred presence and a *content* of multiple images for the Sacred. Attention to *both* process and content places one in a better position to hear the meaningfulness of feminist imagery, especially if it does not come from her or his own spiritual tradition. Why do some feminists use the word "Goddess" to name the Sacred? Isn't she simply an idol of pagans? Why do others use "She" for the Sacred? Doesn't that fly in the face of a genderless God? These are just a few of the questions that feminist spiritualities raise. If unanswered, they may block our hearing of imagery that brings us toward the Sacred presence we seek. This is why a spirituality for feminists calls for a map that traces *how* feminists interpret the experience of Sacred presence as well as *what* names they use to re-present the Sacred. An understanding of these radical shifts in feminist spiritualities may help us to stay in one another's presence as we search for the Sacred.

In order to sketch this activity, we need to take another look at the nature of symbol and its relationship to image, metaphor, and concept. Though several feminist authors use the words "symbol," "image," and "metaphor" interchangeably, I think this is confusing as well as incorrect. Unraveling their meanings provides much needed clarification of the way feminists name and interpret the experience of Sacred presence. Furthermore, the choice to replace or restore symbol systems necessarily raises conceptual issues. These too demand attention.

Symbols of the Sacred

In Chapter 1 we identified the following characteristics of common symbols: (1) they are expressions of people's deepest feelings, attitudes, and values; (2) they arise from the unconscious; (3) they pick up meaning from diverse human experience and offer meaning back to us; (4) they have a life of their own; (5) they guide our lifestyle and behavior; and (6) they die if they hold little cultural relevance or lose power to direct people's future activity. We also said that while *sacred* symbols incorporate these characteristics, their distinguishing feature is to capture the human experience of feeling relatedness with the creative life-force and all reality.

These prior identifications are a good beginning, but the process of naming the Sacred after the feminist critique raises other critical questions. If symbols arise from the unconscious, do we have any control in shaping their meaning? Can we consciously choose a symbol other than "God" to express Sacred presence? Can we invent new symbols that will have the same power as the old? Are images of God symbols of God? These are not issues simply for the theologians, thealogians, philosophers, and hermeneutical theorists. They are live questions for feminists who are looking for ways to symbolize their experiences. For most this is a radical change, since religious symbols were usually received without question. Their own experiences never comprised the content of religious symbols. So, the constructive path is little traveled and there is need for some kind of markers on the way.

A History of Meaning Symbols carry a history of meaning; they are a "cumulative reality."[24] This is, perhaps, one of their most distinguishing traits when comparing them with images or metaphors. Symbols pick up meaning from diverse human experience over a long period of time. Catherine Keller, drawing on the interpretation theory of Paul Ricoeur and the theology of Nelle Morton, affirms that symbols "evoke a more stable order of experience" because they "signify a heavier weight of past experience and interpretation."[25] Their history bestows an established status on them. Consequently, their meaning does not change easily, and, as we have already seen, they contain the power to guide our lifestyle. The symbol "mother," for example, is solidly rooted in our cultural and personal psyche; its meaning shifts very slowly because of its established character. Our own experience of mothering or being "mothered" is largely influenced by what "mother" has meant throughout the history of our culture and social order. So, too, when it comes to the symbol "God." Our own experience of relationship with "God" is significantly affected by the meaning that past peoples have given to "God." "God" comes with a very heavy history. Our God-relationship is necessarily tied to—influenced by—this cumulative meaning of "God." Symbols bind us, then, to the history from which they arise.[26]

A Surplus of Meaning In developing a theory of religious symbols, several authors refer to the work of Paul Tillich. Carol Christ and Anne Carr, for example, affirm Tillich's assertion that religious symbols provide us with access to the transcendent; they are a dynamic path to the Sacred. We need symbols of the Sacred, then, to draw us into participation with transcendent reality, a reality that is distinguishable but not separate from humanity and the world.[27] Symbols such as "Yahweh," "the Blessed Mother," "shalom," "Jesus," and "Earth Mother" have empowered varied peoples throughout history to be in the presence of the Sacred. Furthermore, sacred symbols should participate in the reality that they signify. This means that a symbol for the Sacred must re-present *authentic* characteristics of the Sacred. This is a key point. If a symbol is sacred because it truly re-presents the Sacred, then the choice of *which* symbols can do this becomes a central concern. Will the traditional symbols "God," "Holy Spirit," "covenant," and "Passover" always re-present the Sacred? Even if they did in the past, can they continue to do so?

These are keenly felt questions for feminists. Answers may be found if we investigate another significant characteristic of sacred symbols:

The symbol itself *never* can be fully identified with the reality it represents. Anne Carr insists that "the transcendent or unconditioned always transcends every symbol of the transcendent."[28] The sacred symbol is not the Sacred itself. Not even "God" re-presents all of the transcendent Sacred. This may appear blasphemous, but the Jewish and Christian traditions have always held that the Sacred *cannot* be captured fully in any human symbol. There is always more to the Sacred than the symbol's meaning. There is always more to the Sacred than "God," or "Jesus," or "Yahweh." Likewise, there is always more to the Sacred than "Goddess."

This lack of identification between symbol and referent[29] brings us to the crux of how symbolism operates in feminist spiritualities. In order to elucidate this process, Anne Carr refers to Paul Ricoeur's analysis of a symbol's "surplus of meaning." The sacred symbol's surplus contains what Ricoeur calls "regressive" and "progressive" elements.[30] The regressive component of symbol is meaning that does not truly re-present the Sacred. Because it is the nature of symbol to pick up meaning from diverse human experience, it is possible that some of the meaning is false as well as true. Within patriarchal history, for example, "God" has contained the meaning male and not female. Therefore, this is a regressive element of the symbol "God." One of the tasks of feminist theology, according to Carr, is to identify any regressive meanings of "God" and reject them. But how does one determine what is "regressive?" Carr implies that we must analyze how the meaning (e.g., the maleness of God) functions in history. The meaning must be left behind if it functions to "denigrate the humanity of women."[31]

The "progressive" element of sacred symbols refers to "the genuinely transcendent meaning of symbols . . . ."[32] If the symbol participates in the reality that it signifies, it holds an abundance of *truthful* meaning (though this may often be obscured by the symbol's regressive elements). The second task of feminist theology, then, is to restore truthful meaning to the symbol. Once again, the truth of the meaning is determined according to how the symbol operates in history.

Yet, how can biblical feminists claim that "God" contains truthful meaning about the Sacred while simultaneously acknowledging the symbol's destructive dimensions? As Carr astutely asserts, religious symbols have been *life-giving* as well as detrimental for many historical and contemporary women. In spite of the exclusive maleness of "God," many Christians have felt empowered to be liberators, prophets, and care-takers of humanity and the earth. For example, Elisabeth Schüssler Fiorenza demonstrates that the "God" of early Christian communities invited relationships of mutuality between women and men, poor and rich, slaves and free.[33] Their worship of the "God" of Jesus encouraged women's liberation and leadership. Their "God" (whom Schüssler Fiorenza names Sophia—the Greek word for wisdom) challenged them to have an inclusive table community; the table of Christians should have enough food for *everyone*. Because the "Sophia" God of Jesus was concerned about those who were least or last in the social order, so too should those who follow Jesus. This "God" envisioned all of humanity to experience and care for the bounty of the earth. Likewise, feminist historians such as Rosemary Ruether, Eleanor McLaughlin, and Francine Cardman have documented Jewish and Christian women of the past who were powerful and prophetic in the presence of the Sacred they named "God."[34]

The polysemic nature of "God" (that is, the symbol "God" holds multiple meaning, acquired throughout history), coupled with the ways in which their human experience has empowered meanings of this symbol, prompts several women today to restore transcendent meaning to "God." Rooted in their contemporary experience of self-integrity and interdependence, Jewish and Christian women cull their sacred stories to discover a "God" who will sustain the be-coming of woman and the interrelatedness of all. Let us examine a few examples of this restorative work.

Rosemary Ruether lifts up the prophetic element of God's meaning within the tradition. "God" is the one who consistently calls for humanity to struggle against the acquisition of privilege within the status quo. "God" sides with social outcasts; so too should the followers of "God." She also claims that the "God" of her heritage can be described as

> ...the Holy Wisdom who is the foundation of our being/new being [and] does not confine us to a stifled, dependent self nor uproot us into a spirit trip outside the earth. Rather he/she leads us to the converted center, the harmonization of self and body, self and other, self and world. She/he is the *shalom* of our being.[35]

Here we see that "God"—imaged as Holy Wisdom and shalom of

our being—signifies a power that sustains and harmonizes all forms of life. This "God" impels humanity to hope for wholeness.

In probing the Hebrew and Christian Scriptures, Letty Russell discovers a God who partners with humanity to bring forth a new creation. Jesus Christ reveals such a "God" by inviting his followers to establish *koinonia* (mutual relationships) through living life in common. Because God partners with humanity, Christians are called to partner with one another in order to establish justice, peace, and freedom for all.[36] But the struggle for liberation through just relations involves considerable suffering, as many women know. Anne Carr notes that biblical sources reveal a God who *suffers with* humanity throughout this process. Even though "one does not know fully what it means to say that God suffers in the suffering world," this meaning for the "God" symbol is "revealed in the symbol of the cross, a central Christian symbol and an important one for Christian women who experience the pain of exclusion and denigration in their own religious heritage."[37] Once again "God's" meaning functions as a way to guide behavior and lifestyles in human experience. Though not to be intended for its own sake, suffering seems to be a constitutive component of establishing peace and freedom in the world. Along with liberation and political theologians, Carr claims that the partnership between God and humanity means that both will continue to suffer.

It is God, however, who ultimately sustains journeying toward the new creation of which Russell speaks. Marcia Falk provides a provocative example of restoring this meaning to the "God" symbol. She has composed *b'rakhot*—new blessings in Hebrew and English—by selecting biblical images and metaphors that correct Jewish over-reliance on imperialistic imagery for "God." She records:

> When I set out to compose a blessing to be said before eating, I considered the traditional blessing over bread: *Barukh atah adonay eloheynu melekh ha-olam/ha-motz; lehem min ha-aretz,* "Blessed are you, Lord our God, king of the world,/who brings forth bread from the earth."
>
> . . . the formulaic God-images opening the traditional blessing struck me as particularly inappropriate to the occasion. For it was certainly not as "lord" or "ruler" that I apprehended divinity at the moment before beginning a meal, but as nurturer, the source of all nourishment.[38]

So she culled the Hebrew Scriptures to find more appropriate imagery for this meaning. In Deuteronomy 8:7, Falk found what she was looking for and wrote the following prayer to bless the bread: "*N'varekh et eyn ha-hayyim/ha-motziah lehem min ha-aretz,* 'Let us bless the *source of life*/that brings forth bread from the earth.'"[39]

We can see from these selected examples that biblical feminists are restoring "progressive" elements to the "God" symbol. For them, "God" contains a surplus of meaning rich with imagery and metaphors that empower the hope for wholeness in today's world. Therefore, the "surplus of meaning" theory regarding sacred symbols holds a great deal of truth for some feminists. However, not all symbols continue to hold a surplus of meaning for everyone. The rhythm of regressive/progressive elements in sacred symbols is often shattered as some feminists find traditional symbols simply regressive and lifeless. Mary Daly, Starhawk, Carol Christ, and the women they represent would argue that the regressive elements of the symbol "God" have been so destructive in their own lives and society that its progressive elements are bankrupt. The ways "God" has and continues to function in persons' psyches and social systems means that the surplus on "God" has run out. For some, the "redemptive"[40] power of the symbol "God" has expired; "God" no longer draws them into participation with mystery and transcendence.

The fact that sacred symbols do not have an infinite source of "progressive" elements for all people is further substantiated by Caroline Bynum's insistence "on the complexity of symbols." With Ricoeur's interpretation theory she reasons that people appropriate symbols in very different ways.[41] Not only does a symbol contain various levels of meaning, each person may find different meanings in the same symbol. Bynum says, "meaning is not so much imparted as appropriated in a dialectical process whereby it becomes subjective reality for the one who uses the symbol."[42] This is to argue that our human experience radically affects the way a symbol will mean—and function—in our own lives and the world we live in. However, Bynum doesn't appear to accept the possibility that certain human experience may eventually extinguish the "surplus of meaning" that symbols contain. Like Ricoeur, she implies that symbols always hold potential to refer to the reality that they re-present[43]—the "beyond" toward which they point is openended. I disagree. "By taking female symbol-users seriously"[44] it is evident that some sacred symbols lose their open-endedness for some people.[45] For many feminists, the Sacred's "surplus" will only be restored if the symbol is *replaced*.

But if symbols are replaced, does this mean that they can be generated at will? If "God" loses its redemptive power can we create new symbols that will participate in Sacred reality? Most of our authors—including myself—accept Tillich's assertion that symbols grow out of the unconscious; they cannot be produced artificially. We receive sacred symbols, yet consciously shape their ongoing meaning and function. Although Carol Christ claims that feminists are creating the symbol "Goddess,"[46] I believe she is *receiving* "Goddess" as a symbol arising from the unconscious of an evolving feminist culture. *Because* the symbol has surfaced in the lives of contemporary feminists, they are able to interpret its meaning. And in this way "Goddess" replaces "God." To the extent, however, that the "Goddess" was dead—dismembered by a patriarchal culture—Christ and others are creating or re-creating her.

The rebirth of the "Goddess" symbol begins as women go "in search of Her."[47] Some begin the journey with a powerful personal experience of the Sacred within. Carol Christ describes it as "the night when I expressed my anger at God and heard a still, small voice saying 'in God is a woman like yourself. . . .'"[48] For others, their experiences of female power through self-integrity lead them to name the Sacred "Goddess."[49] Merlin Stone's work has been very influential in the symbol's rebirth. Several years ago she said, "At the very dawn of religion, God was a woman. Do you remember?"[50] Stone's claim—and question—prompted feminists within various disciplines and from diverse religious backgrounds to remember the God who was woman. Starhawk, Carol Christ, Charlene Spretnak, Christine Downing, Naomi Goldenberg, and others have studied the myths, prayers, and archaeological artifacts of ancient peoples who worshiped Goddess as supreme. The archaeological research of Marija Gimbutas and James Mellart, and the cultural and historical studies of Gerda Lerner, Riane Eisler, and Monica Sjöö and Barbara Mor provide increasing evidence of Goddess as the primary sacred symbol of paleolithic and neolithic peoples.[51]

Paleolithic art furnishes important "psychic records" of the ways these people interpreted the mysteries of life and death. Riane Eisler surveys the archaeological findings of this period. The imagery in wall paintings, cave sanctuaries, and burial sites all suggest that "an integral component of [the paleolithic] sacred tradition was the association of the powers that govern life and death with woman."[52] They also indicate a belief that humans, animals, and all other forms of nature emerged from the same life source. And the imagery re-presented ancient people's wonderment with the awesome mystery of "the fact that life emerges from the body of woman."[53] Sjöö and Mor's work contains two striking images from this period: a rock drawing of a woman giving birth, from Sha'ib Samma in Yemen, and the Venus of Laussel, from Dordogne, France.[54]

Paleolithic imagery of the link between woman and the mysterious powers of life and death may be early representations of the highly developed Goddess religion of Neolithic peoples. Marija Gimbutas's collection of neolithic imagery (6500-3500 B.C.E.) leaves little doubt regarding the primacy of "Goddess" as the "Giver and Taker of Life." Some images show the Goddess begetting her son, often represented as a bull. Gimbutas suggests that whereas the feminine principle—namely, Goddess—represented the creative force, the male principle—often imaged as a bull or divine son of Mother Goddess—represented the stimulating force, without which nothing in nature would grow or thrive.[55]

Everything comes from the womb of Goddess, including maleness. In this sense, then, the Goddess reigned supreme, even though several scholars argue that this did not mean that women dominated men within the social history of these times. One of the remarkable things about neolithic imagery for the Sacred was the use of animals to represent different aspects of Goddess. Bees, serpents, butterflies, and birds are just some of the images associated with Goddess. She is the Lady of the Animals, life-giver and care-taker of all. Her intimate relationship with natural life is further imaged in reliefs and sculptures of the Bird Goddess and the Snake Goddess. Amid such abundance of imagery, Gimbutas offers the following interpretation:

> There were, in my opinion, two primary aspects of the Goddess (not necessarily two Goddesses) presented by the effigies. The first is "She Who Is the Giver of All"—giver of life, of moisture, of food, of happiness—and "Taker of All," i.e., death. The second aspect of the Goddess is her association with the periodic awaken-

> ing of nature: She is springtime, the new moon, rebirth, regeneration, and metamorphosis. Both go back to the Upper Paleolithic.[56]

She is Creator, Mother, Virgin, Maid, Crone, and She has many names. She gives life, She takes life; She is the source of birth and rebirth.

This Goddess and all her imagery were suppressed by the powerful force of patriarchal cultures.[57] "But though the Goddess suffered, she was never destroyed. And though her memory was denigrated and hidden, it was never forgotten."[58] Starhawk maintains that an oral tradition of Goddess sacred stories was passed on throughout the ages.[59] The Wiccan tradition continues today as Starhawk and others interpret Sacred presence with the imagery of Goddess. There are several reasons for this choice of imagery. Primary among them is their belief that the sacred symbol Goddess has been reverently filled with the concrete imagery of nature as a way of affirming Sacred presence *within* the natural cycle of life and death. Starhawk says:

> To Witches, the cosmos is the living body of the Goddess, in whose being we all partake, who encompasses us and is immanent within us. We call her Goddess not to narrowly define her gender, but as a continual reminder that what we value is life brought into the world.[60]

Unlike the symbol "God" of patriarchal culture, Goddess unequivocally affirms the immanence of the Sacred in every form of spirited matter. She re-presents the experience of interconnectedness and the acceptance of death as part of the natural cycle. While she exists within, she is also a personal power who is consistently invoked in prayer and ritual. The rituals of witches demonstrate their belief that Goddess hears and responds to their prayers.

A personal Goddess who symbolizes the sacredness of nature is not only rooted in ancient traditions but is also discovered within the experience of struggling for a world without weapons. A deep reverence for life is demanded from those who pray to Goddess. This is a central meaning of Goddess for Carol Christ as well. Only Goddess appropriately symbolizes her conviction and experience that the earth is holy. She records:

> I found in Goddess spirituality an image that affirmed my own experience of the holiness of nature as a significant element in the divine reality.
>
> To me, Goddess is a symbol of the waxing and waning, life and death powers that are reflected in all human activities. To me, Goddess is a symbol for my connection to nature and for my creative processes that lead to cultural activity . . . .[61]

Both Christ and Starhawk provide clear examples of the ways in which meanings of the ancient symbol Goddess are appropriated in the lives of contemporary women. Their concern with the threat of nuclear holocaust encourages the choice of a symbol that re-presents the Sacred's presence within life on earth.

The Goddess symbol contains several other meanings for those who name her to re-present the Sacred.[62] Perhaps the most significant meaning is the most obvious one: "Goddess" re-presents the sacredness of woman. At the end of her analysis of Hindu female deities as a resource for the rebirth of "Goddess," Rita Gross concludes: "As I look at her now, what seems most significant is . . . her sheer presence *as female*. By being there as female she validates me as I am. It is good to be in the image of the Goddess."[63] "Goddess" signifies the goodness of female power. In the presence of "Goddess" many feminists feel valued *as woman* and experience inclusion within Sacred life as they never have before.

As we can see, the symbol(s) one uses to name the Sacred is indeed a complex activity. There is a radical challenge in all of this, though, that moves beyond the issue of personal choice or particular human experience. In a spirituality for feminists, *the language we use and how we use it must encourage interdependent living.* Will a restored "God" and/or recreated "Goddess" do this for our culture? This is a question that all feminists must keep to the fore.

Images and Metaphors

Perhaps one reason why few authors distinguish *symbol* and *image* is because they share certain characteristics. Images, like symbols, often arise from the unconscious, impact our behavior, and function in different ways for different people. In addition, images sometimes become symbols, as in the case of "mother." Our culture gives us the symbol "mother" that merges with our own image of what "mother" means. There are some differences, however, that are important to point out in weaving a theory of naming Sacred Presence.

Images Shape Symbols of the Sacred We do not receive sacred symbols baldly; they come to us filled with the concrete content of imagery.[64] "God the Father," "Christ the King," the "Blessed Virgin Mary," "Yahweh the Liberator," and "Mother Earth" are just a few examples of the ways images have shaped the meaning of symbols. Much of the feminist critique questions the imagery coupled with sacred symbols. A central concern, as we have seen, is how the use of imagery limits the Sacred and diminishes woman. So, feminists return to sacred stories and—guided by their hope for wholeness—select imagery for sacred symbol(s) that will sustain their hope. This is not enough, however. Another step is called for in shaping sacred symbols, whether this involves restoring or replacing them. A spirituality for feminists compels an attentiveness to imagery surfacing within the contemporary experience of presence to the Sacred.

How do we image new presence to the Sacred? How do we image something *new* ? To understand this process, we must take a few steps backward. Very early in life, we receive images from our unconscious, some of which are God-images. How do these images find their way to the unconscious? This is an extemely complex psychological process. Nelle Morton refers to the work of Jean Piaget, which provides certain clues: "Jean Piaget observed that a child forms an image out of her imitation of that outside which imposes a concrete value, style of life, or perception of reality on the child."[65] These cultural images then somehow become part of the unconscious and may remain there for life unless the person consciously affirms the imagery or attempts to exorcise it. For example, in a patriarchal culture, male imagery has been valued over and against female imagery for God. As children, we take this imagery in at an unconscious level. If it remains within our unconscious, it guides our valuing of maleness over femaleness in countless subtle ways. As Catherine Keller says, "Inasmuch as they [images] function as unconscious cultural implants they prefabricate our consciousness."[66] If we bring this imagery to consciousness instead, we can choose to affirm or reject it.

Rejection of cultural and religious imagery is again an intricate and lengthy process comprised of at least two dynamics. The first is a conscious awareness of the detrimental effects of certain imagery. This may be obtained through theoretical study as well as psychological and social analysis. In these ways we can identify or isolate images that deaden our own selves and/or the direction of life within society. The second dynamic involves the actual shattering of oppressive imagery. Nelle Morton claims that "concepts can be corrected and changed, not so images. They must be shattered or exorcised."[67] Although she does not explicate *how* this happens, her autobiographical stories contain an important clue: Imagery within us can be exorcised by hearing the imagery of others. Morton records a poignant element of her own story that demonstrates this kind of exorcism. This is what she says about the experience of viewing Emily Culpepper's short film "Period Piece":

> When Emily's vulva was flashed on the living room screen all my Southern primness surfaced. She could have used a picture from a book on physiology! I guess that is what Emily thought too. She too is Southern. It wasn't a picture of some unknown woman she had to deal with. It was herself. By the time the first "pure red blood" dropped from her vagina I was in tears. In one brief moment she had shattered the deep internalized patriarchal image within me, and I *knew*, not from my head but from the pit of my stomach, what Judy Chicago, Adrienne Rich, and Emily Culpepper were saying to me. . . . I knew that if ever I laughed at a "dirty" joke or condoned pornography in any way I would be laughing at myself and making my sacred images more distorted. I am indebted to these women and others who have made me see more clearly.[68]

Morton's patriarchal image of "woman" was shattered as she viewed Culpepper's self-identified image.

But how was Culpepper's image formed? *Emily was present to her self.* She opened all of her senses to a self with integrity and discovered a radically different image of "woman" from what she had received from a patriarchal culture. Morton reminds us that "deep in the experience itself is the source of *new* imaging."[69] Deep in *her* experience of menstruation, Culpepper sensed a *new* image of woman that shattered the old. The importance of our senses cannot be underestimated. As Keller notes: "The image, one might say, is the sensuous face of human expression. In the image sensory experience in the world has been taken into depth, made the object of imagination."[70]

As we said above, shaping sacred symbols requires an attentiveness to imagery that surfaces within the contemporary experience of presence to the Sacred. An experience of transformed presence happens, though, through sensing and imagining something new in relation to our selves. Sacred imagery expresses *relationship* with the Sacred, not the Sacred's inner nature. Presence to a powerful, integrated self or presence to the majesty of trees in a forest precedes words that describe an image of Sacred presence.[71]

Moving beyond Piaget, Morton insists that "an image is *not just* a picture in the mind's eye but a dynamic through which one communicates publicly or which communicates oneself."[72] This dynamic is what I am calling "presence," and it prompts an abundance of words (or artistic representations) that shatter old images and draw us toward the reality underneath the image.

Nelle Morton records several examples of how this happened in her own life. Let us consider one of them.

In 1976 Morton boarded a plane to New York. She describes the terror she usually feels when flying, but this day it was particularly bad because the sky had turned dark and they were experiencing significant turbulence. In times past, she would pray to God the Father to keep the plane safe. However, this day she experienced a turning point in her spiritual journey.

> The thought came—what would happen if I invoked the Goddess! How does one call on the Goddess anyway? And which Goddess? I no sooner had such a thought than I leaned back in my seat and closed my eyes. Suddenly, it was as if someone had eased into the vacant seat next to me and placed her hand on my arm. "Relax," she said. "Let go of all your tightness. Feel your weight heavy against the seat and your feet heavy on the floor. The air has waves as does the ocean. You can't see them, but if you let yourself be carried by them you can feel their rhythm—even in turbulence. . . Let yourself become a part of the rhythm."
>
> I did as she directed. Fear left my muscles. I did indeed feel the rhythm. Soon, I was enjoying the ride. . . .

She had gone. I began to feel such power within, as if she had given me myself. She had called up my own energy. I was unafraid. Nor have I been afraid in a plane since that day.[73]

Morton's story exemplifies—even at the beginning—her presence to a self with integrity. To be true to her self, she knew that she could no longer call on "God the Father" to save the day. This integrity prompted the choice of another image—Goddess—to re-present the Sacred's protection of her. As she experienced the image, Sacred presence no longer meant parental protection. Rather, the Sacred invited her to find a power within that would effect relaxation. The image "Goddess" had transformed her experience of Sacred presence.

Carter Heyward also offers several examples of new imagery surfacing for the Sacred she names "God." Her writings depict how the experience of mutual, reciprocal relationships led her to image God as "co-creator" (instead of Creator) and "power in the relation" (instead of the "All-Powerful"). Heyward's mutual, passionate presence to others in the struggle for justice enables her to image and know that God's presence happens when humanity loves one another. Her experience also enables her to image and know that God's presence does not happen when relationships are violated and humanity is too afraid to use its creative power. The following poem contains words that express her experience of this new imagery:

Violation of Relation
We are afraid
to see
the world
We are afraid
  to know humanity

The world is created by us, we who are friends of God, we who make God in-carnate. We are afraid to bring God to life.

Co-creation is our effort to live and die together, a mutual effort, enabled by a common choice, effecting common benefit. We are afraid to be common. We are afraid to live and die . . .

> Co-creators, we god in love, a common awareness that no one of us is alone, and that in the relation between subject and subject, there is power. We are afraid to be alone, we are afraid to be together, we are afraid of power.
>
> Our power is effective. We are afraid to be effective.
>
> Our power is good. We are afraid to be good.
>
> We god toward justice, moved by and moving the God given voice by the prophets, the God moving transpersonally in history, by us, through us. We are afraid of justice, we are afraid of the prophets, we are afraid of history.
>
> So it is in the beginning. We are afraid to re-member ourselves.[74]

These are words that shatter old images and draw Heyward and others toward the reality of a transformed Sacred presence amid the imagery. The imagery "we begin to speak will round out and create deeper experiences for us and put us in touch with sources of power and energy of which we are just beginning to be aware."[75] These images, rooted in the concrete experience of presence, shape the meaning and function of sacred symbols in our lives.

It is important to remember that sacred symbolic imagery operates in different ways for different people. The same words take on different meanings for people with diverse backgrounds and experiences of the world. Linda Mercadante brings to our attention that "choices of imagery that may be understandable from a white perspective, may be quite alienating when viewed from a black perspective. . . .For instance, it is a distinct advantage for a group with little power in society to know that a powerful God is on its side."

In contrast to the immanent sacred imagery of white feminists, "the transcendence and independence of God means that no matter how powerful the forces of evil, no matter how hopeless-looking the situation, God has the latitude to maneuver and is free enough to clearly perceive and work out the ultimate plan."[76] Naming the Sacred together is as important as naming the Sacred out of our own individual experiences. A spirituality for feminists requires it even though we barely see the horizon where it will lead.

Metaphor: A Special Kind of Image Metaphors are often the most appropriate language for interpreting our experience of transformed Sacred presence. Metaphors are a unique genre of image and they shape sacred symbols in more revolutionary ways than non-metaphoric images. Morton tells us that "an image cannot become metaphoric until it is on its way. . . . "[77] Metaphors both express and enable *movement* in an experience of presence. The dynamism contains two related activities: Metaphor (1) breaks apart a culturally acceptable image of the experience and (2) offers a radically different way of imagining presence.[78] Both the choice for and the use of metaphoric imagery interrupt the power of past symbolic imagery and provide another way of viewing reality. Morton speaks of the "iconoclasm" of false or oppressive imagery and the "epiphany" of a new horizon. "God as Mother," "God as Partner," "God as Lover," are examples of metaphors that may exorcise past symbolic imagery of the Sacred and invite a new form of presence. But metaphor only encourages this type of movement because one feels tension between the image (for example, "mother") and the referent (for example, "God"). The tension exists because "metaphor always rubs some fresh possibility against some status quo. . . ."[79] This is why for Morton, "God the Father" no longer contains metaphoric power.

This brings us to a central concern of all feminist spiritualities. Will our male image of the Sacred, so inextricably bound to the traditional sacred symbols, truly be shattered without using some female metaphors to name Sacred presence? Several feminists within diverse spiritual traditions argue that we must name God "She," and/or the Sacred "Goddess," in order to exorcise the male "God" that has taken hold of all our imaginations since childhood.[80] In proposing the use of female God-language in a Jewish context, Rita Gross writes:

> Why does everyone cling to the masculine imagery and pronouns even though they are a mere linguistic device that has never meant that God is a male? *If we do not mean that God is male when we use masculine pronouns and imagery, then why should there be any objections to using female imagery and pronouns as well?* [81]

Along with several others, Gross insists that use of the female pronoun to refer to God is needed to shatter our unconscious image (and belief) that God is exclusively male, though our theology tells us "he" is not. Naomi Janowitz and Maggie Wenig offer an example of metaphoric iconoclasm and ephiphany in the following Sabbath prayer:

> Blessed is She who spoke and the world became. Blessed is She.
> Blessed is She who in the beginning, gave birth.
> Blessed is She who says and performs.
> Blessed is She who declares and fulfills.
> Blessed is She whose womb covers the earth.
> Blessed is She whose womb protects all creatures.
> Blessed is She who nourishes those who are in awe of Her.
> Blessed is She who lives forever, and exists eternally.
> Blessed is She who redeems and saves. Blessed is Her Name.[82]

If the Sacred's true essence is beyond gender, why should we not drop the use of pronouns, or use "it" to refer to the Sacred? The majority of feminists claim that pronouns—not "it"—most appropriately image a *personal* Sacred, a being who knows and responds to us in some way.[83] If this is true, should we use both "he" and "she," or exclusively "she?" There are some who argue that the use of both enables male *and* female experience to image the Sacred. Furthermore, the exclusive use of "she" may have similar detrimental effects on personal psyches and social systems as did the exclusive use of the male pronoun. While the first statement is true and the latter a very distant possibility, we must be careful not to sidestep the necessary iconoclasm of male imagery for the Sacred. We may need to call God "she" in countless prayers and rituals before the Sacred can be imaged beyond maleness. Then, "what has been destroyed as an idol can return as an icon, evoking the presence of God."[84]

The metaphoric potential of the sacred symbol "Goddess" invites several feminists—within as well as outside biblical traditions—to name the Sacred "Goddess." We have already seen some of the ways in which Goddess-centered feminists are shaping the meaning of this ancient symbol. In addition, Mary Jo Weaver documents "the willingness of female Catholic liturgists to invoke the Goddess in their search for new ways to express their personal and collective experience of the divine."[85] Judith Plaskow holds that "Goddess" is an appropriate and necessary image for the Sacred, and it must be spoken again within

Judaism. She asserts: "Acknowledging the many aspects of the Goddess among the names of God becomes a measure of our ability to incorporate the feminine and women into a monotheistic religious framework."[86] Rosemary Ruether proposes the image "God/dess" for Christian feminists, as a way of incorporating both male and female dimensions within the Sacred while still maintaining the Sacred's oneness.[87]

These are some examples of how feminists demonstrate a need for the revolutionary potential of metaphor to sense the Sacred anew.[88] We also need metaphors to interpret sacred symbols, says Sallie McFague, because they help us to name the unfamiliar and new in terms of the familiar and old.[89] Naming "God" as "Mother" gives us a way of talking about our new experience of Sacred presence in terms of that familiar image. The "thread of similarity" between "God" and "Mother" helps us to image what "we do not know how to think or talk about"[90]—namely, our transformed sense of the Sacred—but we must also remember that "God" *is* and *is not* a mother. Metaphors for the Sacred can never be identified with the Sacred. Metaphors bring two unlikes together by naming their common ground. The use of metaphoric imagery always reminds us that language never fully re-presents the experience of Sacred presence. At the same time it provides us with an alternative way of interpreting the presence of the Sacred in our world.

A spirituality for feminists challenges us to use metaphors in our public and private language for the Sacred. Metaphoric imagery shocks us; it unsettles our ties to the symbolic imagery we wish to leave behind. To speak of "God" as "She" produces tension. Yet this tension is precisely what enables us to discover that "God" is not literally a "He." And tension spurs us to new vistas where we image the Sacred out of experiences of integrity and relatedness with the life-force that runs through all reality. Furthermore, the "is/is not" character of metaphors powerfully reminds us that several metaphors are needed to interpret relationship with the Sacred. There can be no idols in a spirituality for feminists.

Concepts

Throughout the past thirty years feminists in religion have focused their critique on the sacred symbols and images of a patriarchal culture. These analyses pinpointed in an altogether crystal manner the intrinsic connection between *image* and *concept*. Shifting sacred imagery necessarily raises conceptual issues. To speak of "God as lover or friend"[91] challenges underlying conceptions of the Sacred that are coupled with "God as father or judge." Not only did we receive the symbolic imagery of our religious traditions, but we were also handed *ideas* of the Sacred's power, transcendent character, and inner nature.

In being with people as they journey through the "dark night of the soul," I have been very struck by the powerful impact that *ideas* of God have on their *images* of God. While attractive from several angles, the image of God as mother does not settle well with people's concept of God's omnipotent and transcending power. "Goddess"—while unequivocally affirming the value of femaleness—disrupts the notion that God does not possess gender. To name the Sacred as "God" and "Goddess" upsets the concept of the deity's Oneness. These are just a few examples of the interdependence between imagistic and conceptual language. They also point out, I think, the importance of re-conceiving the Sacred's nature as it relates to us. This, too, is part of the feminist spirituality journey.[92]

McFague's analysis is helpful for us here. She defines concept as an abstract notion or idea. Conceptual language is secondary (as compared with the primary language of image and metaphor) and as such continues the interpretive process that imagistic language initiates. For McFague, "imagistic language does not just tolerate interpretation but *demands* it."[93] Though concepts cannot *explain* images, "they raise questions of their meaning and truth in explicit ways."[94] Concepts attempt to clarify the meaning contained in imagery, but they also interpret the use of competing imagery. For example, how can God be both "mother" and "father?" Or, how can "Goddess" incorporate a male dimension within the Sacred? With the images received, we question their adequacy and appropriateness as well as the ways in which they critique traditional concepts of the Sacred. A renewed conceptualization of the Sacred-human relationship is as important as the re-imaging process in our effort to name the Sacred.

As we hear the sacred imagery of others and image our own anew, several conceptual issues will surface in a spirituality for feminists. I list them here as questions, and suggest that they represent a healthy uprooting of past assumptions and beliefs, especially for those who inherited the stories and symbols of biblical religions.

1. To what extent does God depend on humanity for the continuation of life on earth? Is the Sacred *All-Powerful*?

2. How can the Sacred *transcend* our human experience and still exist *immanently* within it?

3. Is *monotheism* better than *polytheism?* Is the Sacred one or many?

4. Are *anthropomorphic* images of the Sacred suitable? Are they enough? Should we image an exclusively *personal* Sacred?

5. Are all images, metaphors, and symbols of the Sacred equally good? Are there some that are better than others? What are our criteria for determining the truthfulness of our imagery?

Most likely, we will not be able to answer any of these questions once and for all. They are the perennial conceptual issues of theology and spirituality, recurring with great force during times of transition and transformation. Ours is such a time. And the challenge presented by a spirituality for feminists invites all people—not simply professional theologians, thealogians, and philosophers—to live with these questions and their provisional answers in the spiritual journey. It is important to remember, however, that "the overall goal of interpretation is to *return to the experience* the primary language expresses."[95] Our attempt to name the Sacred with symbols, images, metaphors, and concepts is successful only if it continuously enables renewed presence to the Holy.

— 5 —

Homemaking: The Earth-Human Relationship

Over the past several years I have had a growing interest in the worldwide ecological movement. My entry point was not so much the intermittent media coverage of developing environmental crises as it was a lifestyle being shaped by the insights of feminist spirituality. Feminism invited me to rethink the earth-human relationship. A patriarchal culture not only subjugates woman, it also severely abuses the world of nature. There must be a connection between the two, as many feminists have argued.[1] My own exploration of that connection, however, dawdled and even limped at times, especially when compared with my strong interests in woman's self-development, mutuality as the ideal genre of human relationships, and feminist imagery for the Sacred. I knew that we humans had done some terrible things to the earth and I knew that the environment needed much more care if we were going to survive. So I promised myself to keep reading, but to let the ecologists practice the clean-up and earthcare. I was already involved in enough "issues."

I think such reticence—perhaps even resistance—is not uncommon. There are several reasons why this is the case: There were two that were particularly pertinent for me. I have already hinted at the first reason: the belief that ecology is just one more issue to fight for, and I'm already part of enough struggles. I was worried about the greenhouse effect, the destruction of the rain forests, and the build-up of nuclear arms. I did think a lot about the land, the trees, organic gardening, and how to recycle waste. But I viewed each of these concerns as possible future projects; my present work was theology and education.

I am unable to pinpoint when "the penny dropped" for me, or how the seed planted by various feminist writers eventually took root in my own consciousness and activities. I do know that several things nurtured the seed along its way. Living in the Dublin mountains, daily walks through a nearby forest, caring for thirteen hens, two dogs, two cats, four Jacob sheep, and a large flower garden were all certainly part of the process. These activities were coupled with more and more reading in ecological biology, ecofeminism, earth-based spiritualities, and the religions of indigenous cultures. Still, it is hard to say how all of this fed the sprouting realization that the earth-human relationship is an *integral concern* of an interdependent lifestyle. Furthermore, by cultivating this awareness it occurred to me that "homemaking" could be a provocative metaphor for characterizing this relationship.

Radical changes in present cultural, social, and personal patterns are required for us to make our homes with and on the earth. We have already considered many of these in our previous chapters. What I suggest here is that living with a powerful sense of self and engaging in mutual relationships in the midst of difference is part and parcel of creating harmony and balance with and upon the earth. At the same time, these kinds of changes in personal and social behavior challenge us to look at how alienation from ourselves and one another replicates humanity's alienation from the earth. All is not well with the earth. Many feminists intuit that this has a lot to do with how we have imaged ourselves as essentially separate from and eminently superior to the natural world. Ecological crises are the logical extention of such imagery. Exploitation of the earth's resources "fits with" a culture that values certain people over others. Homemaking with the earth, then, is not simply another project to be done; it is part of the entire enterprise of developing a sustainable culture. Perhaps we could say that this involves "naturalizing humanity" (and naturalizing culture) by making the earth our home. I will return to the "homemaking" metaphor throughout this chapter as a way of re-imaging the earth-human relationship with the resources of various feminist spiritualites. First, however, it is important to mention the other reason for my initial reticence with regard to the ecological dimension of a spirituality for feminists.

I believe that a *Christian* spirituality must include a deep awareness and practice of humanity's interdependence with the natural world, but the traditional beliefs of the Christian religion itself have often hindered this. The salvific process, for example, has usually been interpreted to mean the sanctification of humanity with little concern for the rest of nature. Only humans have souls, we were told as little children, so when our cats and dogs died they could not possibly make it into heaven. The image of heaven itself, as described by orthodox Christian doctrine, encouraged an undervaluing of this world. Ultimate holiness and salvation could not be experienced on earth. Our true home was some *place* else. Sacraments also supported this exclusion of the nature world from our most intimate and ultimate concerns. They reconciled us with God and one another but did little to heal humanity's alienation from the earth. My Christian heritage, then, has significantly inhibited my ecological sensibilities.

I am fully aware of the contemporary scholarship on Christian ecological theology and creation-centered spirituality.[2] It (correctly, I believe) argues that not *all* of the Christian heritage is incompatible with our present ecological concerns. Though predominant interpretations of Scripture and tradition have devalued the nature world and encouraged humanity's "mastery of the earth," there are other (less dominant) aspects of the heritage that allude to the earth's intrinsic worth and beauty. For example, Kathleen Fischer reminds us that Psalm 104 lifts up the immanent value of all species on our planet:

> God, what variety you have created,

arranging everything so wisely!
Earth is completely full of things you have made:

among them vast expanse of ocean,
teeming with countless creatures,
creatures large and small (vv. 24-25).[3]

Fischer maintains that Yahweh's covenant with creation is renewed by Jesus' redemptive action that extends to the whole creation. She cites Romans 8:19,22 as evidence for this claim: "Indeed the whole creation eagerly awaits the revelation of the children of God . . . Yes, we know that all creation groans and is in agony even until now."[4] This interpretation of sacred texts echoes the thirteenth-century mystic/environmentalist Hildegarde of Bingen who was inspired to write: "God desires that all the world be pure in his sight. The earth should not be injured. The earth should not be destroyed."[5] Through her meditations on scripture, this medieval theologian proclaims the holiness of the earth and God's wish for its health. She also senses the interdependent character of all that is with the musing: "God has arranged all things in the world in consideration of everything else."[6] While these examples are only a small sampling of Christian ecological theology, they indicate a significant aspect of this contemporary research.

There *are* elements within Christianity that subvert its dominant theological devaluation of nature and its anthropocentric (human-centered) character of redemption. Retrieval of these is key for the transformation of Christianity as well as this world religion's transformative potential within an era threatened by ecocide. I am very glad to know this—I could not remain Christian otherwise. *However*, it is just as urgent for Christians to admit that the sanctification of the nature world (or, in non-theological terms, the greening of the earth) is *not* central to the Jesus story. While it may not be incompatible, I think it is dishonest to argue that it was at the core of Jesus' words and deeds. This may be another reason why I could not see clearly that the earth-human relationship is an integral piece in the hope for wholeness—my Christianity blurred that vision.

This is not all bad news, particularly in the development of a spirituality for feminists. Throughout this book, I have argued that our collective hope for wholeness—for ourselves, each other, the sacred, and the earth—is dependent on the recognition of truths within our own spiritual traditions and a willingness to converse with members of other traditions. The conversation, the exchange is vital if we really do believe that diversity feeds universal love and knowledge. The conversation nurtures images of and activities toward wholeness that could not happen otherwise. No tradition contains all of the answers in an interdependent world. As a feminist and a Christian, it seems to me that re-imaging the earth-human relationship is one of the most critical and timely opportunities for the practice of ecumenism and interreligious dialogue. Though some Christian feminists are doing provocative work with an ecological orientation, we also need the revelations and insights of earth-based and Goddess feminist spiritualities.[7] We need to hear the thorough-going biophilic philosophy of Mary Daly. Traditions and contemporary philosophies rooted in an unambiguous love for the earth provide essential resources for feminists to image the earth as our home.[8]

The Demise of Woman and Nature

Multiple ingredients have blended together to form the contemporary mindset and subsequent activities that poison our environment and threaten universal extinction. As in most baked goods, the ingredients of this mindset are not immediately apparent. If the finished product requires any changes, however, it would be important to know what went into the mixture in the first place. Re-imaging the earth-human relationship must begin with such a search. We need to ask: How did we get where we are?

Several feminists provide a pivotal clue for unlocking the complexities of our present ecological crises. They maintain that the demise of nature goes hand in hand with sexism. An integral connection exists between woman's inferior status and viewing the earth as an object to be used and abused. Theologies, philosophies, socioeconomic mechanisms, and the science of a patriarchal culture coalesce to ensure that the oppression of woman will support the exploitation of the nature world. Rosemary Radford Ruether was one of the first to insist that the ecological crisis will not be averted until women are free. The process of all women's freedom must happen as an integral part of ecological harmonization.[9] As Judith Plant contends in her book on ecofeminism,

"Taking the feminist critique of human relationship and putting it side by side with an analysis of human and non-human relationships, show[s] that both women and the earth have been regarded as the object of self-interested patriarchs. . . ."[10] Changing the present earth-human relationship, then, includes investigating how both woman and nature were used at the expense of a world that may end.

Philosophical Ingredients

As we saw in Chapter 1, philosophical dualism imaged reality as two essentially separate levels of existence. The higher level of supernature and spirit transcended the lower level of nature and matter. The human mind, with its intellectual powers of consciousness and intentionality, symbolized the higher realm; the body, with its make-up of matter and emotions, belonged to the lower sphere of nature. Greek philosophy—as exemplifed in the works of Plato and Aristotle—identified maleness with the transcendent and femaleness with the earth.[11] Man was "above" (along with God) and woman was "below" (close to nature).[12] As Susan Griffin baldly states through the voice of patriarchal culture: "It is observed that women are closer to the earth."[13] Thus humanity—that is, male humans—imaged itself as separate from and superior to the world of nature (and the world of woman).

Aristotelian biology bolstered man's wish to dominate nature and control woman. The reproductive process was understood to be activated by the male semen, which formed the passive matter (contributed by the female), in order to create the embyro. "The female, as female, is passive, and the male, as male, is active, and the principle of movement comes from him."[14] The real cause of new human life came through the male's action. Females were needed simply to receive and nurture the life that was given. This vision of reproduction reinforced the philosophical separation of spirit and matter as well as the view of matter as passive and lifeless. In addition, the presumed inferior essence of woman was integral to the image of matter as inert.

Dualistic philosophy contained other important ingredients that contributed to the simultaneous demise of woman and nature. As may already be obvious, it proposed an ontology with a chain-like character. The "chain of being" (as it came to be known) pictured the different kinds of beings in hierarchical sequence. God was at the top of the chain, followed closely by celestial beings and spirits, with the links continuing in the order of males, females, animals, plants, and nature-matter. The being at the top held the most value and "he" was imaged as pure spirit. God's essence was absolutely non-material, as were angels and archangels, though they were of less value than God because God had created them. Continuing down the chain, human beings were comprised of bodies and souls. Their souls, the spiritual and most real part of their being, separated from the body at death and lasted forever. Although this was as true for woman as it was for man, woman's body was viewed as containing more nature-like characteristics than man's. Animals were perceived as more material than humans, since their spirits died along with their bodies. Plants and the rest of nature were even more matter-filled than animals and the lowest forms of nature were absolutely spirit-less. In this kind of schema value resided with the spiritual.[15]

Chain-of-being ontology necessarily affected an understanding of how humanity discovers knowledge. Dualistic philosophy viewed humanity's ability to think and make choices as characteristics of its spiritual essence. Knowledge, truth, and goodness best came through the process of pure theoretical speculation. The more hampered one was by feelings or subjective desires, the less truth and goodness were found. Sexual passion and feelings of attraction or connection especially obstructed the pursuit of knowledge and the practice of morality. They, above all other emotions, represented the activities of the body. What was connected with the body could not possibly provide any source of what humanity needed to know for the good life.

All of these philosophical ingredients added up to numerous forms of alienation. An alien is one who is not at home, somewhat suspect because she or he really belongs someplace else or is not quite made of the same stuff as the natives. Alienation, as used here, is similar to that. Man was not quite made of the same stuff as woman. Man was more human-like; woman was more nature-like.[16] Neither man nor woman was quite at home in his or her body (though woman was more at home than man). Their real selves—their spirits—belonged someplace else. Their bodies were alien. In the same way, humanity as a whole was not part of nature. The earth was alien to humanity's truest essence. Everything alien was perceived as not only inferior but in need of control, used for the benefit of humanity's (especially man's) search for its true home.

Cosmology and Science: The Mechanistic Ingredients

Prior to the seventeenth century, most Europeans viewed the universe as one dynamic organism. Though dualistic philosophy existed, the Renaissance understanding of the cosmos was deeply influenced by the lifestyles of ordinary folk. At the beginning of her classic study, Carolyn Merchant writes:

> In 1500, the daily interaction with nature was still structured for most Europeans, as it was for other peoples, by close-knit, cooperative, organic communities. Thus it is not surprising that for sixteenth-century Europeans the root metaphor binding together the self, society, and the cosmos was that of an organism.[17]

The experience of daily life, coupled with organic philosophical and scientific theories, shaped people's image of an interdependent cosmos. At the heart of this image was the identification of nature, especially the earth, with a nurturing mother. Renaissance literature contained countless images associating nature and the earth with the female sex. The earth was alive and often pictured as a mother who provided and nurtured life. Stoic philosophy particularly supported the idea that the world itself was an intelligent organism, and that the force of growth or the potential for life existed *within* the nature world.

As Merchant points out, the prevalent metaphor of nature as nurturing mother effectively functioned to restrain human and social behavior that would impair the earth. "As long as the earth was considered to be alive and sensitive, it could be considered a breach of human ethical behavior to carry out destructive acts against it."[18] She documents a heated debate about the morality of mining the earth, carried on during the sixteenth century, as a key example of how cosmology affects the ethical choices of peoples and societies in a practical way.

All of this dramatically changed with the scientific revolution of the seventeenth century. Scientific theories of men like Francis Bacon, René Descartes, and Isaac Newton laid the foundations for a revolution in cosmological imagery. Crucial also to the shift was the rise of capitalism and a market-oriented economy. Science and economics merged to break the organic image. Nurturing mother was replaced by the image of nature as machine-like.

Several dimensions of this metaphor promoted nature's demise.

First, the earth—like machines—can be controlled.[19] Machines' operations are knowable and predictable. The developing science of mathematics was rooted in the assumption that mathematical laws and formulas could predict the movements of the universe and eventually provide humanity with absolute control. Second, machines are lifeless. They do not contain an animating spirit. They must be activated from without in order to work and produce. Newton's physics supported this notion of the lifeless earth. Matter was perceived as passive; it could not move itself. Motion or force was understood to be external to rather than immanent within matter. And third, nature—again, like machines—was imaged as being made up of various components that could be put together and taken apart. "Things [particles of matter] rather than relations are the ultimate reality. . . . "[20] Susan Griffin aptly summarizes this mechanistic cosmology:

> It is decided that matter is dead.
> That the universe acts as a machine which can be described by describing the actions of particles of matter upon other particles according to immutable mechanical laws.
> That the particular (like the parts of a machine) may be understood without reference to the whole.[21]

The Economic Ingredients

The mechanistic worldview flourished not simply because scientists were extremely persuasive men. Its forceful credibility was also stimulated by changing economic systems. As previously indicated, transitions in economic life significantly contributed to the "death of nature" and the control of woman. Merchant provides a detailed analysis of how this came about. Her argument centers on the shift from "peasant control of natural resources for purpose of subsistence [an agrarian economy] to capitalist control for purpose of profit [a market-oriented economy]."[22] As science "birthed" the machinery necessary for industry, a surplus of products provided resources to initiate a market economy. Mechanization was the basis for the development of economic exchange beyond the farm, manor, and village. Machines for factories, mining, agriculture, the timber and other industries subtly yet deeply affected ordinary folk's perception of the universe.

All of these factors blended into "cultural sanctions for the denudation of nature."[23] Now nature could be experimented on, mined, logged, and used in whatever way required for the expansion of commercialization and industrial development. The earth was composed of dead matter. This view justified its manipulation and rationalized its expendability. Merchant succinctly concludes, "living animate nature died, while dead inanimate money was endowed with life."[24]

Nature's death was not the only prerequisite for the emergence of capitalism, however. Woman's economic role decreased considerably as factories developed, businesses expanded, and crafts and trades became oriented for market production. Medieval economy was based in the home (economics originally meant "functions of the home"). Women, regardless of class, were integral to the management and production of food, clothing, commodities, and aesthetic items. As the economic workplace moved from the home to the factory and market, women's productive role declined and her reproductive role became central.[25] As Rosemary Ruether writes:

> For the first time women as a group became marginal to production and economically dependent on male work for survival. Even though many poor women went out to work in the factory at this time, they were still tied, as women, to providing the procreative and domestic support systems of male work.[26]

Woman—like the earthmachine—needed to be controlled. Because of her passive and inferior nature, she was restricted from entering the work force except for the lowest-paid and most menial forms of work. Management of her activities—again, just like nature—was central to a capitalist economy.[27] This meant, on the one hand, that the process of pregnancy and birth would be controlled by the male medical establishment. No longer would woman herself, with the assistance of a female midwife, be seen as the primary agent in reproduction. On the other hand, it meant that woman would rear children and ensure that all domestic activities were looked after. She would "make the home," without man and without economic recompense. It was this form of management, then, that provided man with the time and energy to make profit at the expense of nature. Woman becomes locked in the home, while man alienates humanity from the earth. "Home" is a psychic resource for man, and humanity's safe place from nature. This notion of homemaking supports ecological destruction. For the earth to survive, homemaking must be turned on its head.

Christian Symbols and the Genesis Myth: The Religious Ingredients

Throughout this book we have documented innumerable ways in which the Christian religion sustained woman's inferior position in society and in the spiritual journey. Her association with nature, sexuality, and the body made her own sanctification process considerably more difficult than man's. Just think of how many official female saints there are compared to the number of officially sanctified men, and note how many of those women saints were described as "virgins" compared to the men. Woman's association with the natural level of existence also excluded her from imaging the true God. Her experience rarely formed imagery and metaphors for the Sacred. She could not—by virtue of her sex—re-present Christ, the incarnate one, in the office of the priesthood.[28]

So, too, earth and the nature-world did not fare well under the influence of principal interpretations of Christian symbols and the Genesis myth.[29] Care-filled reverence for the earth was subtly undermined by the ways in which certain symbols and narratives shaped the Western image of the earth-human relationship. In addition to philosophy, science, and economics, religion played a formative role in nature's demise.

In the previous chapter I indicated some ecologically rooted concerns regarding the Christian symbol "God." Feminists of all spiritual persuasions have analyzed the environmental implications of this powerful symbol. Now let us examine in more detail how God-imagery affects humanity's perception of the earth. First of all, God's being or essence is imaged as *pure spirit*. God does not have a body; God is matter-less. This absolutely spiritual God creates the earth through thoughts. These thoughts are represented in the Genesis narrative by the words that God declares. "God said, 'Let there be light,' and there was light" (Genesis 1:3). God creates the earth through words. God is not imaged as creating nature from anything natural.[30]

God's essence as pure spirit emphasizes the transcendent character of God. God is not at home in creation. God transcends—exists beyond—the earth. However, God has created humanity in "his image and likeness." Humanity images God because women and men possess souls, their animating force. The spirits of human beings image God who is pure spirit. Consequently, God relates to men and women. God reveals Godself within history, within the lives, struggles, and joys of women and men. The transcendent God is then also the immanent one because God reveals intentions and offers love within the daily existence of human beings. However, this same God does not exist within nature. God's immanent character is excluded from anything that does not possess an eternal soul. God is close to humanity and distant from the earth.

Finally, God's nature is perceived as absolutely omnipotent. As we have already seen, King-imagery for God accentuates God's way of controlling the world through domination or benevolence.[31] The God who is an all-powerful King not only creates and controls the world, but is the one who will bring about its end. No matter what humanity does, the earth and the nature world will die. Sallie McFague asserts, "The Judeo-Christian traditions' triumphalist imagery for the relationship between God and the world . . . does not support human responsibility for the fate of the earth but shifts the burden to God. . . ."[32] And, in this scenario, *humanity* will exist forever, somewhere beyond the earth and all its fruits.

This multi-faceted picture of the Christian God endorses the devaluation of nature and everything associated with it (like woman, the body, and sexuality). Such sacred imagery contains obvious, and logical, consequences for the religious symbol of "salvation." All that has been created will not be redeemed. The earth and nature (that is, all non-human existence) is not worthy of salvation. In fact, humanity must distance itself from its own "matter"—the body—in order to be saved. In describing the trajectory of humanity's alienation from nature, Rosemary Ruether shows how salvation from nature is central to humanity's redemptive process. "Only by extricating mind from matter by ascetic practices, aimed at severing the connections of mind and body, can one prepare for the salvific escape out of the realm of corruptibility to eternal life."[33] As well as lacking the possession of eternal spirits, the rest of created reality does not have the intellectual ability needed to transcend material existence—much of creation will not make it "home."

Two other religious ingredients are key in a feminist analysis of the contemporary ecological crisis. They have to do with how Christianity has answered two of the most basic questions human beings have ever asked: "How did it all begin?" and "What about the end?"[34] As we know, Christian interpretation of the Genesis myth has provided an extremely influential answer to the question of origins. There have been diverse interpretations of this story, but we want to focus on the predominant one. Portions of this version are what the twentieth century inherited and what still shapes—if only at an unconscious level—how we view our relation with everything non-human.

In fact, the Genesis creation myth is the joining together of two very different stories. The oldest narrative, from the Yahwist tradition, is found in Genesis 2-3. It was written in approximately 1200 B.C.E. The second story, found in the first chapter of Genesis, was written in 500 B.C.E. out of the Priestly tradition. It seems that both stories were included in the Hebrew Scriptures because both were considered to have revelatory authority. Though they contain common elements, they also differ significantly. Yet, the prevailing Christian interpretation conflated the stories to produce one set of theological truths.

These "truths" are now brought into question in light of humanity's behavior on the planet. Elizabeth Dodson Gray criticizes the myth's picture of male-female relations as well as human/non-human relations. According to her, the Genesis myth supports two large conceptual errors: (1) it identifies maleness with humanity; man is the norm and therefore superior to woman; (2) it asserts humanity's superiority over the rest of creation.[35] With regard to the first error, she points out the obvious but oft-overlooked reality: The Genesis myth reverses the normal processes of birth—man is not born of woman but woman is born from the body of man.[36] This model of superior-inferior relationship is projected onto humanity's view of itself in relation to the rest of creation. "Be fruitful and multiply, and fill the earth and subdue it; and have dominion over . . . " (Genesis 1:28).[37] Humanity's domination of the nature world supports a hierarchical model of existence, a chain-of-being ontology. Such a picture ranks the diverse beings of creation and images humanity's absolute independence from everything else in the Garden.[38]

Interpretation of Genesis 3:1-20 sustains and consolidates an image of the beginning times that justifies a hierarchical ontology with sexist and ecocidal implications.[39] Woman falls first and tempts man to follow suit. Woman's deed maims human existence for all times. Her punishment is her inferior status. But her deed causes an even greater punishment for both herself and man. They must now die. Death is pictured as their greatest enemy. The underside of such an image is the theological assertion that death is unnatural. The Adam and Eve story in Carol Christ's view, provides us with an expectation of "life after death in which limitations of finitude are overcome." This "denial of our finitude," she continues, supports a nuclear mentality. Because *we* don't die, what does it matter if the entire earth explodes?[40]

The Christian doctrine of original sin, as formulated by Augustine, proclaims the universal implications of the mythic first fall. Death is not humanity's only punishment. Adam and Eve's original sin is passed on to every generation. Each human being is born with the taint of Adam's sin. This substantially weakens humanity's efforts to create the original Paradise that has been lost. In fact, original sin renders humanity powerless in establishing ecological balance and societal justice.[41] If we can't ever do it, why should we try?

The doctrine of original sin presumes a very specific picture of Paradise. Original happiness had little to do with the cyclical character of nature's life, death, and rebirth. It had little to do with the ebb and flow of human beings' self-development. Absent as well was the peace/happiness-conflict/pain pattern of our relationships with the earth, the Sacred, and one another. The cyclical quality of all our relationships and the seasonal pattern of nature appear to be "unnatural" to the picture of a *perfect* beginning. In fact, the first indication of a shift in the stasis of blissful existence is interpreted to mean that the perfect beginning has passed. Original harmony was imaged as static, only to be rediscovered in a life after death.

Well then, "what about the end?" Christian eschatology—the theology of the end-time—answers this question in ways that support a dualistic worldview with all of its anti-nature assumptions. Orthodox Christian end-time imagery presents a picture of heaven that is both like and unlike the initial Paradise. Non-human beings are absent. The seas, skies, birds, plants, rocks, and four-legged animals present at the beginning eventually drop out of the picture of harmony. Such a scenario is quite unlike the myth of origins, though it is the logical extension of asserting humanity's superiority. It betrays the dualistic influence of Platonism, which also dictates a similarity between the beginning and the end. The quality of heavenly harmony is comparable to the stasis of Paradise referred to above. In the fourteenth century, Aquinas developed the concept of "beatific vision." This, for him, describes the ultimate experience of happiness an individual obtains after entrance into heaven. As Mary Daly points out, the happiness produced by this vision is emotion-less, passive, and powerless. It consists in an operation of the intellect alone—we unite with God through our mind—and it happens only by God's initiation and maintenance.[42]

Aquinas's picture of the end is quite different from the "prophetic eschatology" of the Hebrew Scriptures. The prophets present end-time imagery about justice, peace, and harmony in *this* world, not after it. Commenting on Isaiah 65, Rosemary Ruether remarks:

> Here no immortality is envisioned, but rather a new age when the evils that prevent the enjoyment of human life within its full temporal life span are overcome. The blessed will work and enjoy their harvests for the "ideal" life span of a hundred years, without calamities of disease or warfare that sweep away the fruits of one's life and toil.[43]

However, an "apocalyptic eschatology" eventually develops within Jewish thought. People begin to hope for a better life after death, after history. The Book of Revelation in the Christian Scriptures is an example of late Jewish apocalyptic hope. Merged with Jesus' own discourse on the time of final judgment (Matthew 25), and the growing influence of Hellenistic dualism, mainstream Christian eschatology becomes other-world oriented. Orthodox imagery—a significant influence on Western culture—contains three central elements: (1) the world *will* end and God will bring it about;[44] (2) there will be a final judgment that rewards the good and punishes the evil forever; and (3) our individual consciousness/ego will continue eternally; we are essentially immortal.

To question any of these beliefs may be considerably unsettling to many of us. It challenges us at a very fundamental level to rethink the meaning of our own lives and the lives of those we name beloved. What should we and they be doing with our lives on earth? What is the meaning of life in light of the inevitability of death? Is death a natural or unnatural part of life? What happens to us after death? These questions may even impede our ability to work out the ecological implications of beliefs about the end-time. For example, has our concern with life after death been so primary that it functions (subtly, no doubt) to lessen interest in gifting our descendants with a livable future on earth? Is real communion with the Sacred something that happens outside of time, history, and the natural world? Can we move beyond a dualistic worldview and still logically claim that our individual consciousness exists without our bodies? If spirit can be separated from matter at death, and that matter goes through some form of spiritualization process (as suggested by biblical reflection on the resurrected body of Jesus), is this not the ultimate denial of the goodness and naturalness of matter and the human body? If heaven is our true home, why bother to homemake with and on the earth? And, if there is no earth in heaven, what value does the nature-world really hold?[45] All of these questions must be faced if we are to re-image the earth-human relationship.

Homemaking: The Spiritual Praxis of Feminists

The restoration of our planet includes as many ingredients as it took to place its life at risk. The recipe, however, must change dramatically. The process demands that we dislodge our former relationship with the earth and recreate one that will provide every natural element with a healthy place to dwell. If we image the relation as "homemaking," this may enable us to purge past perceptions and at the same time usher in something substantially different. As a metaphor, I think that it can assist us in naming the unfamiliar and new (a life-affirming relationship with nature) in terms of the familiar and old.

Homemaking has to do with creating and managing a home. The word "home" itself has several meanings. It is also a word that conveys feelings as well as images. Just think of the multi-layered response that happens inside of us when someone asks: "Where are you from?" or "Where is home?" Home can be a place, a physical location where one dwells. Usually it contains additional meaning, since the word "house" more precisely describes a material setting. For example, when we speak about the "homeless" we mean more than those without a house. Home is often a setting wherein one feels safe, comfortable, and at ease. Though not necessarily a physical space, it is usually a stable environment that provides nourishment for growth and a haven for grief, suffering, and loss. When we feel "at home" in a place or with a certain group of people we experience a deep sense of kinship and belonging.[46]

Homemaking is all the activities that go into creating this kind of kinship, sense of belonging, and nurturing context. Since the women's liberation movement, "homemaking" has been used more frequently than "housekeeping." This indicates a shift going on in people's perception of the value associated with these kinds of activities. From a feminist perspective, homemaking includes housekeeping, but it connotes something far more valuable and integral to human development and wholeness. In suggesting homemaking as a metaphor for the earth-human relationship, I want to emphasize that I am not talking about housekeeping, though the mundane and often tedious tasks of cleaning, waste disposal, and general upkeep are part and parcel of making a good home. At the same time, I think that those who have been "housekeepers" in the past (and those who are still forced to do others' housework in order to survive economically) hold key roles in re-imaging the "nature of nature" and humanity's relationship with it.[47] Furthermore, the liberation of those who have and continue to "keep house" is essential for the continuance of the natural cycle of life and death.

The movement from housekeeping to homemaking in the domestic sphere holds several clues to what homemaking might mean when we use it to characterize the earth-human relationship. We can no longer make a home simply within our own houses. Such individualistic activity has encouraged the creation of comfort within the private domain at the expense of the public; a safe and indulgent place for humanity at the cost of killing the earth. Instead, we ought to ask: How can we create an environment that sustains everything on earth? The answer, I think, lies in phrasing the question differently: How can we make our homes *with* as well as *on* the earth? Or, how can our homemaking activity become biocentric rather than anthropocentric?[48]

Part of the answer includes two important convictions developing within the feminist spiritualities. First, the elements of nature and the non-human animals hold intrinsic value. They are inherently valuable apart from their worth to us. This "sensibility toward the cosmos," writes Sallie McFague, "is one that values what is unselfishly with a sense of delight in others for their own sakes."[49] This is a challenge to recognize the *independence* of non-human nature. And it is a prerequisite for imaging our *interdependence* with the rest of the natural world, the second feminist conviction. Homemaking *with* the earth calls us to be co-creators, to be partners with the earth. On the one hand, this means that we are dependent on nature for certain things. Elizabeth Dodson Gray comments that although we need the plants for the photosynthetic process, they do not need us.[50] On the other hand, it means that human action upon the energy cycles within the biosphere ought to be for the benefit of all. What we do ought to have good effects beyond humanity.

To co-create the earth as home for all, however, radically challenges one central meaning to the present definition of "earth." According to the *Concise Oxford Dictionary*, the meaning of "earth" includes: "the planet on which we live, the present abode of man *[sic], opposite heaven or hell as places of future existence. . . .*" Homemaking on the earth requires new ways of imaging heaven and hell. If they continue to be perceived as "places" opposite the earth, then we cannot call the earth our home. In addition, the preceding definition of earth implies that only the *human* life cycle will ultimately be able to regenerate itself. This essentially undercuts any perception of interdependence. If the earth is our home only up to a certain point, or place, or time, then it is not really our home at all. This is not doing away with "heaven" or "hell," but it is recognizing that re-imaging the earth-human relation as homemaking necessarily incorporates finding new images for old symbols of judgment.

For any of this to happen, though, homemaking (inclusive of housekeeping) must be done by men as well as women. It must be done by rich as well as poor, white as well as black. The nurturing and the cleaning, the responsibility for health through kinship as well as washing, childcare, and earthcare ought to be done by all. Otherwise there will always be groups who are blind to the consequences of the mess they make. Or there will always be some people who will nurture at the absolute expense of themselves. And the gap between the messmakers and the cleaners will continue to grow. As Judith Plant reminds us, "Taking care of the environment is about learning an entirely new lifestyle and wishing for a whole new set of systems."[51] The re-valuing of woman and nature through shared homemaking is the heart of our ecological challenge. The question is: How?

The Nature of Culture

We have seen already how a patriarchal culture defined woman as "closer to nature" than man, and we have analyzed how this cultural formula of woman's essential connection with nature promoted sexism on the one hand and ecological destruction on the other. Feminist theory holds that the harm produced by this connection was and is due in large part to the nature/culture dualism. Patriarchy defines "culture" as that which goes beyond, or transcends, the nature-world. Culture is the sum total of what humanity produces through its intelligence, moral activity, and aesthetic abilities. Culture is superior to and essentially separate from everything non-human. The natural world holds considerably less inherent value than the cultural world of humanity.

Consequently, feminists of divergent spiritual traditions by and large agree that the nature/culture dualism must be shattered for the liberation of women and nature.[52] Nature can no longer be imaged as all that is opposite to culture (and vice versa). Again, the question is: How? Considerable difference exists in the feminist answer. Traditional lines have been drawn between a "radical or cultural" and "socialist" feminist position. Much of the feminist spirituality movement grew out of radical or cultural feminism.[53] This analysis sought to break the dualism by *accepting* the woman/nature relation. That is, women began to explore the ways in which they felt a deep connection with nature and how experiences of "embodiedness" enabled them to image the interdependence of body and spirit. They celebrated rituals and practiced meditations highlighting the relation between woman's menstrual cycle and the cycles of nature and the seasons. They lifted up the "spiritual" and "personal" character of nature, especially through remembering ancient Goddess traditions. In effect, they attempted to deepen their experiences of communion with nature in order to create a culture that would value humanity's interdependence with the nature-world.

The present analysis of this earlier manifestation of "nature feminist spirituality" criticizes some of its apparent assumptions. Are women really closer to nature than men? Joan Griscom comments:

> I find it difficult to assert that men are "further" from nature because they neither menstruate nor bear children. They also eat, breathe, excrete, sleep, and die; and all of these, like menstruation, are experiences of bodily limits. Like any organism, they are involved in constant biological exchange with their environment and they have built-in biological clocks complete with cycles.[54]

Closely allied with this concern is a question about the apparent biological determinism of cultural feminism. Does woman's biology determine her destiny? Will the new culture created through this approach maintain the patriarchal assumption of an essential difference between masculine and feminine characteristics? Will a feminist culture still reserve the world of nature for women? Carolyn Merchant asserts, "Any analysis that makes women's essence and qualities special ties them to biological destiny that thwarts the possibility of liberation."[55] A third criticism centers on the (again) apparent inference of women's superiority to men. Do men have anything to contribute to a new, life-affirming culture? What, in fact, is the ultimate objective of radical feminism—an inclusive culture or a women's culture?

These criticisms are voiced especially by those whose primary concerns have been class and race as well as gender. The "socialist feminist" perspective has substantially influenced the spirituality of feminists. Traditionally, socialist feminist theory has centered its critique on a *capitalist* patriarchy. It has been concerned with how the socioeconomic system ought to change so that women from the working or jobless class, third world women, and women of color can have an adequate share in the world's resources. It has been concerned less with the exploitation of nature, except how its abuse is required for a capitalist system. The critique roots itself in a vision of nature as historically and socially constructed—that is, nature has little identity apart from its usefulness to humanity. Therefore, a socialist feminist position would be more likely to argue that woman has no essential connection with nature; the relation has been constructed by a capitalist and patriarchal culture. The relation benefits capitalism and sexism; consequently, it ought to be broken.

Today, the feminist spirituality movement still contains very different ways of trying to break the nature/culture dualism. However, cultural and socialist concerns *are* coming closer together in the theory and praxis of most feminist spiritualities. Ynestra King and Carolyn Merchant both argue that the "ecofeminist" movement provides a canopy under which the socialists can dialogue with the radicals. Though, as King says, cultural feminism emphasized the nature component of the dualism and socialist feminism focused on the cultural/historical element, we need each perspective to incorporate the insights of the other in order to break the dualism once and for all. A spirituality for feminists must be concerned with "history as well as mystery."[56] That is, the health of the earth is dependent on socioeconomic analyses that challenge the cultural practice of nature-abuse *and* spiritual praxis that highlights the independence of nature and humanity's inseparability from it. King's words aptly summarize these sentiments: "The crisis of this civilization which has led us to the brink of nuclear annihilation, is spiritual as much as it is economic."[57]

What, then, is the "nature of culture"? Culture, and all of humanity's historical activities that create it, is not reducible to nature. Likewise, nature is not reducible to culture. What this means is that humanity and non-human nature—while comprised of similar elements (namely, the spirited-matter of earth, air, fire, and water)—are not identical in their being. But neither are they absolutely separate from one another. Uniqueness is a prerequisite for interdependence. Our history is intimately bound up with the earthstory. Our culture emerges from and interacts with the earth.

The new culture that surges from such a consciousness bears myths, dreams, historical activity, art, poetry, social change, science, philosophy, etc., that invite humanity to treat the earth as home. Feminist spiritualities are filled with the fruits of this nascent culture. This culture is no longer identified with maleness, yet feminists differ regarding the continued connection between femaleness and nature. Mary Daly, for example, argues for an essential relation between women and the "wild." Her ultimate concern is to fashion a culture that loves women and the earth. Although I agree with critics that her work borders on reversing the dualism, I also want to maintain that her radical philosophy is necessary as *one* significant tool for dismantling patriarchal culture. Her spirituality alone will not foster the interdependence of nature and culture. But it does continue to sharpen the critical and creative edge of every feminist vision.

Representatives of the contemporary Goddess movement root their ecological vision of culture in how they as women sense a deep harmony with the earth. The works of Carol Christ and Starhawk, for example, tend to identify nature as female and view women's experience as a unique source of knowledge about the "nature of nature." However, they do not adopt Mary Daly's essentialist position. Instead they explore how women's *historical* association with nature places them in a position to know it in a distinctly different manner from men. When speaking about her visions of the holiness of the sea, Christ remarks:

> Though these visions come to us through women, they do not belong to women exclusively. They offer insights essential to us all, containing clues to a spirituality that can reawaken our sense of our connection to all living things, to the life force within us and without us.[58]

This is somewhat different again from the spirituality of many Christian feminists. Rosemary Ruether, Beverly Harrison, and Susan Thisthlewaite represent positions that deemphasize the woman/nature connection and focus more on the socio-historical practice that ought to go on in a culture needing naturalization. Other Christian feminists, especially Australians, image a culture of ecology through the body-spirit experience of woman liberated. As I indicated previously, though, the feminist spiritualities of the late 1980s and early 1990s are learning from the perspectives of each other. Though some are more cultural and others more socialist oriented, their combined potential represents one of the most significant resources for re-creating the earth as our home.

The Culture of Homemaking

In 1989, five hundred Australian women gathered at a National Women's Conference in Collaroy. Paula M. Smith, R.S.M., wrote the following poem as a response to the dreaming of these Australian women. It was also read at a feminist liturgy that concluded my own visit to Adelaide.

Poor Woman My Country

Poor woman my country
I rejoice with you
Finding yourself
preparing to give birth
from a womb of life
large enough to encompass
the entire creation.
You are knowing the melodies
and naming your dreaming.
They find expression

in those
moments
when the full moon
mirrored in the Pacific
opens the depths.
They find expression
when flowers
carefully selected
are shared, passed on
and open the divine in self and other.
They find expression
when the mists
begin to rise,
and shapes formerly indefinite
take the form
of Sophia, woman, goddess.
Their condition is far from
dispassionate, no mere linguistic
exercise, devoid of vision
and structured as law alone . . .
    it's the story of the alienation
    the joy of discovery that life can
    be whole after the rape,
    the serenity that personal choice
    and commitment can give,
    the assertion that dignity is
    for all,
    the naming of the pain.
It requires transformation
of consciousness,
continued feminine discourse,
reclaiming of values
that burning indignation asserts
belong to all,
gentle listening,
fidelity to imagination,
the ability to rejoice
while standing on the

edges of a world that must
be explored.
The naming is happening
the rainbow is rising
in strong colors
from the clouds over the Pacific
as you woman
claim your joy,
your pain,
your new way of dancing
to celebrate your womanhood.[59]

Compassion: Where Philosophy Begins The culture of homemaking re-values woman and nature. The philosophies that birth and nurture such a culture originate to a large degree in the experience of compassion. Compassion means to "feel with," to "suffer with" in such a way that we are impelled to participate in the healing of the one in pain. Compassion requires first of all an ability to feel a connectedness with the "other." It means sensing a deep relation. Compassion with the earth has been blocked because "we no longer feel ourselves to be part of this earth."[60] Much of Susan Griffin's work, both her poetic and metaphysical imagery, surfaces as she breaks through the desensitization of patriarchal conditioning. When woman finds the "roaring inside her" (so poignantly depicted by Paula Smith's poem), her capacity to feel deeply returns.

I remember speaking about the need for compassion at a workshop in Dublin on feminism and ecology. I ended the session with a simple meditation that invited participants to remember any experiences of connectedness with nature from their childhood. As they listened to flute music from the Native American R. Carlos Nakai,[61] one woman's face filled with tears. After the meditation she told us that as a child, she used to spend a lot of time in the forest hugging trees. She loved the trees and talked to them as she would to any friends. I asked: "Is that why you are crying?" She paused for a moment and then replied, "No, I am crying because for the last twenty years I completely forgot that I ever hugged a tree." Charlene Spretnak would call this a moment of "awakening."[62] In order to image a worldview beyond the nature/culture dualism, we must allow our senses to feel the life of the nature-world. Or, as my story suggests, we must uncover past moments of feeling a natural bond with other life on earth.[63]

As we recover our ability to sense the life of the "other"—"to move out of the conditioning that keeps [us] so cut off from our grounding in the natural world"[64]—we are more able to feel the pain of the earth. This compassion has "survival value."[65] It is the essence of a new paradigm, a philosophical worldview that theorizes about interdependence rather than dualism. Spretnak writes that "the crying need right now...is for a new philosophical underpinning of civilization. We need an ecophilosophy that speaks the truth with great immediacy in language that everyone can understand."[66] I identified some of the components of this philosophy of interdependence in Chapter 1. Our specific interest here lies with rethinking humanity's essence as interrelated with the natural world. This brings us, as some authors have pointed out, to the realm of *ontology*, the philosophy of *being*. How is it that we as human beings exist?

The ontology for a culture of homemaking contains two fundamental assertions. First, as human beings we are different from other beings of nature. We used to identify the difference in terms of our intelligence, will, and human spirit. But, as we have already seen, we need to rethink the meaning and value of these human characteristics. Is there no element of choice in the natural world? Are we the only species with "spirit?" How is it that "intelligence" can be used to destroy the planet? Thus we need to rethink the meaning of our difference. Second, our being is an essential part of the natural, evolutionary process. This means that "*we* are nature . . . the mind is itself a thing of nature."[67] We exist as natural-historical beings.

Granted, these are only rudiments of a new ontology. But they point us toward a way of appreciating the "otherness" of nature—thus respecting its essence and value apart from us—and acknowledging our own identity as nature. Again, compassion is vital. It not only bears the theory, it also spurs the practice. As we feel the distress of the earth, the pain of our forests, we "see ourselves as answerable and accountable to those who are different from us. . . ."[68] We want to do something about it. This is what Ynestra King means when she says, "Here, potentially, we recover ontology as the ground for ethics."[69] This is an effective, practical ethics. Its potency lies in the motivating force of compassion. A paradox begins to develop, though, precisely within this experience of compassion. Joanna Macy puts her finger on it with the notion of the "ecological self." As we feel the cry of the earth, the anguish of the other, our consciousness of the human way of being starts shifting. Our identity extends beyond past notions of being human: "I am part of the rain forest protecting myself. I am that part of the rain forest recently emerged into human thinking." Macy refers to this as a "spiritual change" that "releases us from a false and confining notion of self."[70] I am suggesting that it also points to the paradox of an ontology of interdependence. We act, then, for the sustainability of ourselves as well as others. If the earth is not a home for every being, it will be home for none.

Science for Life Twentieth-century science provides a powerful source for feminists to re-image humanity's relationship with the natural world. It sparks and supports the fashioning of a new ontology, as described above. There is a strong sense of irony, though. Feminists discover that science can have a mutually beneficial relationship with spirituality. A spirituality for feminists affirms and is confirmed by new developments within the scientific arena. I want to indicate two such developments that are having a marked impact on the feminist spiritual journey, precisely because they replace the mechanistic vision of Newtonian science. In its place, they offer rich possibilities for imaging the earth as home.

The "new physics"—as discussed in the works of Fritjof Capra and David Bohm—present the implications of quantum and relativity theory for a scientific framework beyond the matter/spirit dualism. Elizabeth Dodson Gray's book *Green Paradise Lost* is an invaluable resource for understanding some of the basics in how sub-atomic physics contributes to a spirituality for feminists.[71] She outlines how quantum theory challenged past conceptions of the atom as a collection of solid particles moving through space. Instead, scientists now propose that these "particles" are not in fact "solid." They are "wave-like patterns of probabilities"; they are patterns of energy that can form one way and then another. Relativity theory extends these insights by confirming that the mass of an atom is not a form of substance but a form of energy. And so, what we used to perceive as solid objects—be they sub-atomic, atomic, or molecular—are actually processes. The existence of matter is the activity of energy. Rosemary Ruether incorporates these insights into her own "ecological-feminist theology of nature":

> When we proceed . . . beneath the surface of visible things . . . the visible disappears. Matter itself dissolves into energy. Energy, organized in patterns and relationships, is the basis for what we experience as visible things. It becomes impossible anymore to dichotomize material and spiritual energy.[72]

Furthermore, those who work in sub-atomic physics are helping us to see that we—indeed, everything composed of spirited matter—are connected in the probability patterns of energy that flow through everything equally. What we now discern at the micro level of the very small is a pervasive pattern of sub-atomic energy moving through humans, cats, plants, trees, rocks, butterflies—everything. That same energy connects us because it travels through all of creation. Humanity is embedded within this fundamental energy field.

Developments are taking place within biological science that complement the new physics. I have found the book *The Liberation of Life: From the Cell to the Community* by biologist Charles Birch and theologian John Cobb particularly helpful in this regard. They propose a theory of "ecological biology" that roots itself in the essential relation between an entity and its environment. This theory suggests that such relation exists at the level of molecule and cell as well as organism and human community. This means that, even at the molecular level, the molecule exists *only* in relation to its environment. That relation—between molecule and environment (which is usually other molecules within a cell)—constitutes its existence. That relation enables it to be or exist. Being does not happen before the relation.

The evolutionary process, then, centers on appropriate adaptation to the environment. Yes, there is conflict within the natural process of struggling for existence. But this effort to survive takes place within the overall context of beings in relation to their environment. An ecological vision of evolution does not assert that "only the fittest survive." It reminds us that every new level of life is dependent on what has gone before. We cannot survive without the sun's energy and the plants. Everything is connected to everything else. Diversity within the ecosystems is essential for the planet's survival. Consequently, a harmonious and cooperative relationship between humanity and the earth benefits all. However, the creation of "harmony" will not happen if nature is perceived only as an object for humanity's enjoyment or survival. This kind of attitude, while recognizing the relation, misses its essential character by once again objectifying nature.

How do we move beyond this consistent tendency to utilize nature for our own purposes? Birch and Cobb suggest that each living thing actively takes account of its environment; each level of life has the capacity to experience. And, "for us to say that something experiences is to say that it is not merely an object in our world of experience but also a subject of relations in its own right. It is acted upon and it acts."[73] Does this mean that all living things *consciously* experience their environment? Birch and Cobb do not go that far. Susan Griffin does. I include here the full text of Griffin's reflection entitled, "Forest (The Way We Stand)," one of the last chapters of her book *Woman and Nature*:

> The way we stand, you can see we have grown up this way together, out of the same soil, with the same rains, leaning in the same way toward the sun. See how we lean together in the same direction. How the dead limbs of one of us rest in the branches of another. How those branches have grown around the limbs. How the two are inseparable. And if you look you can see the different ways we have taken this place into us. Magnolia, loblolly bay, sweet gum, Southern bayberry, Pacific bayberry; wherever we grow there are many of us; Monterrey pine, sugar pine, white-bark pine, four-leaf pine, single-leaf pine, bristle-cone pine, foxtail pine, Torrey pine, Western red pine, Jeffry pine, bishop pine. And we are various, and amazing in our variety and our differences multiply, so that edge after edge of the endlessness of possibility is exposed. You know we have grown this way for years. And to no purpose you can understand. Yet what you fail to know we know, and the knowing is in us, how we have grown this way, why these years were not one of them heedless, why we are shaped the way we are, not all straight to your purpose, but to ours. And how we are each purpose, how each cell, how light and soil are in us, how we are in the soil, how we are in the air, how we are both infinitesimal and great and how we are infinitely without any purpose you can see, in the way we stand, each alone, yet none of us separable, none of us beautiful when separate but all exquisite as we stand, each moment heeded in this cycle, no detail unlovely.[74]

I have used this text often in ritual and guided meditation. It never fails to make a powerful impact on all participants. It invites humans to reconsider their place and role on the earth. Griffin's prose offers a mystical interpretation of scientific insights; it images unequivocally the subjectivity of our partners in homemaking.

The Economics of Sustainability Clearly, the present system of international capitalism benefits only those with the most capital. It does not sustain the majority of humanity or its natural environment, yet designing another system to replace it is one of the most perplexing realities facing us today. The task becomes ever more urgent as several communist countries turn democratic, as the USSR attempts to shift toward a market-oriented economy, as the Rome EC summit decides to implement political and monetary union (and as the United States has done in the treaty with Canada to dismantle the trade barriers between the countries and seeks to negotiate a similar agreement with Mexico). Will these moves produce a global economics of sustainability for everyone and the earth?

Strategies for creating an alternative economic reality are beginning to emerge within the feminist spirituality movement. They are, however, a far cry from an adequate theory and integrated international practice of sustainable economics. While most cultural and socialist feminists are convinced that radical changes are called for, this is one of the least developed areas within feminist spiritualities. Recent trends, however, especially within the ecofeminist movement and the writings of ethicians like Beverly Harrison,[75] indicate a growing consciousness that spiritual liberation cannot happen apart from economic democracy.

But where does the hope for this new economic order lie? At the present moment, much of it is located in the creativity of community-based economics experimenting with alternative ways to structure the "functions of the home." Practices include the sharing of domestic duties and childcare between women and men, the creation of community crêches or day-care centers, organization at the local level to stop environmental destruction by corporate industry, the development of various forms of barter systems within limited geographical locales, and several other ways of decreasing a community's dependence on government and national companies to provide economic security. Women's access to the economic sector and men's responsibility for homemaking form integral features of these strategies. At its heart, though, lies the conviction that a sustainable economy cannot emerge unless wealth is produced and shared equally and nature is not abused in the process.

Alternative local economic practices, while necessary, are not sufficient to challenge international economic systems. Much more work needs to be done in the theoretical arena. The publication of titles such as *If Women Counted: A New Feminist Economics*[76] and *The Living Economy: A New Economics in the Making*[77] indicate significant beginnings. It is hoped that more will follow. And it will be important for those on the feminist spiritual journey to read these texts together. This, I think, is key if a spirituality for feminists is to manifest in a genuine way a hope for the wholeness of *all*.

The Religious Ingredients for a Homemaking Culture The diverse traditions of feminist spiritualities converge in their insistence on our need to reimage the Sacred in light of an ecological consciousness. Feminists' peacework, environmental care, and anti-nuclear activism impel a search for Sacred presence on earth. The first step toward encounter here, as we have already seen, involves radical criticism of a matter-less, absolutely transcendent, and distant "God." Past imagery has robbed the nature world of its inherent value and creative potential. But what shall we put in its place? How can we name the Sacred so that she/he/it will empower us to make our home with the earth?

I want to consider two distinct forms of Sacred imagery surfacing within feminist spiritualities. They have some common elements but also manifest irreconcilable differences. In large part, these differences are due to diverse faith stances and spiritual heritages. Once again I suggest that a spirituality for feminists invites us to hear imagery that comes from various traditions as we seek the Sacred. In this way we honor the ecological principle of the necessity for diversity. At the same time, our chosen spiritual heritage will no doubt affect the kind of impact that some imagery has on us over others. Yet we may need to experiment with diverse naming in order to image the Sacred out of a genuinely biocentric consciousness.

In the previous chapter we saw that "Goddess" is the preferred imagery of some feminists because of its potential to affirm Sacred presence in the natural cycle of life and death. The ancient imagery of this symbol fills its contemporary meaning with the power to spark belief in the immanent presence of the Sacred. "He" is no longer "out there"; "She" is here. As Charlene Spretnak insists, "immanence takes the place of transcendence"[78] in an ecofeminist spirituality. Starhawk says "[the] Goddess is embodied in the living world, in the human, animal, plant, and mineral communities and their interrelationships." Why is it so essential to image the Sacred in this way? Starhawk continues:

> For when this world is seen as the living body of the Goddess, there is no escape, nowhere else to go, no one to save us. This earth body itself is the terrain of our spiritual growth and development . . . with the reality of what's going on here. When what's going on is the poisoning and destruction of the earth, our own personal development requires that we grapple with that and do something to stop it, to turn the tide and heal the planet.[79]

No transcendent "God" has the power to stop the cycle of destruction that human beings have set in place. In Starhawk's view, this notion of a "savior God" must be replaced with a sense of the Sacred that impels us to take our own responsibility for healing the earth. The Sacred is here, waiting for us to work with her in the project of re-creation. Furthermore, the Sacred is best represented as female. "Goddess" contains enormous potential to re-value woman and nature together.

Some of these concerns are echoed by feminists working within a Christian tradition. Authors such as Rosemary Ruether and Sallie McFague also reconstruct the primary sacred symbol with an emphasis on immanence, though they are not willing to let go of the transcendent character of "God or God/ess." The heritage of Christianity, I think, afffects their contemporary re-imaging in ways that recover a "God/ess" who is with us here while simultaneously reinterpreting the meaning of her transcendence. Sallie McFague does this by offering a novel and quite unsettling image of God's nature through reinterpreting the appearance stories of Jesus after his death. McFague asks us to reconsider the meaning of these narratives. What if, she queries, we were to interpret the appearance stories not as proof for the bodily resurrection of Jesus (or the future promise of our own bodily resurrections), but as "the promise of God to be permanently present, 'bodily' present to us, in all places and times of our world?"[80] Perhaps in our time, a time that demands the interpretation of sacred symbols with an ecological consciousness, we ought to understand the appearances of Jesus as God's promise to be with us in time and space. She develops this metaphorical interpretation as a way of leading us to image the universe as "God's body," the universe as the "self-expression of God." In this way, the world is also the incarnation of God. But does this mean that God is reducible to nature, that God cannot exist apart from nature? No, answers McFague. God exists within the material universe, but God is not identical with what she has created. God's transcendent character manifests itself in her personal agency to sustain creation as mother, lover, and friend. The natural world manifests God's presence in a "palpable," touchable fashion, but God is also the one who enables the natural life cycle to continue. God cannot be killed if humanity were to destroy the planet.

There are several other examples of feminist imagery for Sacred presence within creation. All attempt to move us through new perceptions of the Sacred beyond the matter/spirit dualism. Each kind of imagery tries to re-present a practical love for the earth of which we are a part. Feminists are convinced that the politics of peace and the sustenance of the earth require this kind of religious work.

Still, there is more work to be done. A spirituality for feminists demands new religious myths of origins and novel ways to answer the question: "What about the end?" Elizabeth Dodson Gray contends that Christian feminists must re-myth their origins so that they will possess a formative sacred story that reflects humanity's interrelatedness with all other creatures of the earth. They need a narrative that asserts the equality of women and men. They need a story that provokes humanity to love and respect the earth.

Will they find this through a reinterpretation of Genesis? Maybe. But perhaps I, a Christian feminist, will also need to listen to the sacred stories of other traditions to spark an imaginative remembering of my own. Starhawk's is one of the most powerful stories of origins told from a feminist perspective. Her book, *Truth or Dare,* starts with "A Story of Beginnings." This is an imaginative picture of how it all began, influenced by contemporary science and her own efforts to save the planet. Its power, I believe, resides in her ability to poetically and prophetically suggest that the beginnnings were not original harmony. Rather, the origin of our earth, ourselves, was a cyclical process of evolution that incorporated movement from conflict to resolution, joy to suffering, death to rebirth. The grandeur and goodness of the beginning was not a static reality of eternal bliss that one fall forever damaged. Instead, the immanent goodness was the power of Goddess and all earthlife to keep evolving through a number of "falls." Starhawk's story is one example of a narrative that remembers the cyclical character of original interrelatedness. Because it is cyclical and not linear, it provides a memory that invites humanity to keep focused on the earth as home.

Is there a way to image the "end" that will do the same? The praxis of homemaking with and on the earth leads to a "this-worldly" interpretation of heaven and hell.[81] The deep communion with the source of life and all others may not be something that happens once and for all in a place out of earth. The horrific disintegration, alienation, and exploitation that kills people and other living things may not be a punishment meted out at the end of time. Suppose that our "hope for wholeness" is not a wish for a final wholeness outside of history but for one that happens every so often on earth, thus giving us the courage to hope and act for it again, to believe that we and the earth will survive? Rosemary Ruether talks about an eschatology focused not so much on individual soul-salvation as one that challenges us to live so that others after us will have a future home here.[82] Catherine Keller proposes that we change the myth of end-time to one of cyclical rebirth.[83] If we image an open and sustainable future instead of an end that will come no matter what we do, maybe this will deepen a belief that what we do makes a difference, now and forever. But what about our own deaths? Will our spirited matter transform in a way that enables our unique identities to go on? If so, where? Maybe our ancestors are genuinely (ontologically) here with us now. Maybe their presence resides in our memories. Whatever way we image their presence after death or our own presence after death, a spirituality for feminists invites us to live now so that earth can be home for the living and the dead.

— 6 —

Embodying Hope for Wholeness: Feminist Ritual

Because I was raised in the Roman Catholic tradition, I was bequeathed a deep love of ritual. One of my favorite memories from early childhood is accompanying my parents to benediction. I can still smell the incense, see the Blessed Sacrament exposed in gold, hear the hushed sounds of silence and sense the awe in the air. At its best, this experience enabled me to feel wholly the presence of the Sacred. The benediction ritual provided a rhythmic form and special space to meet the transcendent God. The sacrament of eucharist also bestowed this possibility. Frequent attendance at the ritual of the Eucharist solidified belief, touched my soul, and drew me into a Sacred presence that nourished a lifestyle guided by Christian faith.

Lex orandi, lex credendi: The way we pray is the way we believe. To put it another way, "the way we pray determines what we believe and what we do."[1] This is the heart of ritual's power at the personal level. But it is also the crux of why feminists have had to distance themselves from the rituals that maintain the patriarchal essence of religions. The rituals of the fathers not only exclude women's experience, they reinforce dualistic beliefs and sacralize the superiority of maleness. Since embarking on the feminist spiritual journey, I, along with countless other feminists, have realized and felt that the rituals of our childhood negate the spiritual insights and practices of living interdependently. Consequently, to continue to seek nourishment and Sacred presence within the rhythm of patriarchal ritual is dangerous to our health.

Something else is going on, though, in addition to the personal impact of ritual. Anthropologists tell us that there exists a dialectical relationship between ritual and culture. The symbols, dreams, and values of a culture shape the structure, themes, and meaning of religious ritual. Likewise, sacred ceremonies sanctify the patterns of valuing, knowing, and behaving within a particular culture. Traditional Jewish and Christian rituals have celebrated and maintained the worldview, symbols, and values of Western patriarchal culture. Ritual's power extends beyond the personal to the political. As defined in the opening pages of our present study, the central and ongoing objective of feminism is to fashion a culture that takes us beyond the vision and activities of patriarchy. The practitioners of feminist spiritualities are keenly aware of the constructive role that ritual can play in this dynamic. The vision, symbols, and values of a feminist culture require that religious ritual be recreated.

I am fully aware of the pain, fear, and confusion that is part of this process. Before feminism there was so much security and familiarity with the rituals; our very relationship with God depended upon them. We knew how and where we could encounter the divine. The formulas were crafted carefully over centuries. No one ever taught us how to fashion our own; we were the passive recipients of others' power to mediate access to the Sacred. This spiritual dependency paralyzed our own ability to imagine language and symbols that could express our experience of the Sacred. I am also cognizant of the radical nature of the invitation to recreate religious ritual. It means far more than putting together a "para-liturgy." The sanctuary has been opened regardless of ordained or non-ordained status. The sacred space is no longer restricted to one particular place or a specified set of actions. This, however, is a necessary and vital part of embodying the feminist hope for wholeness. Let us now consider why.

What Is Feminist Ritual?

One of the most remarkable signs of the health of the feminist spirituality movement is the celebration of rituals by people coming together from different backgrounds and religious traditions. The conversational character of a spirituality for feminists is embodied through the creation of rituals that respect the diversity and interdependence of its participants. This phenomenon, I believe, gives witness to the hope for wholeness that is at the heart of the spirituality paradigm proposed throughout this book. It also directs my choice for the word "ritual" as the most inclusive term for describing what is happening.[2] Though "liturgy," "worship," and "prayer service" are terms also in use, these surface primarily in Jewish and Christian feminist spiritualities, and are employed interchangeably with ritual. By choosing "ritual" I want to indicate a significant part of the common language in a spirituality for feminists. Its use is meant to represent two things: (1) that feminists are and ought to continue celebrating rituals with others from varied traditions and (2) that feminists are and ought to continue creating rituals within their own traditions. In these ways we publicly express the truths that exist in our own traditions and the courage to have those truths enriched or confronted by the spiritual journeys of other feminists.

So, what is feminist ritual? Having participated in various kinds and having examined a number of authors, I offer the following as an effort to identify common threads in diverse tapestries. First, a definition: *Feminist ritual is imaginative symbolic expression of the Sacred movement of life, death, and rebirth.* It is "corporate symbolic action"[3] that expresses the interdependence of self, the Sacred, others, and the earth in artistic form. It is symbolic activity that is above all a revelatory experience. Ritual enables us to reveal our present effort to move toward wholeness through and with the Sacred. Ritual reveals Sacred presence within ourselves, our activities, and relationships with one another and the earth. This process, as Starhawk says, "sustains us as it marks the cycles of birth, growth, decay, and renewal that sustain our lives."[4] The structure of rituals vary from something as simple as opening prayer, meditative music, sharing our imagery of Sacred presence, closing prayer to a larger communal gathering that expresses the specific memories and hopes of a group that has been with one another over a certain period of time.

Many feminists also practice personal rituals. These are moments set aside for individuals to focus on the interior process of deepening self-integrity or personal power. Starhawk, Hallie Iglehart, and Diane Mariechild offer several examples of ritual-work that nourish individual needs and assist the process of integrating body and spirit, sexuality and spirituality, emotion and intellect.[5] The greater number of feminist rituals, though, are practiced within a communal context. Christian feminist base communities, Jewish feminist communities, covens, and women's spirituality groups provide a supportive setting for the public expression of self-love, mutuality in diversity, reverence for the earth, and sensing Sacred presence. In community feminists ritualize their experiences of relationship and their search for justice, love, and peace. Through diverse structures and different traditions feminist ritual enacts communal faith in and hope for wholeness.

Feminist Ritual: Artistic, Creative, Imaginative

There are an infinite number of ways to ritualize the feminist spiritual journey. It is up to each participant to draw on her or his creative ability to image the symbols, words, movement, and music that will express the particular focus of each ritual. For many, this is one of the most difficult challenges of feminist ritual. Not only is it plain, hard work; very few of us have been taught to "tap our own inner imagery."[6] It is true that some will be more naturally gifted than others, yet the richness and effectiveness of ritual will depend on everyone making some effort to contribute. Simple guidelines that facilitate this process include: (1) spend some time individually through silence and/or guided meditation to identify appropriate symbols and images; (2) bring together a number of resources for prayer, music, poetry, sacred texts, and/or body movement; (3) as Diann Neu says, "Discover who the artists are: dancers, musicians, mimists, storytellers, creators of environment, poets, organizers, and invite them to use their talents in the celebration"[7] and (4) select together from the resources inside and outside the group.

Shared creativity is an integral dimension of becoming active participants in the ritual-making process. It also accentuates the equal value of individuals and the nourishing character of interdependent activity. Yet the importance of imagination in feminist ritual travels deeper than this. Much of the deadness in patriarchal religious ritual arises from not calling on the arts. Theological discourse encapsulated in rigid prayer forms emphasizes the superiority of reason over imagination. Feminist ritual attempts to shatter this expression of dualism by becoming "more than words."[8] In describing what they wanted their rituals to accomplish, the authors of *Women's Spirit Bonding* identified the centrality of "enabling individuals to draw upon their physical, emotional, and imaginative powers as well as their analytic skills."[9] The art of individual and collective imagination symbolizes and deepens the wholeness that we seek.

Feminist Ritual: Sensual

Imaginative symbolic expression engages our whole body-spirits. The sacred space of feminist ritual creates boundaries wherein we can sense the depth of spiritual experience. The light of candles and the color of our symbols and environment invite a renewed sense of sight. Incense and flowers enliven smell. Body movements—even such simple gestures as a handshake or blessing the forehead of another—bring forth a different way of knowing our connections with one another. Telling stories and making music raise and quiet energy through hearing. Many rituals incorporate a time for feasting, signifying that "eating food together is a holy action, a necessary luxury."[10] This process of "coming to our senses" offers whole forms of healing. It integrates diverse ways of knowing where we have been and what we ought to do. It reminds us that our participation in the sacred movement of life, death and rebirth is an embodied one.

Because it is a sensual experience, feminist ritual conveys the significance of feelings for spirituality. As Kay Turner indicates:

> In the context of ritual women are creating a space in which to feel better, to feel more, to feel the past as well as the future . . . . Ritual upholds and celebrates the validity of feelings as a mode of revelation, communication, and transvaluation.[11]

It is through feelings as well as thoughts that we discover self-integrity and healthy forms of interrelatedness. Together, emotion and rationality enable self-determination and a lifestyle of interdependence. Ritual supports the integration, not suppression, of feelings. It does this not only through serious and solemn moments. Feminist ritual extends its boundaries to incorporate time for spontaneity, laughter, and play. It is all right to laugh within sacred space. Why? Starhawk says, "The elements of laughter and play keep us from getting stuck on one level of power or developing an inflated sense of self-importance. Humor keeps kicking us onward, to go deeper . . . ."[12]

Feminist Ritual: Repetitive

Repetition has always been a fundamental characteristic of ritual. We often name activities or events "rituals" if we engage in them frequently. Birthday celebrations, having a cup of tea or coffee at a certain time each day, and opening a football game with the national anthem are all examples of what we might designate as "ritual." Religious rituals such as the seder meal or the sacrament of baptism are comprised of prayers, blessings, and stories that are repeated each time the rite takes place. Repetition provides a sense of familiarity and security; it roots participants in their cultural, familial, and religious heritages.

One of the earliest critiques that feminists raised regarding the rituals of their religious traditions, however, was the absence of women's directives in formulating the rites. Futhermore, repetition of men's formulas left little room for the inclusion of women's contemporary experiences. In fact, as they are practiced in many communities today, Jewish and Christian rituals value the past more than the present precisely through the rigid repetition of outdated formulas and prayers. What has this meant for feminist ritual? Initially we veered away from any kind of repetiton, especially by creating prayer services and liturgies that were completely outside of sacramental or Sabbath settings. Or, even as Christian feminists followed the basic structure of sacramental rites we consistently created different prayers, creeds, and blessings. As time has passed, though, I think that we are beginning to reclaim the value of repetition in ritual. Marcia Falk astutely describes the issue at stake:

> One of the deepest challenges for all feminist liturgy, I believe, is to keep our speech, like our thoughts, constantly evolving and re-

> sponsive to change, even as we create forms to be used repetitively to build community and foster tradition.
>
> How to do this successfully—how to create an exciting balance between spontaneity and repeated form—is a question that religious feminists, both "traditional" and "post-traditional," inevitably grapple with.[13]

As Falk indicates, repetition of ritual forms builds community and fosters tradition. This is significant for feminist communities especially as they seek to recreate the religions of their history or create feminist religions rooted in the ancient images and stories of the Goddess. Repeated rites—with extensive space and moments for attention to the present—empower the creation of tradition in a spirituality for feminists. Let us consider some of the new rites that are evolving.

1. *Litanies that remember historical and contemporary women.* The basic formula encourages local communities and/or larger gatherings to remember women whom they name as holy. At the National Conference on Women in the Uniting Church in Australia (1990), they prayed the following "litany":

A Celebration of Women

Leader The color purple is God's gift to us all.
Purple for the dignity of women:
of biblical women, of women in history,
of contemporary women, such as Linda and
Michelle, Carol and Jenny.
We stand up for and commit ourselves to the
dignity of women.

Response We light a purple candle for the dignity of women.

Leader The color white is God's gift to us all.
White for the singlemindedness of women:
Ruth for committing herself to travel with Naomi
and worship her God;
Amelia committed to never giving up until women
could vote;

Muriel committed to writing and speaking
until women may preside at the Eucharist in the
Anglican Church;
Dorothy and Janet committed to speak
until all women may speak and be heard in the
Uniting Church.

Response We light a white candle for the singlemindedness of women.

Leader The color green is God's gift to us all.
Green for the hope of the women's movement:
the hope of biblical women who dared to stand tall;
the hope of women in history
who wrote without a contemporary audience;
the hope of us all for a Church Made Whole.

Response We light a green candle for the hope of women.

Leader The people choose a purple, green, or white candle and speak about which one is chosen and why.

Coralie Ling[14]

2. *Invocation of Sacred Presence.* The invocation calls on the Sacred to be present for the ritual and often identifies the theme of the ceremony. The opening prayer from the Liturgy of the Cork Feminist Spirituality Conference (1988) is one example:

God and Goddess, we gather here
in your name.
and in our name
We have heard the tradition of the centuries
Some of the words that have condemned us to
reject ourselves and one another in your name.
We have been raised
to be distrustful of ourselves
suspicious of other women
limited in our hope

confined in our love.
We acknowledge that
we have learned this lesson well
from our brothers and husbands
lovers and friends
and we have learned this lesson
from one another as well.
And all of this in your name.
We bring the layers of our history
and our life together
and pray to you, God and Goddess, who are both
Mother and Father to us
for the courage to shake the dust
of oppression from our well-worn sandals
For the strength to say no more
to the wedges that
have kept us separate from one another
For the love that will
fertilize our lives so that
We might be reconciled with
one another.[15]

3. *Psalms for Feminists.* This form patterns itself after the basic rhythmic structure of psalms from the Hebrew Scriptures. Usually they reinterpret a traditional psalm with language and imagery from the lives of women. Janet Morley has written the following:

I will praise God, my Beloved
for she is altogether lovely.

Her presence satisfies my soul;
she fills my senses to overflowing
so that I cannot speak.

Her touch brings me to life;
the warmth of her hands makes me wholly alive.

Her embrace nourishes me, body and spirit;

every part of my being responds to her touch.

The beauty of her face is more than I can bear;
in her gaze I drown.

. . . .

Even in chaos you will bear me up; if the waters go over my head,
you will still be holding me.

For the chaos is yours also,
and in the swirling of mighty waters .
is your presence known.

If I trust her, surely her power will not fail me;
nor will she let me be utterly destroyed.

Though I lose all knowledge and all security,
yet will my God never forsake me;

but she will recreate me, in her steadfast love,
so that I need not be afraid.

Then will I praise my Beloved among the people,
among those who seek to know God.[16]

4. Rites for Grounding. The Wiccan tradition and practitioners in the spiritualities of women's power have developed various meditations to assist participants in making the transition from daily activities/ preoccupations to the sacred space of ritual. Starhawk describes grounding as a "means to connect with the earth, with our own centers, with the forces around us and the people who share our ritual. To be grounded also means to be in a particular energy state, calm and relaxed, yet alert: aware of both your own internal energy and the group's energy."[17] The following is an abridged version of a grounding meditation used frequently by Starhawk:

Notice your own energy. How do you feel in your body? In this space? In this circle? How connected or disconnected? How tired? How excited? Just observe your energy; don't try to change it.

Now take a deep breath, down into your belly. Place your hands on your belly. Feel it expand as you inhale, becoming round like the moon.

. . . .

Now imagine your breath sinking down through your hips, your legs, your feet. Imagine yourself as a tree, rooted in the earth, with your breath sinking down through your roots. Feel your roots push down through the living soil. Let them connect you to this spot on the earth; let them tell you what it is like to be rooted here, to be linked to the plants, the animals. Let them tell you about the weather and the seasons.

. . . .

Breathe deep again, and let your roots push deeper, down through the bedrock, down into the core of fire at the heart of the earth. Feel the fire as pure, transforming energy. If you still carry any energy you'd like to let go of, let it go into the earth, to feed the earth, like compost. Let it go with a sound. Let yourself make a bigger sound.

Notice how your energy feels, and how the energy in the room feels. How did it change with your sound?

. . . .

Now let's breathe together, breathing in and out. Letting our breath become one breath, letting ourselves become one living, breathing organism.

. . . .

Now ground the energy by touching the earth with your hands, or by lying down on it. Imagine letting the energy go back to the earth, for her healing and renewal.

. . . .

Now notice how you feel, and how the energy of the group feels. What has changed?[18]

5. Blessing Ritual Participants. Offering a blessing is one form of closing the ritual. Sometimes participants bless each other, wishing one another protection and nourishment for their return to everyday activities, and sometimes (as in the following example) one person also blesses the whole gathering. This blessing is taken from a Good Friday ritual, created by Diann Neu:

Blessing for the Journey

(The blesser invites everyone to stand and gather close in a circle. She offers the blessing in her own words, gathering together the spirit of worship.)

Song: "Blessing Song" by Marsie Silvestro

Bless you my sister . . . Bless you on your way
You have roads to roam . . . before you're home
And winds to speak your name.

So go gently my sister . . . Let courage be your song
You have words to say . . . in your own way
And stars to light your night

And if ever you grow weary
And your heart's song has no refrain
Just remember we'll be waiting
To raise you up again.

And we'll bless you our sister . . . Bless you in our way
And we'll welcome home . . . . all the life you've known
And softly speak your name

Oh we'll welcome home . . . all the self you own
And softly speak your name.[19]

6. Recalling Women's Words. This formula produces diverse creativity. Feminists recall women's words by retelling the stories of biblical women, reading selections from the writings of spiritual and political leaders, and voicing the poetry of past and contemporary women poets. An imaginative remembering of women's words occurs in the following liturgy, "A Seder of the Sisters of Sarah." Ronnie Nevin and Diann Neu chose a Jewish woman's words to introduce the seder rite of

Kindling the Lights

Jewish holidays are ushered in with the kindling of lights, and many Christian celebrations begin by lighting candles. Tonight, before we light the festival candles, we hear the words of Hannah Senesh, a daughter of the Exodus, a Jewish freedom fighter who was captured and executed by the Nazis in 1944. While in prison, she wrote:

Blessed is the match consumed in kindling flame.
Blessed is the flame that burns
 in the secret fastness of the heart.
Blessed is the heart with strength to stop
 its beating for honor's sake.
Blessed is the match consumed in kindling flame.

Hannah Senesh

Let us, as Jewish and Christian women together, light the candles that guide us on our way toward liberation.

One woman at each table lights the candles. (Lights are dimmed.)[20]

This is a sampling, then, of the formulas or ritual units that have been repeated throughout the evolution of feminist ritual. While the basic forms are consistent, their very nature requires that the content be drawn from the spiritual journeys of present participants. Repetition in this fashion circumvents irrelevance and vivifies the memories and hopes of a spirituality for feminists.

What Is Feminist Ritual For?

Above all, ritual should transform its participants. It should heal us so that we can partake in the world's healing. What most feminists find, though, is that ritual's effectiveness for healing is integrally linked to the communal setting that bodies it forth. There must be some form of community, some kind of trust or practice of mutual relationships in order for ritual to work. Healing usually does not take place without some shared vision or in an atmosphere of distrust. Consequently, ongoing feminist communities and/or gatherings of feminists with a common purpose provide the most effective context for ritual. There is another side to this reality: Feminists have discovered over the years that they need spiritual communities wherein the practice of rituals forms an integral part. Rosemary Ruether describes why:

> It is not enough to hold an ideology of criticism and social analysis as an interpretive base, nor to participate in protest and action groups and organizations as vehicles of change. One needs communities of nurture to guide one through death to the old symbolic order of patriarchy to rebirth into a new community of being and living. One needs not only to engage in rational theoretical discourse about this journey; one also needs deep symbols and symbolic actions to guide and interpret the actual experience of the journey from sexism to liberated humanity.[21]

Feminist spiritual communities offer sustenance and support especially through opportunities for ritual-making. Likewise, ritual is a very effective medium for building and maintaining a community's vitality. [22]

The healing power of feminist ritual within community radiates in diverse ways. We recall the real presence of Sacredness through imaginative symbolic expression. Together we mediate access to the deity or, as Starhawk says, we enter the realm of mystery. Through the use of symbols, music, and prayers from a feminist imagination, we deepen our experience of and closeness with mystery. From a Christian perspective, Miriam Therese Winter explains it this way: "Let us never forget that the eternal God is neither male nor female but Mystery, a Presence, Power, Love. Underlying the rituals of *WomanPrayer, WomanSong,* [her book] is the effort to overcome the limitations of language to come to this understanding of God."[23] From the Jewish tradition, Marcia Falk describes it another way: "What shatters a verbal idol? Not hatchets, and not concepts—not the abstract idea that God is neither male nor female—but new living metaphors, verbal images possessing powers of transformation."[24]

The healing continues at the personal level through rituals that celebrate what we value and rites that mourn loss or experiences of suffering and abuse. Rosemary Ruether includes examples of women-church rites of "Healing from Distress of Mind or Body," of "Healing from a Miscarriage or a Stillbirth," and of "Healing for Wife Battering."[25] Rituals can ease times of transition, or mark special moments of the life cycle. Starhawk outlines "rituals of passage," an "Anger ritual," a "Pride ritual."[26] Rituals also offer opportunities for healing the earth-human relationship. Feminists celebrate the turning of the seasons; they symbolically express Sacred presence within the natural world. This deepens an appreciation for the beauty of the earth and encourages ecological politics. Rituals enable the sanctification and healing of each dimension of relationality in our lives. They interpret, celebrate, and continue to fashion a culture of interdependence.

While most group rituals share the intentions outlined above, there are certain underlying differences in purpose because of the make-up of the community. I have already indicated that rituals created by feminists from varied spiritual traditions manifest an intent to respect relational truths from diverse histories. The imaginative symbolic expression of honoring religious difference is a key feature of the feminist spiritual journey. It provides a significant vehicle for acknowledging conflict as well as crossing the boundaries of difference. When these rituals take place through local, national, and international gatherings, they provide space for participants to embody some of the most difficult challenges of an interdependent culture.

When participants share the Wiccan tradition, the underlying objective of ritual, regardless of its particular theme, has to do with raising and shaping energy or psychic power. Starhawk explains: "In ritual (a patterned movement of energy to accomplish a purpose) we become familiar with power-from-within, learn to recognize its *feel*, learn how to call it up and let it go."[27] Wiccan rituals begin by invoking energy from the earth and continue by calling forth the mysterious powers of Goddess and God. The central part, however, focuses on raising the psychic energy of its participants by inviting all to touch their own personal power, contribute it to the group's energy, and eventually return the energy to the earth. Often the symbols of the four elements are used to focus the thoughts and feelings of the group, and rituals usually include music, dance, chants, and storytelling. By following this structure, Craft rituals value the immanence of Sacred power and motivate participants to use that power in creating a sustainable and peaceful planet.

Jewish feminist prayers and rituals also strengthen the connection between the religious faith of its participants and the political work that they undertake. *Tikkun olam*—the repair of the world—is facilitated by the liturgical life of Jewish communities. Judith Plaskow describes this purpose: "To celebrate and ritualize our visions is to locate our political projects in the context of the ongoing work of creation, to take our place in the eternal dialogue between God and creation through which the world develops and unfolds."[28] The structure of their rituals usually follows traditional Jewish forms such as *Shabbat,* the seder meal, and *davenning*. These forms, however, are filled with new content expressing the spiritual insights of feminism. In this way, Jewish feminists ritualize within the tradition in order to preserve the best of it while simultaneously transforming its patriarchal dimensions. In describing her rationale for composing new Jewish blessings, Marcia Falk notes:

> I try to preserve meaningful ties to the historical Hebrew tradition, interweaving images and phrases from a variety of biblical midrashic, liturgical, and poetic sources. At the same time. . . I depart quite deliberately from the traditional prayers in as many ways as I need to.[29]

Remembering and reforming the tradition is central also to the rituals and liturgies of Christian feminists. Members of Protestant denominations create new prayers, blessings, and creeds that are used within traditional prayer services and liturgies. They incorporate biblical stories retold from a feminist perspective. They use a multiplicity of symbols and metaphoric language to celebrate an inclusive God and to lift up the revelatory character of women's experience. Implicit in their ritual-making is the rejection of churchmen's exclusive control of Christian worship. They refuse to be excluded any longer from creating symbolic expression of the sacred movement of life. The same is true for Roman Catholic feminists. The women-church movement in the United States is a prime example of women and men locating ritual and "sacramental power in the community rather than in ordained representatives."[30] They no longer wait for the reforms of churchmen; they create their own rituals—both inside and outside of sacramental settings. They believe that each ritual "effects what it signifies" (the traditional understanding of sacramental power), thus providing the spiritual nourishment necessary to remain in dialogue with the institutions of Christianity.

Feminist ritual, as it is practiced today, embodies the hope for wholeness in diverse ways. Yet, as I have also tried to indicate, common features exist in each kind of feminist spirituality. This furnishes the extraordinary opportunity to ritualize our own experiences of relationship, and to be healed by the ritual activities of others. This, I believe will deepen like nothing else our consciousness of interdependence and prompt action toward the health of all creation.

Epilogue: Whispers of New Hope

Women "hearing each other into speech" has been the primary resource for this book. I have tried to articulate the fruits of such hearing, and encourage new kinds of conversations to take place. The art of good conversation, however, requires all participants to listen as well as to speak. Genuine conversation requires that our speech be interspersed with silence. And yet, the silence after speech will not be empty: the new silence will carry the past hearing as it waits for more.

The movement from silence to speech to silence is a lot like beginning, writing, and ending a book. I have already begun the quietening process that comes with ending. As I embrace the silent side of speech,

I can hear whispers of new hope: markers for the future of a spirituality for feminists. Before I close, then, let me sketch the whispers; perhaps you hear them too.

The most provocative whispers have to do with the experience and meaning of "wholeness." I have talked a lot about wholenesss from several diverse perspectives. But as the crystal of this concept shifts, another set of colors sparkle.[1] How can our understanding of the path to wholeness truly be purged of all the linear vestiges of "perfection"? I have argued that the wholeness which feminists seek (self-integrity and interdependence) is *not* a journey to perfection which can only be experienced once in life after death. If perfection is the primary target of spirituality (or personal development), we will never be good enough until the end. And even that is optimistic in the perfection schema. The ideal is *never* experienced now; we are always falling short. This promotes, I believe, a denial of our own intrinsic value, a restlessness and emptiness within our relationships with others and disbelief in our ability to partner with the Sacred. In short, the desire for perfection leads to despair, not to hope.

How is the search for and the experience of wholeness different from this? As I mentioned in Chapter 2, wholeness has as much to do with experiences of interdependence with others, the earth, and the Sacred, as it has to do with moments of self-integrity. The pursuit of wholeness is not an individualistic activity; it encompasses political, personal, social, ecological and interpersonal concerns. What I want to make more explicit now, however, is the tidal character of this spiritual journey.[2] Seeking and finding wholeness reflects, I think, the ebb and flow of the sea. What this means is that we can and do experience times of wholeness. We do find moments of at-one-ness with self. There are earthcare events that offer health back to members of the environment. Mutual love does happen between people with differences. We do experience the flow of wholeness now, on and with the earth. This does make a difference to our world. We can know our own goodness. We can effectively utilize political and sacred power.

These are the experiences and memories that we carry with us into the ebb times. How hard it is, though, to remember the wholeness in the brokenness. How difficult it is to believe in future happiness and peace amidst tragedy, suffering, loss, and death. We, the earth, and others—especially when broken by social systems—can be violently scarred. Loss of physical, psychic, or spiritual health leaves permanent marks on our embodied spirits. Self-determination is often blocked; many people do hold power over us.

Yet, these experiences do not necessarily stop us from finding self-integrity and interrelatedness once again. I am fully aware that they do stop some people. I am painfully cognizant of how the destruction of interrelatedness in our world robs many of us of opportunities to survive. I know there are species we have killed forever. What I am trying to describe—to whisper—is that wholeness can be experienced again even as we carry our own scars and as we live with a deep awareness of social injustices.[3] Indeed, the flow after the ebb will be substantially different from the one before it. It will be a personal experience or social event of wholeness that has integrated and moved beyond past despair or loss. As the wounds heal, the wholeness that is reborn will carry the ebbmarks of history and earthstory.

What maintains the energy of this tidal movement? And where does it all lead? The feminist spiritual journey happens in the presence of the Sacred. This presence—expressed through myriad images, metaphors, and concepts—enables the movement of holiness. Sacred sustenance will not be effective, however, unless it meets our own willingness to survive. This, I believe, is what the "hope for wholeness" is all about. Here, hope is an embodied virtue that energizes us to find wholeness not once at the end of time, or not because we continue to fall short of experiencing it. Instead, we "hope for wholeness" by imaging what it could be like through remembering what it was, and through remembering how we found it after it was lost.

I no longer look for an end-point to time and space. I do not hope for absolute perfection and a static happiness. I hope that more and more people, in history, will experience the holy movement of ebb and flow, along with the earth. I hope that a spirituality for feminists will bring us closer in this direction.

Notes

Introduction

1. See, for example: Hallie Iglehart, *WomanSpirit: A Guide to Women's Wisdom* (San Francisco: Harper & Row, 1983); Diane Mariechild, *Mother Wit: A Feminist Guide to Psychic Development* (Trumansburg, New York: The Crossing Press, 1981); and D. Mariechild with Shuli Goodman, *The Inner Dance: A Guide to Spiritual and Psychological Unfolding* (Freedom, CA: Crossing Press, 1987); and Charlene Spretnak, ed. *The Politics of Women's Spirituality: Essays on the Rise of Spiritual Power within the Feminist Movement* (Garden City, NY: Anchor Press, 1982).
2. For Jewish feminism see Susannah Heschel, ed., *On Being a Jewish Feminist: A Reader* (New York: Schocken Books, 1983) and Judith Plaskow, *Standing Again at Sinai: Judaism From a Feminist Perspective* (San Francisco: Harper & Row, 1990).

   For Christian feminism see Susan Cady, Marian Ronan, Hal Taussig, *Sophia: The Future of Feminist Spirituality* (San Francisco: Harper & Row, 1986); Anne E. Carr, *Transforming Grace: Christian Tradition and Women's Experience* (San Francisco: Harper & Row, 1988); Denise Lardner Carmody, *Seizing the Apple: A Feminist Spirituality of Personal Growth* (New York: Crossroad, 1984); Joann Wolski Conn, ed., *Women's Spirituality: Resources for Christian Development* (Mahwah, NJ: Paulist Press, 1986); Mary Grey, *Feminism, Redemption and Christian Tradition* (Mystic, CT: Twenty-Third Publications, 1990); Beverly Harrison, *Our Right to Choose: Toward a New Ethic of Abortion* (Boston: Beacon Press, 1983); Carter Heyward, *The Redemption of God: A Theology of Mutual Relation* (Washington, D.C.: The University Press of America, 1982); Mary Hunt, *Fierce Tenderness: A Feminist Theology of Friendship* (New York: Crossroad, 1982); Rosemary Radford Ruether, *Women-Church: Theology and Practice of Feminist Liturgical Communities* (San Francisco: Harper & Row, 1985); Elisabeth Schüssler Fiorenza, *In Memory of Her: A Feminist Theological Reconstruction of Christian Origins* (New York: Crossroad, 1983); Maria Harris, *Dance of the Spirit: The Seven Steps of Women's Spirituality* (New York: Bantam Books, 1989).
3. See Starhawk, *The Spiral Dance* (San Francisco: Harper & Row, 1979)), *Dreaming the Dark* (Boston: Beacon Press, 1982), and *Truth or Dare: Encounters with Power, Authority and Mystery* (San Francisco: Harper & Row, 1987); and Z. Budapest, *The Holy Book of Women's Mysteries* (Oakland: Susan B. Anthony Coven No. 1, 1979/80) 2 vols.
4. See Carol Christ, *Laughter of Aphrodite: Reflections on a Journey to the Goddess* (San Francisco: Harper & Row, 1987); Charlene Spretnak, *Lost Goddesses of Early Greece: A Collection of Pre-Hellenic Myths* (Boston: Beacon Press, 1984); Naomi Goldenberg, *The Changing of the Gods: Feminism and the End of Traditional Religions* (Boston: Beacon Press, 1979); and Merlin Stone, *When God Was a Woman* (New York: Dial Press, 1976). For an excellent bibliographic resource for varied feminist spiritual traditions see Patrice Wynne, *The Womanspirit Sourcebook* (San Francisco: Harper & Row, 1988).
5. This is the name Mary Daly gives to her own feminist philosophy; see especially *Gyn/Ecology: Toward a Metaethics of Feminism* (Boston: Beacon Press, 1978) and *Pure Lust: Elemental Feminist Philosophy* (Boston: Beacon Press, 1984).

6. By "praxis" I mean the dialectical process of gaining knowledge through thinking about one's actions, and having one's actions directed by that reflection. As Jürgen Habermas points out, this process is also directed by specific interests that one holds, and these interests affect the nature and contours of the knowledge discovered. For feminist theologians, their primary interest is the liberation of women and other oppressed groups; this will necessarily affect the theory (theology) that comes from the critical reflection on the activity directed toward that end.
7. The "separarist" character of Mary Daly's philosophy essentially means that she theorizes out of women's experience (though often placing it in dialogue with men's theory) in order to invite women toward self-integrity and deep connection with the earth. She is not interested in theorizing about men's wholeness. She does not, however, deny wholeness as a possibility for men.
8. Heterosexism is the unjust cultural ideology of heterosexual superiority and homosexual inferiority.
9. Quotation from tabloid announcing the Second National Conference of Women-Church: "Claiming Our Power," p. 1 (WATER, Silver Spring, MD). The women-church movement originated in the United States. Mary Hunt defines it as "a global, ecumenical movement made up of local feminist base communities of justice-seeking friends who engage in sacrament and solidarity." See her article, "Defining Women-Church," *WATERwheel* Vol. 3., No. 2 (Summer 1990): 1.
10. From the statement of the journal's "Objectives," Premier Issue, Spring 1984.
11. From the statement of the journal's "Objectives," Issue One, 1985, p. 2.
12. *Sophia: The Future of Feminist Spirituality*, p. 4. It is also to agree with Carol Christ who offers the following insight regarding a scholar's search for truth: "Incorporating personal reflection into our work does not mean that our work becomes solipsistic. I propose that empathy, not objectivity, is the way out of solipsism. As scholars we should strive to constantly remember that we are grounded in particular experiences and histories, while seeking ever to expand the range of our empathy, our ability to imagine the perspective of others."*Laughter of Aphrodite*, p. xvi.

    I want to add that truth based on "empathy" means that relationships are a central source for truth. In this way truth is both relational and historical. My own efforts to "empathize" formally occur in an educational arena that will be discussed in the following section.
13. Developed in conversation with Ann Louise Gilligan.
14. "Socially powerless" people are those conditioned by social structures to perceive themselves as inferior. This is not a *natural* powerlessness; therefore it can be changed.
15. Gustavo Gutierrez, *A Theology of Liberation: History, Politics, and Salvation* (Maryknoll, NY: Orbis Books, 1972) and *The Power of the Poor in History* (Maryknoll, NY: Orbis Books, 1983).
16. See his *On Job: God-Talk and the Suffering of the Innocent* (Maryknoll, NY: Orbis Books, 1987), esp. pp. *xiii–xiv.*
17. What follows has to do with theology rooted in the experience of different sectors of humanity helping one another. This is the kind of reflection I am involved in. However, other feminist theologians write out of a concern for and activity of supporting the natural world. This is equally necessary, though from a practical perspective, theologians usually choose one or two

particular commitments out of which they write and speak. We will see more about the importance of theology coming from an ecological consciousness and activity in Chapter 5.

18. Within this context I teach feminist theology. I use the subject as a vehicle for the conscientization of women and men.
19. I am aware that naming this experience as "privileged" is directly due to the fact that I have chosen it. I did not leave my culture of origin because of war or persecution. This necessarily makes a difference.
20. Daniel Maguire, in conversation and lectures.
21. Patriarchy is not only a cultural system that oppresses females, but every other group that does not fit the norm of "white, male, propertied and educated." See Elisabeth Schüssler Fiorenza in her *Bread Not Stone* (Boston: Beacon Press, 1984), "Introduction," for a similar understanding of patriarchy.
22. Joan Kelly, *Women, History and Theory: The Essays of Joan Kelly* (Chicago: University of Chicago Press, 1984), pp. 65-109.
23. Kelly identifies these positions as: (1) "a conscious, dialectical stand in opposition to male defamation and subjection of women;" (2) "a sure sense that the sexes are culturally, not just biologically, formed"; and (3) "a more universalist outlook than the accepted value systems of the time . . . . they stood for a general conception of humanity." *Ibid.*, pp. 66-67.
24. "Men in solidarity with women" listen to women's experiences of oppression, and commit themselves to join women in the struggle against sexism.
25. Rosemary Ruether also defines feminism as the creation of a new culture. She writes: "The feminism we envision is one that is able constantly to build an integral vision of a new humanizing culture beyond patriarchy without becoming closed or sectarian toward any living cultural option or human community." *Women-Church*, p. 40. In addition, it is important to note that there exists great diversity between feminists in their critique of patriarchy and their alternative vision for a new culture. See Maria Riley's fine analysis of the differences within feminism in her *Transforming Feminism* (Kansas City: Sheed and Ward, 1989); and see Sandra M. Schneiders, *Beyond Patching: Faith and Feminism in the Catholic Church* (Mahwah, NJ: Paulist Press, 1991).
26. See Jon Alexander, "What Do Recent Writers Mean by Spirituality?" *Spirituality Today* 32/3 (Sept. 1980): 247-256, for a fine survey of the contemporary meaning of the term.
27. *Horizons* vol. 13, no. 2 (Fall, 1986): 253-74. See also Joann Wolski Conn's entry, "Spirituality," in *The New Dictionary of Theology*, edited by Joseph Komonchak, Mary Collins, and Dermot Lane, (Dublin: Gill and Macmillan, 1987): 972-986; and Gordon S. Wakefield's entry, "Spirituality," in *A Dictionary of Christian Spirituality*, Gordon S. Wakefield, ed. (London: SCM Press, 1983): 363-363.
28. Schneiders, "Theology and Spirituality," pp. 264-65.
29. *Ibid.*, p. 267. Schneiders's definition follows a sampling of definitions offered by current scholars in the discipline of spirituality. She argues that within each definition there is this emphasis on integration of the self through reference to something beyond the self.
30. I will return to this in more detail in Chapter 1.
31. Therefore, relationship, not self, is the basic unit of spirituality.
32. See my essay, "Christian Feminism: The Spirituality of Bonding," *The Irish Catechist* 8/3 (October 1984): 15-29, where I identify ways in which a dualistic worldview affected Christian women's experience of relationship in their spiritual journey.

33. Anne Carr makes this point in an important article, "On Feminist Spirituality," *Horizons* 9/1 (1982): 96-103.
34. See, for example, Starhawk, *Dreaming the Dark*, p. xiii; Spretnak, *The Politics of Women's Spirituality*, p. 396; Davis and Weaver, "Dimensions of Spirituality," in *The Politics of Women's Spirituality*, p. 370; Ochs, *Women and Spirituality*, (Totowa, NJ: Rowman and Allanheld, 1983), p. 10; Beverly Harrison, *Our Right to Choose*, p. 106-110; Cady, Ronan and Taussig, *Sophia: The Future of Feminist Spirituality*, pp. 3-7.

Chapter 1

1. The *Woman's Bible* has been reissued by Polygon Books, Edinburgh, 1985. Two other significant works from this period indicate that the search for women's freedom in society necessarily affected women's relationships with the God of patriarchal religions. These include Matilda Joslyn Gage, *Woman, Church and State* (originally published in 1895, reissued by Persephone Press, Watertown, MA, 1980) and Charlotte Perkins Gilman, *His Religion and Hers* (originally published in 1924).
2. Margaret A. Farley, "New Patterns of Relationship: Beginnings of a Moral Revolution," *Theological Studies* Vol. 36 (December 1975): 631.
3. Starhawk, "Witchcraft and Women's Culture," in *Womanspirit Rising: A Feminist Reader in Religion*, Carol P. Christ and Judith Plaskow, eds. (San Francisco: Harper & Row, 1979), p. 262.
4. Naomi Goldenberg argues that this is the most appropriate word to describe reflection on the history and symbolization of the deity as Goddess. *Theos* is the Greek word for a masculine god; *thea* is the word for goddess. See her *Changing of the Gods*, p. 96.
5. Carol P. Christ, "Spiritual Quest and Women's Experience," *Womanspirit Rising*, p. 230.
6. "Power" holds several connotations, including many negative ones. By power, I mean *ability to effect change*. Feminists use power to effect personal and social change toward wholeness and freedom.
7. Michele Roberts, "The Woman Who Wanted to be a Hero," in *Walking on the Water: Talking About Spirituality*, Jo Garcia and Sara Maitland, eds. (London: Virago Press, 1983). Another collection of essays wherein women in an American context reflect on their own spirituality is *The Stories We Hold Secret: Tales of Women's Spiritual Development*, Carol Bruchac, Linda Hogan, Judith McDaniel, eds. (Greenfield Center, NY: The Greenfield Review Press, 1986). Also note Linda Hurcombe's *Sex and God: Some Varieties of Women's Religious Experience* (London: Routledge & Kegan Paul, 1987).
8. See, for example, Mary Daly, "A Built-in Bias," *Commonweal* Vol. LXXXI, (January 15, 1965): 508-11; *The Church and the Second Sex* (San Francisco: Harper & Row, 1968); Valerie Saiving, "The Human Situation: A Feminine View," (1960) republished in *Womanspirit Rising*, pp. 25-42.
9. A sampling includes: Rosemary Radford Ruether, *Liberation Theology* (New York: Paulist Press, 1972), *Religion and Sexism* (1974), and *New Woman/New Earth* (New York: Seabury Press, 1975); Letty M. Russell, *Human Liberation in a Feminist Perspective* (Philadelphia: Westminster, 1974); Judith Plaskow, "The Coming of Lilith: Toward a Femininst Theology," (1972) now in *Womanspirit Rising*; Rita M. Gross, "Female God Language in a Jewish Context," (1976) in *Womanspirit Rising;* Elisabeth Schüssler Fiorenza, "Feminist Theology as a Critical Theology of Liberation," *Theological Studies* 36 (1975): 605-

26; Phyllis Trible, "Eve and Adam: Genesis 2-3 Reread" (1972) in *Womanspirit Rising.*

10. Title of a book by Merlin Stone (New York: Dial Press, 1976). Stone was one of the first to recover the ancient religion of the "Goddess" (dating back to 25,000 B.C.E.) as a source for the contemporary experience of women's spirituality. Starhawk and Z. Budapest also published works at this time that started to construct an alternative religion of witchcraft, rooted in pre-Christian, earth-based, and tribal religions of Europe. Starhawk calls witchcraft a "mystery religion" and its central religious symbol is the "Goddess." This symbol encourages the positive use of female power to create a world where the earth and all its people live in harmony and peace. Contrary to popular notions that witches are sources of evil, Starhawk and Z. Budapest argue that witches are "wise women" who explore ways of changing the consciousness and political systems of patriarchy. See Starhawk, *The Spiral Dance: A Rebirth of the Ancient Religion of the Great Goddess* (San Francisco: Harper & Row, 1979) and Z. Budapest, *The Holy Book of Women's Mysteries*, 2 vols. (Oakland, CA: Susan B. Anthony Coven No. 1, 1979).
11. See Naomi R. Goldenberg, *Changing of the Gods*, and Carol P. Christ, "Why Women Need the Goddess: Phenomenological, Psychological, and Political Reflections," in *Womanspirit Rising*, pp. 273-287.
12. The title of Daly's second book (Boston: Beacon Press, 1973).
13. In *Gyn/Ecology: The Metaethics of Radical Feminism* (Boston: Beacon Press, 1978), Mary Daly argues that "there is no way to remove male/masculine imagery from *God*" (p. xi), so she chooses the religious symbol *Goddess* to refer to the creative and sustaining source of all being.
14. Mary Daly, *Pure Lust: Elemental Feminist Philosophy* (Boston: Beacon Press, 1984).
15. Christian feminist theologian Elisabeth Schüssler Fiorenza has recovered these stories of early Christian women in her book, *In Memory of Her: A Feminist Theological Reconstruction of Christian Origins* (New York: Crossroad, 1983).
16. Daly, *Beyond God the Father*, p. 12.
17. This is what Judith Plaskow names as "what has been said about women, mostly by men," in her fine analysis of women's experience as a basis for theological reflection. See her *Sex, Sin and Grace: Women's Experience and the Theologies of Reinhold Niebuhr and Paul Tillich* (Washington, D. C.: University Press of America, 1980), p. 9.
18. See Christ and Plaskow's discussion of this in *Womanspirit Rising*, pp. 5-9.
19. Nelle Morton describes the process: ". . . we have experienced birth, not rebirth, not new birth, or rite of passage or entry, but birth of ourselves for the first time. We have experienced creation, not re-creation, or new creation, but a primordial creation ourselves." See her "The Dilemma of Celebration" in *Womanspirit Rising*, p. 165.
20. I use the word "belief" deliberately, here and elsewhere. Although feminists are engaged in critical analyses, the choice to remain in dialogue with the tradition or not is ultimately a belief stance. At this point in history, there is no way of absolutely proving that feminist dialogue with the tradition will continue to perpetuate patriarchy, or will contribute to its demise.
21. See Schüssler Fiorenza's *In Memory of Her*, especially Chapters 1 and 2.
22. See Ruether's *Sexism and God-Talk*, Chapter 1.
23. Carol Christ, "Why Women Need the Goddess," pp. 276-77. In another important work, Christ argues that women can also find important sources for their spiritual development in women's literature. See her *Diving Deep and*

Surfacing: Women Writers on Spiritual Quest (Boston: Beacon Press, 1980).

24. Goldenberg, "The Return of the Goddess; Psychoanalytic Reflections on the shift from theology to thealogy," *Sciences Religieuses/Studies in Religion* 16/1 (Winter 1987), p. 39.
25. Daly's use of women's experience here would be somewhat similar to Rosemary Ruether's, Letty Russell's, and Elisabeth Moltmann-Wendel's.
26. Daly, *Beyond God the Father*, p. 34.
27. In this way, she is similar to Schüssler Fiorenza, Starhawk, Goldenberg, and Christ.
28. Daly, *Beyond God the Father*, p. 36.
29. *Laughter of Aphrodite: Reflection on a Journey to the Goddess* (San Francisco: Harper & Row, 1987), p. 15, emphasis mine.
30. Feminist authors are not the only ones who have made this discovery. Process philosophers, critical social theorists, physicists, biologists, medical practitioners, liberation theologians, and others have also powerfully argued this point in different ways. This does not take away the importance of the feminist discovery. Rather, it confirms its importance by others who also have the interest of freedom and a whole world at the heart of their theory and praxis.
31. See Ruether's *Liberation Theology*, and *New Woman/New Earth*. For her most recent statement, see *Sexism and God-Talk*, Chapters 2, 3, and 4.
32. See Mary Daly, *Beyond God the Father*.
33. *Ibid.*, p. 19.
34. See how Madonna Kolbenschlag in *Kiss Sleeping Beauty Goodbye* (New York: Doubleday, 1979) and Sandra Schneiders in "The Effects of Womens' Experience on Their Spirituality," *Spirituality Today* 35 (Summer 1983): 100-116 document this.
35. Though shared by all feminists, they may name what is being rejected in different ways. For example, Starhawk calls it the consciousness of "estrangement," or a "patriarchal spirituality." For her, estrangement means that we see ourselves as essentially separate from others and the universe. Relationships are usually characterized by manipulation and domination. See *Dreaming the Dark: Magic, Sex, and Politics* (Boston: Beacon Press, 1982), especially Chapters 1 and 2; and *Truth or Dare: Encounters with Power, Authority, and Mystery* (San Francisco: Harper & Row, 1987), Chapter 1.
36. Carol Ochs suggests: "Women's contribution to spirituality—the insight of their interconnectedness—is that full human maturity must entail coming into relationship with reality." *Women and Spirituality*, p. 10.
37. Cady, Ronan, Taussig, *Sophia: The Future of Feminist Spirituality*, (San Francisco: Harper & Row, 1986), p. 5. See also by same authors, *Wisdom's Feast: Sophia in Study and Celebration* (San Francisco: Harper & Row, 1989), which is the revised and expanded version of *Sophia*.
38. *Dreaming the Dark*, p. 9.
39. Here, I could reference almost every author, but I want to highlight some works that focus their analysis on the interrelatedness of racism, sexism, classism, heterosexism, and colonialism. See, for example, *Women's Spirit Bonding*, eds. Janet Kalven and Mary I. Buckley (New York: Pilgrim Press, 1984); *Women's Consciousness/Women's Conscience*, Barbara Hilkert Andolsen, Christine E. Gudorf, Mary D. Pellauer, eds. (San Francisco: Harper & Row, 1985); *Our Passion for Justice*, Carter Heyward (New York: Pilgrim Press, 1984); *Making the Connections*, Beverly Harrison, ed. by Carol S. Robb (Boston: Beacon Press, 1985); and *The Politics of Women's Spirituality*, ed. Charlene Spretnak.

40. *Sophia: The Future of Feminist Spirituality*, p. 5. Also several essays in Joann Wolski Conn's edited collection, *Women's Spirituality: Resources for Christian Development* speak of the need for women to integrate autonomy and relationship.
41. Mary Daly argues that the philosophy of interconnectedness—which she calls "biophilic consciousness"—is the necessary corrective for patriarchal dualism. Whereas patriarchy dismembers women and the natural world, recognition of the connectedness of all living things will encourage the remembering of those who have been violated, and enable life to generate new life. See her *Pure Lust*.
42. Beverly Harrison, *Our Right to Choose*, pp. 102, 103.
43. Joann Wolski Conn, "Women's Spirituality: Restriction and Reconstruction," in *Women's Spirituality: Resources for Christian Development*, p. 24.
44. See her essay "Why Women Need the Goddess," in *Womanspirit Rising*, pp. 273-287, and "Symbols of Goddess and God in Feminist Theology," in *The Book of the Goddess: Past and Present*, ed. Carol Olson (New York: Crossroad, 1987), pp. 231-251. (Reprinted in *Laughter of Aphrodite*, pp. 135-160).
45. Christ, "Why Women Need the Goddess," p. 274.
46. Naomi Goldenberg identifies a similar dynamic, but she uses the word "image" instead of "symbol." Goldenberg suggests that "the term *image* refers to any pictorial pattern that abides in our mental structures." They come from the conscious and subconscious levels of awareness and structure our activity in the world. Images affect our actions; we live according to what we imagine. See her *Changing of the Gods*, p. 62ff.

    Most of our authors use the terms "image" and "symbol" interchangeably, especially in reference to God and Goddess. Though image and symbol appear to function psychologically and sociologically in similar ways, there are differences between them that warrant further investigation to understand the transformative process that people experience in the feminist spiritual journey. See my Chapter 4, especially pp. 93-110.
47. *Ibid.*
48. I use the word "common" to denote symbols that have been shaped by the experience of many people and/or hold meaning for several groups.
49. Mary Daly makes this point when she is discussing the symbol of Mary in Christian theology. See *Beyond God the Father*, Chapter 3.
50. *Beyond God the Father*, p. 18.
51. In much patriarchal theology, the distinction was not made between the symbolic expression of divine reality and the deity itself. Although the tradition of the *via negativa* existed (all words for God are inadequate expressions of who God actually is), the theological preoccupation with orthodoxy often led to an identification of God with the human language for God. This is why many people believe(d) that God *is* male, *and* a Father. For further elaboration of this, see Sallie McFague's *Models of God: Theology for an Ecological, Nuclear Age* (Philadelphia; Fortress Press, 1987), esp. pp. 23ff.
52. "Mysticism, Liberation and the Names of God: A Feminist Reflection," *Christianity and Crisis* 41 (June 22, 1981): 182.
53. *Sophia: The Future of Feminist Spirituality*, p. 76.
54. Ruether, *Women-Church*, p. 2.
55. Christ offers a powerful analysis of women's experience of nothingness in her *Diving Deep and Surfacing*, pp. 1-26. See also Constance Fitzgerald's article "Impasse and Dark Night," in *Living With Apocalypse: Spiritual Resources for Social Compassion*, Tilden H. Edwards, ed. (San Francisco: Harper & Row, 1984), pp. 93-116.

56. "Why Women Need the Goddess," p. 275.
57. We shall see how they do this in the chapter on the Sacred.
58. *Women-Church*, p. 3.
59. Starhawk, *Truth or Dare*, p. 48.
60. Various methods or approaches to the tradition have been employed by feminists. The primary difference in method is between feminists who search for liberating insights and activity in the history "underneath the texts," (for example, Schüssler Fiorenza) and those who look for revelatory principles within the texts themselves (for example, Ruether, Trible, and Russell). Schüssler Fiorenza argues that the activity of women and men struggling to live a "discipleship of equals" is what provides powerful inspiration for feminists today. Though biblical texts *are* androcentric (that is, male-centered), they also allude to sacred stories of women like Mary Magdalene who appeared to confront the patriarchalizing dynamic within the early Christian communities. Ruether, on the other hand, argues that certain principles like the prophetic-liberative tradition or the proscription against idolatry—both contained in the androcentric texts—are provocative guides for feminists. She proposes that the texts themselves provide redemptive possibilities. Carol Christ provides a fine analysis of the similarities and differences of feminist methods in her essay "Symbols of Goddess and God in Feminist Theology," *op. cit.*
61. *God and the Rhetoric of Sexuality* (Philadelphia: Fortress Press, 1978).
62. *Human Liberation in a Feminist Perspective: A Theology* (Philadelphia: Westminster Press, 1974).
63. *Sexism and God-Talk*, pp. 61-71; 22-27.
64. *In Memory of Her*; and *Bread Not Stone* (Boston: Beacon Press, 1984).
65. For example, *Women and Religion in America*, vols. 1 & 2, edited by Rosemary Radford Ruether and Rosemary Skinner Keller (San Francisco: Harper & Row, 1981, 1983).
66. See, for example, selections in Conn's *Women's Spirituality*; Rosemary Haughton, *The Recreation of Eve* (Springfield, IL: Templegate Publishers, 1985); and *Women of Spirit, Female Leadership in the Jewish and Christian Traditions*, ed. by Rosemary Radford Ruether and Eleanor McLaughlin (New York: Simon and Schuster, 1979).
67. *Changing of the Gods*, p. 18.
68. *Laughter of Aphrodite*, pp. 73-82.
69. See, for example, Gerda Lerner's *The Creation of Patriarchy* (New York: Oxford University Press, 1986), esp. Chapter 1.
70. See Ruether's article, "Goddesses and Witches: Liberation and Countercultural Feminism, *The Christian Century* (Sept. 10-17, 1980), and the response of Charlene Spretnak in *The Politics of Women's Spirituality*, "Introduction," and Carol Christ, *Laughter of Aphrodite*, pp. 57-72.
71. From Starhawk, "A Story of Beginnings," in *Truth or Dare*, pp. 2,3.
72. See Starhawk, *The Spiral Dance* (record of Wicca religion); and *Dreaming the Dark* (contemporary feminist Wicca that promotes peace in our world).
73. See esp. Chapter 10 of *Laughter of Aphrodite*.
74. Nelle Morton, *The Journey Is Home* (Bosoton: Beacon Press, 1985), esp. pp. 147-175.
75. *Truth or Dare*, pp. 40-70.
76. *Ibid.*, p. 33.
77. Daly, *Gyn/Ecology*, pp. 107-312.
78. Daly, *Pure Lust*, p. 35.
79. *Ibid.*, p. 356.

80. See Heyward's *The Redemption of God*, esp. Chapter 2, "Re-imaging Jesus: Power in Relation."
81 *Womanspirit* magazine, published quarterly between 1974-1984, was one of the first journals to document the birth of these spiritualities.
82. Joanna Rogers Macy, *Woman of Power*, Issue 1, p. 10.
83. Charlene Spretnak's *The Politics of Women's Spirituality* is a significant work that represents the diversity and common themes of spiritualities of women's power. Her own introduction and editorial comments throughout the work provide an extremely helpful analysis. The book includes an extensive bibliography of women's spirituality of those feminists who are working outside Western religious frameworks. Another significant and more contemporary resource in this arena is the journal *Woman of Power: A Magazine of Feminism, Spirituality and Power* (P. O. Box 827, Cambridge, MA 02238). Its quality of production, articles, artwork, and poetry, as well as its effort to represent a broad range of strands in feminist spirituality, make it one of the most important resources for feminist spirituality today.
84. See esp. Charlene Spretnak's book, *The Spiritual Dimension of Green Politics* (Santa Fe, NM: Bear & Co., 1986) and her article, "Ecofeminism: Our Roots and Flowering," in *Woman of Power* Issue 9 (Spring 1988): 6-10.
85. Hallie Iglehart, "Expanding Personal Power Through Meditation," in *The Politics of Women's Spirituality*, p. 297.
86. See Nancy F. W. Passmore, "A Consciousness Manifesto," (pp. 163-171) and Barbara Starrett, "The Metaphors of Power," (pp. 185-193) in *The Politics of Women's Spirituality.*
87. Sally Gearhart represents a separatist position. She argues that our culture needs some women to separate themselves from men in order to find energy that is uniquely woman's. She believes this provides an essential resource in fighting the patriarchal worldview and culture. See her essay, "Womanpower: Energy Re-sourcement," in *The Politics of Women's Spirituality*, pp. 194-206.
88. Diane Mariechild (with Shuli Goodman), *The Inner Dance: A Guide to Spiritual and Psychological Unfolding* (Freedom, CA: The Crossing Press, 1987).
89. *MotherWit: A Feminist Guide to Psychic Development* (Trumansburg, NY: The Crossing Press, 1981). See also Margo Adair's *Working Inside Out: Tools for Change* (Berkley: Wingbow Press, 1984).
90. Juanita Weaver, "Images and Models—In Process," in *The Politics of Women's Spirituality*, p. 249.
91. See her *Womanspirit: A Guide to Woman's Wisdom* (San Fransico: Harper & Row, 1983).
92. Iglehart, "Expanding Personal Power Through Meditation," p. 297.
93. See, for example, Kay Turner's excellent article, "Contemporary Feminist Rituals," in *Politics of Women's Spirituality*, pp. 219-33; Hallie Iglehart, *Womanspirit*, and Diane Mariechild, *MotherWit* and *The Inner Dance*. For feminist rituals, see Marge Sears, *Life-Cycle Celebrations for Women* (Mystic, CT: Twenty-Third Publications, 1989).

Chapter 2

1. This chapter focuses on the changes that have taken place within *women's* lives as they experience self-integrity and interrelatedness. A similar analysis of men's lives would be an important contribution to the praxis of imaging wholeness.
2. See pp. 13-26. Christ notes that her description is a phenomenological one,

"derived from literary analysis and reflection on the relation of experiences depicted in literature to life" (p. 138). It is, therefore, not intended to describe *all* women's experience.

3. *Ibid.*, p. 15.
4. *Ibid.*, p. 21.
5. Daly usually capitalizes "Self" (beginning in *Gyn/Ecology*) to emphasize the ultimate value of women's be-ing for life on this planet to continue.
6. *Beyond God the Father*, p. 11.
7. *Ibid.*, p. 23.
8. *Ibid.*, p. 31.
9. *Gyn/Ecology*, p. 7.
10. *Beyond God the Father*, p. 32.
11. This is a large part of what Daly demonstrates in *Pure Lust*.
12. *Gyn/Ecology*, Chapter 9.
13. *Pure Lust*, p. 370-371.
14. *Gyn/Ecology*, p. 338.
15. Chapter 2 of *Beyond Anger: On Being a Feminist in the Church* (Dublin: Gill and Macmillan, 1986).
16. *Ibid.*, p. 8.
17. *Ibid.*, p. 15. I think that this is an unfortunate sentence. In a previous paragraph Osiek states that anger can "never be completly put aside" (p. 15). If this is true, it cannot really be a "step or stage" that one ultimately passes through as Osiek implies with her schema. Although anger is part of the process, I do not think it is simply one stage of it. It is present at all stages as long as the self journeys through an oppressive environment.
18. Osiek herself describes the "breakthrough process" in Chapter 3 of her book. This involves a process of personal conversion and structural transformation of the Christian church. The latter part of this chapter will explore the patterns of breakthrough as it appears from the lens of various feminist spiritualities, including, though not limited to, Christian feminism. Also we'll look more specifically at how woman's relationship with symbols of God and Jesus affects self in the chapter on the Sacred.
19. First Irish Christian feminist conference in May 1988. See account in *Womanspirit: A Resource for Those Interested in Feminist Spirituality* (Dublin), Vol. 2, No. 2 (Summer 1988), p. 15.
20. Title of song by Meg Christian.
21. Sometimes authors, such as Joann Wolski Conn, use the terms "independent" or "autonomous" to refer to women's experience of wholeness within themselves. I prefer the term "self-integrity," since integrity means "the experience of organic unity" and does not carry the individualistic connotations that "autonomous" does. The problem is to find language that symbolizes the differentiation process of becoming a unique self while remaining within the overall context of interdependence. Catherine Keller argues that this "requires a reformulation of the concept of self," in her *From a Broken Web: Separation, Sexism & Self* (Boston: Beacon Press, 1986), p. 161. See also how the authors of *Sophia* tackle this issue, esp. pp. 4-8. On the other hand, Elisabeth Moltmann-Wendel in *A Land Flowing with Milk and Honey* uses the term "autonomy" but argues that it is a concept that "does not denote a rationalistic, individualistic self-determination, but self-determination within a context of relationship" (p. 9).
22. This is also true for women of color. See, for example, Dolores Williams, "The Color of Feminism: Or Speaking the Black Woman's Tongue," *The Journal of Religious Thought*, Vol. 43, No. 1 (Summer 1986): 42-58; Katie Gene-

va Cannon, *Black Womanist Ethics* (Atlanta: Scholars Press, 1989).

23. "Parenting, Mutual Love, and Sacrifice," in *Women's Conscience: Women's Consciousness*, p. 191.
24. Heyward, "Is a Self-Respecting Christian Woman an Oxymoron? Reflections on a Feminist Spirituality for Justice," *Religion and Intellectual Life* 3/2 (Winter 1986): 48.
25. Charlene Spretnak, *The Politics of Women's Spirituality*, p. 161.
26. *Truth or Dare*, see esp. pp. 64-67.
27. *Ibid.*, p. 66.
28. *Ibid.*
29. See Chapters 5-9 where Starhawk discusses each of these in turn, and how women break free from the power of the king. Mary Daly speaks about the need for women to exorcize the "internalized God-father," see *Gyn/Ecology*, p. 2.
30. *The Redemption of God* (Washington, D.C: The University Press of America, 1982), p. xv.
31. "Women's Spirituality: Restriction and Reconstruction," in Joann Conn, ed. *Women's Spirituality* (Mahwah, NJ: Paulist Press, 1986), p. 12. (This article was originally published in 1980).
32. Saiving's essay in *Womanspirit Rising;* Judith Plaskow develops this thesis in her work *Sex, Sin and Grace*. Mary Daly analyzes the dynamic in *Beyond God the Father*. Rosemary Ruether refers to it in *Sexism and God-Talk*, pp. 185-86.
33. *Truth or Dare*, p. 15.
34. Naomi Goldenberg develops this in a slightly different way by arguing, "The death of father-gods could mean the onset of religious forms which emphasize awareness of oneself and tend to understand gods and goddesses as inner psychic forces."*Changing of the Gods*, p. 41. In this way, perhaps theology turns into psychology.
35. "Expanding Personal Power Through Meditation," *The Politics of Women's Spirituality*, p. 295.
36. See pp. 43-47 in Iglehart's *Womanspirit* for directions of this guided meditation.
37. Within the Christian and Jewish feminist tradition, several books are published that record woman's ritual-making: eds. Linda Clark, Marian Ronan, Eleanor Walker, *Image-Breaking, Image Building: A Handbook for Creative Worship with Women of Christian Tradition* (New York: Pilgrim Press, 1981); eds. Janet Kalven and Mary Buckley,*Women's Spirit Bonding;* Miriam Therese Winter, *Woman Prayer/Woman Song* (Oak Park, IL: Meyer Stone Books, 1987); Rosemary Ruether, *Women-Church: The Theology and Practice of Feminist Liturgical Communities;* Martha A. Acklesbert, "Spirituality, Community and Politics: B'not Esh and the Feminist Reconstruction of Judaism," *Journal of Feminist Studies in Religion* 2/2 (Fall 1986): 109-120. Within the Goddess tradition: Starhawk, *Dreaming the Dark* and *Truth or Dare*; Hallie Iglehart, *Womanspirit;* Diane Mariechild, *The Inner Dance.*
38. Alice Walker, *In Search of Our Mother's Gardens* (New York: Harcourt Bruce Jovanovich, 1983), p. xii
39. See Chapter 3 of Ruether's *Sexism and God-Talk*, "Woman, Body and Nature: Sexism and the Theology of Creation," pp. 72-92.
40. *Ibid.*, p. 79.
41. Mary Daly provides several examples of what this means for woman's Self. She names the reality "sado-spirituality" and analyzes how patriarchal dualism within Christian theology imposes asceticism on woman—disciplines that dull her mind and usurp the Self. See Chapter 1 of *Pure Lust.*

42. Ruether, *Sexism and God-Talk*, p. 259.
43. Hallie Iglehart, "The Unnatural Divorce of Spirituality and Politics," *The Politics of Women's Spirituality*, pp. 411-413. See also exercises for self-healing and healing of others in Diane Mariechild's *MotherWit: A Feminist Guide to Psychic Development*, Chapter 5.
44. Starhawk, *Truth or Dare*, p. 118.
45. See Ruether, *Women-Church*, Chapter 9; Sears, *Life-Cycle Celebrations for Women*.
46. *Ibid.*, pp. 204-206.
47. Elisabeth Moltmann-Wendel, *A Land Flowing with Milk and Honey*, p. 159.
48. Starhawk, *Dreaming the Dark*, p. 138. Mary Daly speaks about woman's "pure lust" as her vigor, fertility, amazing hope, and pure passion that strives in every way for an abundance of be-ing. See her *Pure Lust*, pp. 2-4.
49. Beverly Harrison, *Our Right to Choose* (Boston: Beacon Press, 1983), p. 106.
50. Heyward, *Our Passion for Justice*, p. 86.
51. This is one of the most radical aspects of women's search for personal power through self-integrity. The dualistic split between sexuality and spirituality—and women's identification with the former—has been a primary roadblock for women's experience of wholeness. Mary Condren, in *The Serpent and the Goddess: Women, Religion, and Power in Celtic Ireland* (San Francisco: Harper & Row, 1989) demonstrates how this dualism—within the Hebrew and Christian traditions—derives its destructive power from the Adam and Eve story. See esp. pp. 2-33.
52. This criticism is also being developed by feminist psychologists, notably Jean Baker Miller and colleagues, see their collection of essays, *Growth in Connection*, (Wellesley, MA: The Stone Center, 1991). Carol Gilligan's work also challenges the individualistic bias of the dominant psychological concept of self, though she doesn't go as far as Miller. See Conn's selection of developmentalists in her *Women's Spirituality*, pp. 63-127.
53. Starhawk, *Dreaming the Dark*, p. 37. Charlene Spretnak speaks about the connection between wholeness within the self and interrelatedness with reality when she says of feminist spirituality: "Inner development is encouraged as a profound adventure, but only within the sphere of oneness and the realization that all our fates are inextricably linked." See her *The Politics of Women's Spirituality*, p. xvi.
54. This is akin to a "process philosophy" conception of self. Several feminists are exploring the possibilities of combining process and feminist insights to develop a "relational self." See Sheila Greeve Daveny, *Feminism and Process Thought*, and Catherine Keller, *From A Broken Web: Separation, Self and Sexism* (Boston: Beacon Press, 1986).
55. Catherine Keller, *From a Broken Web*, p. 213.
56. *Ibid.*, p. 155.
57. Charlene Spretnak, *The Politics of Women's Spirituality*, p. *xvii*.
58. See the essays on "Women and Poverty," in *Women's Spirit Bonding*, Kalven and Buckley, eds., pp. 1-38.
59. See the essays on "Racism, Pluralism, Bonding," in *Women's Spirit Bonding*, pp. 67-136; the articles in *Woman of Power*, Issue Four (Fall 1986) entitled "Women of Color: A Celebration of Power."
60. See Starhawk, *Dreaming the Dark* and *Truth or Dare*; Gina Foglia and Dorit Wolffberg, "The Spiritual Dimensions of Feminist Anti-Nuclear Activism," in *The Politics of Women's Spirituality*, pp. 446-461; "Greenham Common Wimmin's Camp," Kalioaka in *Woman of Power*, Issue Seven (Summer 1987): 57-59.

61. See articles in *Woman of Power*, Issue Nine (Spring 1988), entitled "Nature"; essays on "Women and Nature: Violence or Interdependence," in *Women's Spirit Bonding*, pp. 39-66.
62. See essays on "Lesbianism and Homophobia," in *Women's Spirit Bonding*, pp. 239-262; Carter Heyward, *Our Passion for Justice*; Beverly Harrison, "Misogyny and Homophobia: The Unexplored Connections," in *Making the Connections*, Carol Robb, ed., pp. 135-151.
63. Diane Mariechild, *The Inner Dance*, p. 23. The intention to be deeply united with the whole of life lies behind much of the mystical tradition.
64. Cady, Ronan, Taussig, *Sophia: The Future of Feminist Spirituality*, p. 5.

Chapter 3

1. *The Concise Oxford Dictionary*, ed. J. B. Sykes, (Oxford: Oxford University Press, 1974), p. 506.
2. In his dictionary entry on "Redemption," Francis Schüssler Fiorenza notes that "salvation refers to a healing, a bringing to health or a making whole and well" *The New Dictionary of Theology* , Joseph A. Komonchak, Mary Collins and Dermot A. Lane, eds. (Dublin: Gill & Macmillan, 1987), p. 836. Christians believe that the salvation of humanity has taken place through Christ. *How* Christ effects salvation for all, and *humanity's* role in this process has been a central subject of theological investigation throughout the centuries. As feminist and other contemporary forms of theology—especially political and liberation theologies—move beyond the philosophical base of dualism, the meaning of salvation demands radical reinterpretation once again. This, of course, has immediate consequences for one's understanding of spirituality, especially if spirituality is described as movement toward wholeness. See Schüssler Fiorenza, *ibid.*, esp. pp. 847-851; and Anne E. Carr, *Transforming Grace: Christian Tradition and Women's Experience* (San Francisco: Harper & Row, 1988), Chapter 9, "The Salvation of Women: Christ, Mary and the Church."
3. We can still see the effects of this kind of spirituality operative today. Liberation theologians have come to describe it as "charity without justice," namely, a love that does not challenge the unjust status and conditions of individuals, a love that does not empower people to work with others so that they can provide and care for themselves. In addition, this dynamic manifests itself when socially powerful people are with the socially powerless and initially relate to them in a patronizing manner.
4. Margaret Farley argues a similar point when she writes, "It is possible to affirm all persons as persons in such a way that maintains a gradation among persons. All are loved as equal before God but not necessarily as equal before one another." See her "New Patterns of Relationship: Beginnings of a Moral Revolution," *Theological Studies* 36 (December 1975): 633.
5. Starhawk, *Dreaming the Dark*, p. 37.
6. Throughout her book, *Pure Lust*, Mary Daly argues that women are not looking for equality within patriarchal space, because it is not possible for women to be equal to men in patriarchy, and because Daly is much more concerned with women empowering them Selves—*this*, not equality with men, is the goal. While I agree that equality within patriarchal space is not possible, I am claiming that genuine experiences of male/female equality can happen through a transcendence of patriarchal values, and in fact provides an essential source to change the culture. Just as women can move

from the foreground to the background, so too can women and men, by their very way of relating to one another, move beyond the present culture and place a wedge in it at the same time.

7. Starhawk, *Truth or Dare*, p. 132.
8. Certainly this is the case when churchmen discuss the nature and role of woman.
9. Elisabeth Moltmann-Wendel, *A Land Flowing With Milk and Honey*, p. 147.
10. Heyward, *Our Passion For Justice*, p. 127.
11. *A Land Flowing With Milk and Honey*, p. 138.
12. *Ibid.*, p. 139.
13. Carter Heyward, *The Redemption of God: A Theology of Mutual Relation*, p. 168, emphasis mine.
14. See Starhawk's comparison of "power-over" and "power-from-within" in *Dreaming the Dark*, chapter 1, and *Truth or Dare*, chapter 1.
15. Riane Eisler, *The Chalice and the Blade: Our History, Our Future* (San Francisco: Harper & Row, 1987).
16. Heyward, *Redemption of God*, p. 44.
17. In *A Passion For Friends: Toward a Philosophy of Female Affection* (Boston: Beacon Press, 1986), Janice G. Raymond argues that our past and present societal context encourage "hetero-relations," namely, "the wide range of affective, social, political, and economic relations that are ordained between men and women by men" (p. 7).
18. Mary E. Hunt, "Friends in Deed," in Linda Hurcombe, ed., *Sex and God: Some Varieties of Women's Religious Experience* (London: Routledge and Kegan Paul, 1987), p. 48. See also Mary Hunt's development of these ideas in her *Fierce Tenderness: A Feminist Theology of Friendship* (New York: Crossroad, 1991).
19. Mary Daly, *Beyond God the Father*, p. 133.
20. *A Passion For Friends*, p. 205.
21. "Friends in Deed," p. 48.
22. *A Passion For Friends*, p. 6.
23. Mary Daly, *Gyn/Ecology*, p. 366.
24. "Friends in Deed," p. 49.
25. Raymond, op. cit., p. 35.
26. First suggested to me by Ann Louise Gilligan, lectures, 1988.
27. *Truth or Dare*, p. 319.
28. Janet Kalven, "Epilogue," *Women's Spirit Bonding*, p. 366.
29. *Truth or Dare*, p. 318-321.
30. Margaret Farley, *Personal Commitments* (San Francisco: Harper & Row, 1986), p. 18.
31. *Ibid.*, p. 19.
32. *Ibid.*, p. 33.
33. *Ibid.*, chapter 4, "The Way of Fidelity."
34. *Ibid.*, p. 44.
35. Sometimes these commitments break down. See Farley's chapter, "Discerning Obligation: A Just Love," where she outlines ethical reasons for changing or breaking committed relationships.
36. Harrison, "Human Sexuality and Mutuality," in Judith Weidman, editor *Christian Feminism: Visions of a New Humanity* (San Francisco: Harper & Row, 1984), p. 150.

37. Farley, *Personal Commitments*, p. 130.
38. *Ibid.*, p. 119.
39. *Ibid.*, p. 132.
40. See *The Redemption of God: Toward a Theology of Mutual Relation.*
41. Elisabeth Schüssler Fiorenza, *In Memory of Her: A Feminist Theological Reconstruction of Christian Origins* (New York: Crossroad, 1983), esp. pp. 130-140. Cady, Taussig et al, *Sophia: The Future of Feminist Spirituality*, pp. 38-54.
42. Rosemary Ruether, *To Change the World: Christology and Cultural Criticism* (New York: Crossroad, 1981).
43. "Epilogue," *Women's Spirit Bonding*, p. 364.
44. See Starhawk, "Toward Community," *Truth or Dare*, pp. 256-288; Martha Ackelsberg, "Spirituality, Community and Politics: B'not Esh and the Feminist Reconstruction of Judaism," *The Journal of Feminist Studies in Religion* Vol. 2 (Fall 1986): 109-120. And my essay "Is There a Feminist Ethic?" in *Ethics and the Christian*, ed. by Sean Freyne (Dublin: The Columba Press, 1991) for a description of my own supportive community at the Shanty.

Chapter 4

1. *The Journey Is Home* (Boston: Beacon Press, 1985), p. 227.
2. See Chapter 1, pp. 22-23.
3. Judith Plaskow and Carol Christ, eds., *Weaving the Visions: New Patterns in Feminist Spirituality* (San Francisco: Harper & Row, 1979), p. 3.
4. Caroline Bynum provides a helpful distinction between "sex" and "gender": "All human beings have gender as well as sex (difference between men and women that can be attributed to biology), and this gender is culturally constructed. . . . what people understand themselves to be qua male and female is learned and shaped within culture . . ." in *Gender and Religion: On the Complexity of Symbols*, edited by Stevan Harvell, Paula Richman, and Caroline Bynum (Boston: Beacon Press, 1986), p. 7.
5. My choice of *Sacred* instead of *God* in this chapter is an attempt to recognize and affirm the diversity of feminist symbols. At the present moment in history, it seems to be a word that can include within it God, Goddess, deity, utlimate authority, Powers of Be-ing, the fundamental energy, transcendence, and immanence. I think it is a word that we can use in conversation with one another, while also choosing another word to represent our own experience of spirituality. The need for such an inclusive term comes out of my experience as an educator—how can I include everyone who is with me in the process of learning?
6. Title of Part 2 of *Weaving the Visions*.
7. See Mary Daly, *Beyond God the Father*.
8. See Carol P. Christ, "Why Women Need the Goddess," in *Womanspirit Rising*, especially pp. 275 ff. and Nelle Morton, *The Journey Is Home* where she spends a considerable amount of time exploring the impact of male God-imagery on the lives of women in a patriarchal society.
9. See Sallie McFague, *Metaphorical Theology: Models of God in Religious Language* (Philadelphia: Fortress Press, 1982), pp. 145-192; Rosemary Ruether, *Sexism and God-Talk*, pp. 66ff.; and Mary Daly, *Beyond God the Father*.
10. See Judith Plaskow, "The Right Question Is Theological," in *On Being a Jewish Feminist: A Reader*, edited by Susannah Heschel (New York: Schocken Books, 1983), p. 229. We shall see how Plaskow proposes to include female God-language in an upcoming section of this chapter.
11. By this I do not mean that all feminists eventually rejected *belief* in God. Rather, this phrasing suggests that as feminists distanced themselves from

the meaning of a patriarchal "God," most felt the real absence of a *personal being* (albeit one with a patriarchal nature), rather than the absence of a symbol. Likewise, the feminist theological reconstruction of the symbol "God" usually happens once again within the experience of presence to a personal being, yet one whose nature is radically different from the "God" of their inheritance.

12. In Chapter 1 I indicated that one of the reasons that sacred symbols must change is because they have encouraged humanity's powerlessness before God. As Carol Christ demonstrates in her fine analysis of "Symbols of Goddess and God in Feminist Theolgy," the second component of the feminist critique of God symbolism centres on the concept of divine power that has been distorted because it "is based on an alienated male experience of power," in *The Book of the Goddess: Past and Present*, edited by Carl Olson (New York: Crossroad, 1987), p. 237.
13. *Dreaming the Dark*, p. 4.
14. See Sallie McFague, *Models of God: Theology for an Ecological, Nuclear Age* (Philadelphia: Fortress Press, 1987), pp. 16ff.
15. Gerda Lerner, *The Creation of Patriarchy*, especially chapter seven; Starhawk, *Truth or Dare*, especially chapter 2.
16. Sallie McFague critiques this at length in *Models of God* and proposes another image in its place: the world as God's body.
17. *Truth or Dare*, p. 49.
18. See Sallie McFague's development of this idea in her, *Models of God*, esp. pp. 63-69.
19. *Laughter of Aphrodite*, pp. 73-82.
20. *Ibid.*, p. 75. Initially, I found this criticism to be quite shattering. I do think she is right that Jewish and Christian feminists need to directly confront the mixture of "liberator" and "warrior" imagery that is part of those sacred stories we wish to retain as truthful in our lives. On the other hand, is there something to learn here about how imagery functions?
21. The *purgation* before the *illumination*.
22. This may not be true in a passive kind of spirituality. Namely, we accept the God-imagery of our tradition and never question its relevance or truth. Once we begin the critical process, however, we have an active form of spirituality and must couple our own search with that of others in order to be in the presence of the Sacred.
23. *The Journey Is Home*, p. 225.
24. Catherine Keller,"Goddess, Ear, and Metaphor: On the Journey of Nelle Morton," *Journal of Feminist Studies in Religion* Vol. 4, No. 2 (Fall 1988): 58.
25. *Ibid.*, p. 57.
26. Paul Ricoeur speaks about the "bound" character of symbols when he distinguishes them from metaphor. On the one hand, Sallie McFague accepts Ricoeur's distinction when she says:

    "Symbols exist at the level of *bios*, metaphors at the level of *logos*: symbols bind us to the cosmos while metaphors are the linguistic play that interprets symbols and brings them to expressive availability. Symbols unite us harmoniously to our roots in the world while metaphors redescribe reality . . ." (*Metaphorical Theology*, p. 213, ft. 23).

    On the other hand, Catherine Keller (as she interprets Nelle Morton) rejects Ricoeur's assertion that metaphors are rooted in the universe of words *(logos)* and not life (*bios*). She asserts:

    "For to trim the roots away from metaphor, to cut off its earthy origin in the loam of life being lived, is to dislocate our own life stories. Metaphors dangle their roots—muddy with our life-situations, our body, our cosmos. Otherwise they lack the sensuality of *image* (as does Ricoeur's theory). For if we look for the tie that binds word to life only in the established symbol, with its susceptibility to institutional purgation and self-perpetuation, then doesn't a spirituality of the status quo threaten to overwhelm the vigor of the spirit?" ("Goddess, Ear and Metaphor," p. 59).

In my own proposition that symbols bind us to the *history* from which they arise, I accept insights from both McFague's and Keller's interpretation of Ricoeur. I agree that symbols arise from *bios;* they come from diverse people's histories within the cosmos. Even as they bind us to that cumulative history, though, they are distant from our own immediate experiences. That is to say, the meaning of symbols in the present does not easily shift because the cumulative history of their meaning is so powerful. How does our contemporary meaning get into symbols? Through metaphor (and imagery), I think. Metaphors (which are words or *logos*) arise from our *bios,* in order to redescribe reality. In this way, metaphors "dangle their roots—muddy with our life-situations," and their tie is more immediate to *us,* thus containing the power to "redescribe reality" in a way that will affect our behavior and interrupt the historical power of the symbol. Metaphor does this as it interprets the symbol (Ricoeur). In other words, I accept that metaphor interprets the symbol, but can only do this because it is rooted in contemporary life experience. See Paul Ricoeur, *Interpretation Theory: Discourse and the Surplus of Meaning* (Ft. Worth: Texas Christian University Press, 1976).

27. See Carol P. Christ, *Laughter of Aphrodite,* pp. 136ff. and Anne E. Carr, *Transforming Grace,* p. 101.
28. *Transforming Grace,* p. 101.
29. "Referent" means the reality to which the symbol refers—in this case the referent is the Sacred. Whereas our authors may differ in their beliefs about the *nature* of the Sacred, namely, some believe that it exists as a personal being while others believe that it exists as an elemental life-force, they all believe in the *existence* of something Sacred.
30. *Transforming Grace,* p. 102.
31. In commenting on Carr's proposal, Elizabeth Johnson makes a crucial point: "The meaning of symbol cannot be separated from the use made of that symbol in the praxis of the community." "Review Symposium of *Transforming Grace*" in *Horizons* Vol. 15 (Fall 1988), 373. I agree with Johnson and therefore question Caroline Bynum's proposal to examine the meaning of symbol, outside of a consideration of its function. See her *On the Complexity of Symbols,* especially when she says: "Our question is, How do symbols mean, not What produces them? or How do they function?" p. 5.
32. Carr, *op. cit.,* p. 102.
33. See *In Memory of Her* and *Bread Not Stone.*
34. Ruether and McLaughlin, *Women of Spirit;* Ruether and Keller, *Women and Religion in America,* 3 volumes. See for example, Ruether and McLaughlin, eds. *Women of Spirit: Female Leadership in the Jewish and Christian Traditions* (New York: Simon and Schuster, 1979); Rosemary Radford Ruether and Rosemary Skinner Keller, eds., *Women and Religion in America* (San Francisco: Harper & Row, 1983); Francine Candman, "Acts of the Women Martyrs," *Anglican Theological Review 70:* (April 1988): 144-150.
35. "Feminist Theology and Spirituality," in Weidman, ed., *Christian Feminism: Visions of a New Humanity* (San Francisco: Harper & Row, 1984) p. 18.
36. See Russell, *The Future of Partnership.* (Philadelphia: Westminster Press, 1979), pp. 17-20, 51-53.

37. Carr, *Transforming Grace*, p. 153.
38. "Notes on Composing New Blessings: Toward a Feminist-Jewish Reconstruction of Prayer," in *Weaving the Visions*, p. 133.
39. *Ibid.*, emphasis mine.
40. Nelle Morton uses this phrase in *The Journey Is Home.*
41. Bynum, *Gender and Religion*, pp. 9-22.
42. *Ibid.* p. 9.
43. Unless of course they "die." What I am arguing is (1) they do not die for all people simultaneously and (2) the interpretation of human experience can consciously call for the death of a symbol.
44. *Ibid.*, p. 15.
45. This is to argue that human experience has more power than symbol. Ultimately, it is human experience that seems to have the edge, even within the dialectical process. How else do people and society experience transformation? It is also to argue that symbols have an existence only in relation to us; they do not exist somewhere out there in themselves.
46. *Laughter of Aphrodite*, pp. 137ff.
47. Christine Downing, *The Goddess: Mythological Representations of the Feminine* (New York: Crossroad, 1981), p. 3.
48. *Laughter of Aphrodite*, p. 100.
49. This is true for several authors in Charlene Spretnak's edited work, *The Politics of Women's Spirituality*.
50. Merlin Stone, *When God Was a Woman* (New York: Dial Press, 1976), p. 1.
51. See Gerda Lerner,*The Creation of Patriarchy*; Riane Eisler, *The Chalice and the Blade*; Marija Gimbutas, *The Goddesses and Gods of Old Europe: Myths and Cult Images* (Berkeley: University of California Press, 1982); James Mellart, *Catal Huyuk* (New York: McGraw-Hill, 1967); and Monica Sjöö and Barbara Mor, *The Great Cosmic Mother: Rediscovering the Religion of the Earth* (San Francisco: Harper & Row, 1987).
52. Eisler, pp. 1, 2.
53. *Ibid.*, p. 6.
54.*The Great Cosmic Mother*, pp. 43, 87 respectively. The paleolithic period spans 30,000 and 10,000 B.C.E.
55. *The Goddesses and Gods of Old Europe*, p. 216.
56. "Woman and Culture in Goddess-oriented Old Europe," in *The Politics of Women's Spirituality*, p. 28.
57. Among the many feminist authors who document this, see Marija Gimbutas, Gerda Lerner, and Riane Eisler.
58. Starhawk, *Truth or Dare*, p. 310.
59. This is disputed, especially by Rosemary Ruether.
60. *Truth or Dare*, p. 7.
61. *Laughter of Aphrodite*, p. 67.
62. These meanings are often gleaned from studying Goddesses within various cultures and religions. See *The Book of the Goddess: Past and Present*, ed. by Carl Olson (New York: Crossroad, 1987).
63. "Hindu Female Deities as a Resource for the Contemporary Rediscovery of the Goddess," in *The Book of the Goddess*, p. 229.
64. Metaphors are a special kind of image—we will consider these momentarily—and so contain the same characteristics as images.
65. *The Journey Is Home*, p. 33. Morton is referring specifically to Piaget's *Play, Dreams and Imitation in Childhood*, trans. G. Gattegno and F.M. Hodgson (New York: Norton, 1962). Several imagery theorists call this "reproductive imagery."

66. "Goddess, Ear and Metaphor," p. 55.
67. *The Journey Is Home*, p. 143.
68. *Ibid.*, p. 123.
69. *Ibid.*, p. 127, emphasis mine.
70. "Goddess, Ear and Metaphor," p. 55.
71. A feminist consciousness of interdependence also affects our dreams and fantasies. This is why dreams and "wishful thinking" also contain significant imagery for interpreting the Sacred's presence in our lives.
72. *The Journey Is Home*, p. 131.
73. *Ibid.*, pp. 157-158.
74. *The Redemption of God*, p. 153.
75. *Ibid.*, p. 87.
76. See her contribution to the "Roundtable Discussion on Racism in the Women's Movement," in *Journal of Feminist Studies in Religion* Vol. 4, No. 1 (Spring 1988): 96, 97.
77. *The Journey Is Home*, p. 152.
78 *Ibid.*
79. Keller, p. 54.
80. Judith Plaskow, Rita Gross, Carol Christ, Sallie McFague, and Nelle Morton.
81. "Female God-language in a Jewish Context," in *Womanspirit Rising*, p.170.
82. "Sabbath Prayers for Women," in *Womanspirit Rising*, p. 176.
83. There are some feminists, however, who do not accept the reality of a *personal* Sacred. Rather, they believe in an energy force or sustaining power(s) that support the natural cycle of life and death on earth. And, for some, they use the metaphor "Goddess" to symbolize this reality. In other words, there are feminists who do not mean that the Sacred is a being, "out there" or even a personal being within, but still use the word "Goddess" to re-present their experiences of integrity and interdependence. See some authors in *The Politics of Women's Spirituality*.
84. Elizabeth A. Johnson, "The Incomprehensibility of God and the Image of God Male and Female," *Theological Studies* 45 (1984): 465. Naomi Goldenberg makes a similar point when she says, "I do not expect that the continued presence of male gods will be harmful to women. Women experience psychic oppression only when father-gods are touted as the sole images of the highest religious value in a society. . . However, when father-gods are present within a panoply of psycho-religious images, they can no longer enforce their former tyranny. Women will be free to reconsider Christ and Yahweh and find new places for them" (*Changing of the Gods*), p. 82.
85. *New Catholic Women: A Contemporary Challenge to Traditional Religious Authority* (San Francisco: 1986, Harper & Row), p. 185. This is close to the intent of the authors of *Sophia* who invoke "Sophia," "a goddess-like figure in the Hebrew and Christian traditions" in their rituals as a way of imaging their contemporary experience of Sacred presence. See especially Chapter 6, "Sophia and the Future of Feminist Spirituality," *Sophia* (Cady, Ronan, and Taussig).
86. "The Right Question is Theological," in *On Being a Jewish Feminist*, Susannah Heschel, ed. (New York: Schocken Books, 1983), p. 230.
87. While recognizing its *theological* value, Nelle Morton challenges the metaphoric potential of the image "God/dess." Morton says that it does not have sufficient iconoclastic power. *The Journey Is Home*, p. 151.
88. Some feminists—through *theoretically* convinced of the need for "Goddess" imagery to disrupt personal presence to an all-male God—find its use in ritual and prayer meaningless. It does not *feel* revolutionary; in fact, its use

does not produce much feeling at all. What is going on here? Several things, no doubt. I want to suggest one possibility. If we're convinced that it is important "to resurrect the Goddess imagery in the psyches of women" (Ann Louise Gilligan, in conversation) then we must be prepared to be patient. As Mary Condren's analysis in *The Serpent and the Goddess* persuasively argues, it took several centuries for patriarchal culture to eradicate the symbol of the Goddess. Furthermore, a careful strategy employed was the creation of religious imagery that pictured the *destruction* of the Goddess. As Condren points out:

"The Fathers of the church never tired of repeating the fact that the Serpent had been crushed by Mary. Although the Serpent originally symbolized the mysterious and ambivalent secrets of the Goddess, Christianity identified the Serpent with the Devil....For Christendom, the serpent/ Goddess...represented the enemy par *excellence.* Rather than eliminating the symbol altogether, Christianity promoted the image, but always as the subjugated, shadowside of the spiritual or military hero." (p. 132).

Is it any wonder, then, that the metaphoric potential of "Goddess" is not felt by some? It may take consistent use of "Goddess" in prayer and ritual—over a long period of time—to unleash its inherent metaphoric power.

89. *Metaphorical Theology*, p. 18.
90. *Ibid.*, p. 15.
91. See Sallie McFague, *Models of God*.
92. Though I agree with authors such as McFague and Morton that images affect our behavior more immediately than concepts, I am saying here that concepts, too, must be changed if new imagery is to emerge and hold power in our lives. In fact, I think that if the concepts do not change, this will block new imagery from surfacing.
93. *Metaphorical Theology*, p. 22.
94. *Ibid.*, p. 26.
95. *Ibid.*, p. 121.

Chapter 5

1. The classic work that persuasively demonstrates the link between woman and nature's domination is Carolyn Merchant, *The Death of Nature: Woman, Ecology and the Scientific Revolution* (San Francisco: Harper & Row, 1980). See also another classic by Susan Griffin, *Woman and Nature: The Roaring Inside Her* (San Francisco: Harper & Row, 1978).
2. See, for example, Denis Carroll, Sean McDonagh, John Carmody, and the works of Matthew Fox.
3. *Reclaiming the Connections: A Contemporary Spirituality* (Kansas City: Sheed & Ward, 1990), pp. 39-50.
4. *Ibid.*, p. 43.
5. *Meditations with Hildegarde of Bingen*, versions by Gabriele Uhlein (Santa Fe: Bear & Co., 1983), p. 78.
6. *Ibid.*, p. 65.
7. This could also be said for many of the tribal religions. Many feminists use these as significant resources in their own spirituality.
8. These traditions and philosophies also provide resources for Christian feminists to transform their heritage of dualism and anthropcentrism. Creation-centered spirituality similarly argues for this kind of ecumenism and inter-religious dialogue. It is important not only to converse with members of

other traditions; such conversation has the potential to help us reconstruct our own traditions as well as recognize their limitations. As I read Starhawk's works, it appears that it is easier for pagans to do this than Christians. Thus, the potential for a pagan gift to Christianity.

9. See *New Woman, New Earth: Sexist Ideologies & Human Liberation* (New York: Seabury Press, 1975). Part and parcel of her argument is an insistence that our current worldview provides the rationale for every societal pattern of domination and oppression. Racism, sexism, classism, and technological power all rest on the same base of the dominating and alienating direction of Western civilization. We need to know this in order to successfully challenge any single pattern.
10. *Healing the Wounds: The Promise of Ecofeminism*, Judith Plant, ed. (Philadelphia: New Society Publishers, 1989), p. 2.
11. As Carolyn Merchant notes, "In Platonic and Neoplatonic symbolism . . . both nature and matter were feminine, while the Ideas were masculine." *The Death of Nature*, p. 10.
12. Elizabeth Dodson Gray, names this "above-below" scheme as the "anthropocentric illusion." See her *Green Paradise Lost* (Wellesley, MA: Roundtable Press, 1979).
13. *Woman and Nature*, p. 7.
14. Aristotle, as quoted in Merchant, *The Death of Nature*, p.13.
15. The "chain of being" ontology sanctioned a "chain of command" behavior. The being with the highest spirit and value could command, control and dominate, all others, and so on, down the line. Therefore, this ontology justified man's control of woman and humanity's subordination of the earth. See a discussion of other implications of the relation between chain of being and chain of command in Letha Dawson Scanzoni's essay, "The Great Chain of Being and the Chain of Command," in *Women's Spirit Bonding*, Janet Kalven and Mary Buckley, eds. (New York: Pilgrim Press, 1984), pp. 41-55.
16. See Sherry Ortner's classic essay, "Is Female to Male as Nature Is to Culture?," where she proposes from an anthrolopological perspective why woman has been perceived as closer to nature than man. In *Woman, Culture and Society*, Michelle Zimbalist Rosaldo and Louise Lamphere, eds. (Stanford, CA.: Stanford University Press), pp. 67-87.
17. Merchant, *The Death of Nature*, p. 1.
18. *Ibid.*, p. 3.
19. While machines obviously have no gender, nature's association with the female gender persisted as part of the mechanistic view of nature. Women—like chaotic and disorderly nature—needed to be controlled. See Merchant's chapter on "Nature as Disorder," *op. cit.*, pp. 127-148.
20. *Ibid.*, p. 282.
21. *Woman and Nature*, p. 18.
22. *The Death of Nature*, p. 43.
23. *Ibid.*, p. 2.
24. *Ibid.*, p. 288.
25. Merchant provides several examples of the restriction of woman's economic role. One outrageous example: "By 1511, women had been forbidden to weave, because strength was needed to operate the looms." See her chapter on "Production, Reproduction and the Female," pp. 149-163.
26. Ruether, *New Woman, New Earth*, p. 8.
27. Susan Griffin provides a brilliant, provocative, and poignant example of capitalism's need for this dual control when she juxtaposes the management of female office staff with the management of a timber industry. The

principles of male control and exploitation of the "object" (woman in one case, nature in the other), operate in both management systems. See her *Woman and Nature*, "Timber: What Was There for Them," pp. 56-64.

28. In an advertisement sponsored by a number of members of the Church of Ireland—prior to the historic 1990 Synod vote for the admittance of women to the priesthood—we find a concrete example of how woman's association with the body and sexuality continues to bar her from officially representing Christ. The ad, titled "Ten Reasons Why Women Should Not Be Ordained to the Priesthood," lists as the sixth reason: "There are serious practical difficulties: Who looks after the Parish whilst the Rector is having a baby?" Of course, they do not raise the question regarding who looks after the Parish if the male priest is absent, for whatever reason. See *The Church of Ireland Gazette* (4 May 1990): 13.
29. In my introduction to this chapter, I already referred to the existence of another much less influential legacy of the Christian tradition that lifted up the beauty of the earth and God's covenant with all of creation. These strains of the tradition did not, however, infiltrate the overriding cultural values of the Western world. They are only having a significant impact in our present century.
30. See Rosemary Ruether, *Sexism and God-Talk*, pp. 76ff.
31. See Sallie McFague, *Models of God*, pp. 65ff.
32. *Ibid.*, p. ix.
33. *Sexism and God-Talk*, p. 79.
34. See Anne Primavesi, *From Apocalypse to Genesis: Ecology, Feminism and Christianity* (Minneapolis: Fortress Press, 1991) for another Christian feminist analysis of these questions.
35. See her "Eden's Garden Revisted: A Christian Ecological Perspective," in Patricia Altenbernd Johnson and Janet Kalven, eds., *With Both Eyes Open: Seeing Beyond Gender* (New York: Pilgrim Press, 1988), pp. 24-57.
36. See her *Green Paradise Lost*, p. 20. Though Genesis 1 does not offer this picture of female birth, Genesis 2-3 contains this imagery and usurped the more equal image of male-female relations in Genesis 1.
37. As Ruether points out, Genesis 2-3 does not present this same picture of humanity's superiority and independence from the nature world (*Sexism and God-Talk*, p. 76). However, once again, in relation to an important component, one interpretation rather than the other became the one lifted up and remembered: The elements lifted up were those that supported the patriarchal culture that had already been formed.
38. Humanity's superiority appears to be bolstered as well by the verse, "Let us make man in our image, after our likeness; and let them have dominion over the fish of the sea . . . " (Genesis 1:26). Does the story imply that the natural world—other than humanity—cannot image the sacred one? Unlike several ancient religions of prehistoric times, and unlike religions of several indigenous tribal people, the transcendent monotheistic God of the Hebrew and Christian people was not imaged by birds, serpents, owls, butterflies, and other creatures of the natural world.
39. The following interpretive elements come from Augustine. Elaine Pagels provides a fascinating discussion of how other Christian theologians disagreed with much of Augustine's interpretation of the myth. For example, both Pelagius and Julian of Eclanum challenged Augustine's notion of the "unnatural" character of death and humanity's essential depravity due to "original sin." See Elaine Pagels, *Adam, Eve and the Serpent* (London: Weidenfeld and Nicolson, 1988), pp. 127-154.

40. See her essay, "Finitude, Death, and Reverence for Life," in *Laughter of Aphrodite,* pp. 217ff.
41. See Gray, "Eden's Garden Revisited," p. 40.
42. See Daly, *Pure Lust,* pp. 337ff.
43. *Sexism and God-Talk,* pp. 238-39.
44. Catherine Keller provides a persuasive argument that apocalyptic literature subliminally inspires and justifies a nuclear holocaust. She argues that "the end-time myth serves as sine qua non of the present end-time threat. . . ." Imaging an end lays the foundations for bringing it about. This raises the very fundamental question: does our earth necessarily have to end? And how many of us live with the conviction that this will eventually happen? See Keller, "Women Against Wasting the World: Notes on Eschatology and Ecology," in Irene Diamond and Gloria Feman Orenstein, eds., *Reweaving the World: The Emergence of Ecofeminism* (San Francisco: Sierra Club Books, 1990), pp. 249-263.
45. During my lecture tour in Australia, one of my hosts, Sr. Pauline Smoothy, a great lover of the exquisite natural beauty of Australia, remarked: "I can't believe that there won't be earth in heaven!"
46. This exploration of the meaning of "home" has to do with what it ought to be. Indeed, for many people, "home" carries with it experiences of abuse, suffering, lack of caring, and being at risk. Question: Is this where the metaphor breaks down, or only works for a certain group of people? And yet, isn't everyone searching for some kind of stable environment and deep sense of kinship?
47. Susan Thisthlethwaite argues that black women's experience contributes something substantially different from white women's experience to this reimaging process. Because black women have been relegated to the sphere of "the natural" more than white women, their struggle for survival brings them face to face with the conflictual and chaotic characteristics of the natural world. White women tend to emphasize the harmonious and healing aspects of nature. See *Sex, Race and God: Christian Feminism in Black and White,* (New York: Crossroad, 1989), pp. 60-76.
48. Ursula King asserts: "To restore ecological justice and balance, our attitude needs to be biocentric rather than anthropocentric, life rather than human-centred." *Women and Spirituality: Voices of Protest and Promise* (London: Macmillan Education, 1989), p. 219.
49. *Models of God,* p.11.
50. See "Nature as an Act of Imagination," *Woman of Power* (Spring 1988): 21ff.
51. *Healing the Wounds: The Promise of Eco-Feminism,* p. 247.
52. The "liberal" feminist position appears, however, to accept the nature/culture dualism. It argues that women ought to sever their connection with nature by gaining more positions of social power within the fields of law, politics, science, and economics. In this way, they can participate in reforming social, scientific, and political practice that creates and sustains environmental crises. There is no critique, however, of an image of culture that is separate from nature. This liberal position is virtually absent from the feminist spirituality movement.
53. See Ynestra King's essay in *Reweaving the World: The Emergence of Ecofeminism,* esp. pp. 111ff.
54. "On Healing the Nature/History Split in Feminist Thought," in *Women's Consciousness, Women's Conscience,* p. 96.
55. "Ecofeminism and Feminist Theory," in *Reweaving the World,* p. 102.

56. Ynestra King, "Ecofeminism: On the Necessity of History and Mystery," *Woman of Power*, (Spring 1988): 42- 52.
57. As quoted in U. King, *Women and Spirituality*, p. 218.
58. Christ, *Laughter of Aphrodite*, p. 226.
59. Published in *Listen: Journal of the Institute of Sisters of Mercy of Australia* (Vol. 8, No. 2, 1989): 12.
60. Susan Griffin, "Split Culture," in *Healing the Wounds: The Promise of Ecofeminism*, p. 7.
61. *Journeys: Native American Flute Music*, distributed by Canyon Records, Phoenix, Arizona.
62. "Ecofeminism: Our Roots and Flowering," *Woman of Power* (Spring 1988): 7ff.
63. Mary Daly speaks a lot about re-membering these kinds of natural connections as part of the background work that radical feminists must do. Her biophilic philosophy originates in memories and present experiences of deep harmony with the creatures of the earth. She calls this "metamemory" as a way of overcoming amnesia. See especially *Pure Lust*, pp. 354ff.
64. C. Spretnak, "Ecofeminism: Our Roots and Flowering," p. 7.
65. Starhawk, "Feminist, Earth-based Spirtuality and Ecofeminism, " in *Healing the Wounds*, p. 178.
66. C. Spretnak, "Ecofeminism: Our Roots and Flowering," p. 9.
67. Susan Griffin, "Split Culture," *The Promise of Ecofeminism*, p. 11.
68. Starhawk, *op. cit.*, p. 180.
69. "Ecofeminism: On the Necessity of History and Mystery," p. 44.
70. "Awakening to the Ecological Self," in *Healing the Wounds: The Promise of Ecofeminism*, p. 202. I do think, however, that Macy borders on being reductionistic. She tends toward the argument that the other is the self, or that the world is our body. I talk about the "paradox" as a way of avoiding the reductionism.
71. *Green Paradise Lost*, see especially chapters 7 and 8.
72. *Sexism and God-Talk*, p. 86.
73. Charles Birch and John B. Cobb, *The Liberation of Life* (Cambridge: Cambridge University Press, 1981), p. 127.
74. *Woman and Nature*, pp. 220-21.
75. See especially her essays in *Making the Connections*.
76. Marilyn Waring (San Francisco: Harper & Row, 1988).
77. Paul Ekins, ed. (London: Routledge & Kegan Paul, 1986).
78. *Healing the Wounds*, p. 113.
79. "Feminist Earth-based Spirituality and Ecofeminism," in *Healing the Wounds*, pp. 179, 180.
80. *Models of God*, p. 60.
81. See Mary Daly, *Pure Lust*, p. 9.
82. See *Sexism and God-Talk*, pp. 235-258.
83. "Women Against Wasting the World: Notes on Eschatology and Ecology," in *Reweaving the World: The Emergence of Ecofeminism* eds. Irene Diamond and Gloria Feman Orenstein (San Francisco: Sierra Club Books, 1990), pp. 249-263.

Chapter 6

1. Martha Ann Kirk, in *Liberating Liturgies*, compiled by members of The Women's Ordination Conference (Fairfax, Vir.: WOC, 1989), p. 10.
2. See the discussion in *Women's Spirit Bonding*, Janet Kalven and Mary Buckley, eds., pp. 345-46, that identifies their reasons for choosing "ritual" as the

most inclusive term, pp. 345-46.

3. The definition offered by Linda Clark, Marian Ronan, and Eleanor Walker in *Image-Breaking/Image-Building: A Handbook for Creative Worship with Women of Christian Tradition* (New York: Pilgrim Press, 1981), pp. 33-34.
4. *Truth or Dare*, p. 99.
5. See, for example, Starhawk's *The Spiral Dance, Dreaming the Dark*, and *Truth or Dare*; Hallie Iglehart, *Womanspirit: A Guide to Women's Wisdom*; and Diane Mariechild, *Motherwit, Crystal Visions*, and *The Inner Dance.*
6. A phrase used often by the authors of *Image Breaking/Image Building.*
7. *Women and the Gospel Traditions: Feminist Celebrations* (Silver Spring, MD: WATERworks Press [The Women's Alliance for Theology, Ethics and Ritual], 1989), p. ii.
8. The full title of this resource is *More than Words: Prayer and Ritual for Inclusive Communities*, by Janet Schaffran and Pat Kozak (Oak Park, IL: Meyer Stone Books, 1988).
9. *Women's Spirit Bonding*, p. 345.
10. Diann Neu, *Women and the Gospel Traditions*, p. ii.
11. "Contemporary Feminist Rituals," in *The Politics of Women's Spirituality*, Charlene Spretnak, ed., p. 226.
12. "Ritual as Bonding: Action as Ritual," in *Weaving the Visions*, Judith Plaskow and Carol Christ, eds., pp. 326-27. Barbara Walker echoes these sentiments by declaring that "laughter is not hostile to spirituality, play can have profound resonances in human psychology." See her *Women's Rituals: A Sourcebook* (New York: Harper & Row, 1990), p. 7.
13. "Notes on Composing New Blessings: Toward a Feminist-Jewish Reconstruction of Prayer," in *Weaving the Visions*, p. 136.
14. From *The Church Made Whole: National Conference on Women in the Uniting Church in Australia 1990*, Elizabeth Wood Ellem, ed. (Melbourne: David Lovell Publishing, 1990), p. 73.
15. *Womanspirit: A Resource for Those Interested in Feminist Spirituality* (Dublin) 3/2 (Winter 1988): 11.
16. From *All Desires Known: Prayers Uniting Faith and Feminism* (Wilton, CT: Morehouse-Barlow, 1988), p. 50 (first published in Great Britain by Movement for the Ordination of Women).
17. *Truth or Dare*, p. 101.
18. *Ibid.*, pp. 101-03.
19. From *Women Church Celebrations: Feminist Liturgies for the Lenten Season* (Silver Spring, MD: WATERWorks Press, 1989), p. 28.
20. From *A Seder of the Sisters of Sarah: A Holy Thursday and Passover Feminist Liturgy*, created by Ronnie Levin and Diann Neu (Silver Spring, MD: WATERworks, 1986), pp. 6-7.
21. *Women-Church: The Theology and Practice of Feminist Liturgical Communities* (San Francisco: Harper & Row, 1985), p. 3.
22. See Martha A. Acklesberg's description of the various conflicts and rewards of creating ritual within a Jewish feminist community, in her article "Spirituality, Community and Politics: B'not Esh and the Feminist Reconstruction of Judaism," *Journal of Feminist Studies in Religion* 2/2 (Fall 1986): 109-120.
23. *WomanPrayer, WomanSong: Resources for Ritual* (Oak Park, IL: Meyer Stone Books, 1987), p. 7.
24. Falk, "Notes on Composing New Blessings," p. 132.
25. *Women-Church*, chapter 8.
26. *Truth or Dare*, pp. 127, 135, 297.
27. *Dreaming the Dark*, p. 155.

28. *Standing Again at Sinai: Judaism from a Feminist Perspective* (San Francisco: Harper & Row, 1990), pp. 237-38.
29. "Notes on Composing New Blessings," p. 135.
30. Mary Jo Weaver, *New Catholic Women*, p. 257, n. 32. See also Marjorie Procter-Smith, *In Her Own Rite: Constructing Feminist Liturgical Tradition* (Nashville: Abingdon Press, 1990).

Epilogue

1. The following discussion was inspired by conversations with Anne Dickson, author of *A Woman in Her Own Right* (London: Quartet Books, 1983) and *The Mirror Within* (London: Quartet Books, 1986).
2. Ann Louise Gilligan suggested this metaphor to me.
3. My sister, Suzanne Zappone Hoover, has taught me this.

Index

Aquinas, 127
Aristotle, 77, 118

Babylonian creation myth, 37-38
Beyond God the Father (Daly), 19, 22, 47-48
body, 58-62, 71, 119; in ritual, 151-52
Bynum, Caroline, 98

Cardman, Francine, 96
Carr, Anne, 94-95, 97
Christ, Carol, 21, 23, 27-28, 32, 37, 46-47, 90, 94, 98-102, 126, 133-34
Christian feminism, 2, 167 n. 2, 33, 39-40, 162
The Church and the Second Sex (Daly), 22
classism, 2, 63
committed relationships, 80-81
communities, feminist, 54, 61, 84-85
compassion, 136-41
concept, 110-12
Condren, Mary, 178 n. 51, 186 n. 88
Conn, Joann, 27, 54
Culpepper, Emily, 104
creation-centered spirituality, 115
culture, 131-34

Daly, Mary, 3, 19-20, 22, 29, 32-33, 37-38, 40, 46-49, 54, 77, 84, 90, 98, 127, 133
Diving Deep and Surfacing (Christ), 46
Downing, Christine, 99
dualism (as a worldview), 12, 24-25, 58-59, 68-70, 118-19

earth-human relationship, 113-45
ecofeminism, 117-18, 132-33
economics, 121-23, 141-42
education, 6, 8
Eisler, Riane, 75, 99-100
elemental feminism, 2, 167 n. 5, 17, 19, 22, 33, 37-38
eschatology, 4, 126

Falk, Marcia, 97, 152-53, 160, 162
Farley, Margaret, 80-81, 83
Father-God, 17, 24, 26, 89, 108
feminism, definition of, 8-10
feminist spirituality, definition of, 12-13, 17
feminist theology, 6, 17, 19, 21, 24, 32, 35, 40
Fischer, Kathleen, 115-16
friendship, across social boundaries, 8, 43-44, 51-52, 57-58, 64, 79-80; female, 49, 76-78

Geertz, Clifford, 27
Genesis myth, 123, 125-26
Gimbutas, Marija, 99-101
God, as a sacred symbol, 2, 19, 24, 30, 32, 83, 88-91, 93-99, 118-119, 123-24, 143-44
Goddess, as a sacred symbol, 19, 32-33, 99-102, 111, 142-43; stories of, 36-37, 39, 41, 54-55
Goddess religions, 2, 167 n. 4, 32, 36, 40
Goldenberg, Naomi, 21, 36, 99
Gray, Elizabeth Dodson, 125-26, 130, 138, 144
Green Paradise Lost (E.D. Gray), 138
Griffin, Susan, 118, 121, 136, 140-41
Griscom, Joan, 131
Gross, Rita, 102, 108-109
Gudorf, Christine, 52
Gutierrez, Gustavo, 5
Gyn/Ecology (Daly), 22, 48

Harrison, Beverly, 61, 81-82, 134, 141
heaven, 115, 126-28, 130, 145
heterosexism, 2, 168 n. 8, 64, 179 n. 62
Heyward, Carter, 40, 52-54, 61-62, 74, 83-90
Hildegarde of Bingen, 116

homemaking, 128-45
Hunt, Mary, 76-77

Iglehart, Hallie, 42, 50, 55, 59, 149
image, 91-92, 102-107
immanence, 25, 37, 143
interdependence (as a worldview), 8, 11-13, 24-27, 40-42, 69-70

Janowitz, Naomi and Maggie Wenig, 109
Jesus, 28, 74-75, 83-84, 96, 143-44
Jewish feminism, 2, 18, 97-98, 108-109, 161, 167 n. 2
The Journey Is Home (Morton), 87
Jung, Carl, 27

Kalven, Janet, 84
Keller, Catherine, 63, 94, 103-105, 145
Kelly, Joan, 9
King, Ynestra, 132-33, 137

Lerner, Gerda, 89, 99
lesbian, 77-78
The Liberation of Life (Birch and Cobb), 139-40
liberation theologies, 4, 97
love of neighbor, 67-70

McFague, Sallie, 90, 110-11, 124, 129, 143-44
McLaughlin, Eleanor, 96
Macy, Joanna, 138
Mariechild, Diane, 41, 46, 50, 55-57, 150
mechanistic worldview, 120-21
meditation, 42, 55-57, 61, 64
Mellart, James, 99
men, in solidarity with women, 9, 40, 169 n. 4; friendship with women, 78-79
Mercadante, Linda, 107
Merchant, Carolyn, 120-22, 132
metaphor, 102, 108-10
Moltmann-Wendell, Elisabeth, 73, 74
Morley, Janet, 154
Morton, Nelle, 37, 87, 92, 94, 103-106
Motherwit (Mariechild), 42
mutual relationships, 16-17, 40, 43-44
mutuality, definition of, 68-82; and intimacy, 75-82

nature, 18, 24-26, 30-31, 59, 69, 101-102; and woman, 117-127; /culture dualism, 131-34
Neu, Diann, 150, 157-59
new physics, 138-39

ontology, 118-19, 137-38
original sin, 126
Osiek, Carolyn, 46, 49-50

patriarchy, definition of, 169 n. 21
perfection, 11, 163-65
Personal Commitments (Farley), 80
Piaget, Jean, 103, 105
Plant, Judith, 117, 130
Plaskow, Judith, 109, 161
poverty, 2, 5-6, 57-58, 63
praxis, definition of 168
Pure Lust (Daly), 22, 48

racism, 63
Raymond, Janice, 76-77
relationality, 12, 16-17
Ricoeur, Paul, 94-5, 98
ritual, feminist 42, 56-57, 59-61; definition of, 149-59; purpose of, 159-62
Ruether, Rosemary Radford, 21, 24, 32, 35, 46, 59, 84, 90, 96, 110, 117, 122, 124, 127, 134, 138-39, 143, 159-60
Russell, Letty, 35, 97

sacraments, 115, 162
sacred stories, 17, 19-20, 34-40
sacred symbols, 17, 19-20, 27-34, 50, 54-55, 92-102
salvation, 67-70, 115, 124
Saiving, Valerie, 54
Schneiders, Sandra, 10-12
Schüssler Fiorenza, Elisabeth, 21, 35, 37, 46, 83, 96
self, development of, 6-7, 12, 45-65; -integrity, 51-62; sacrifice, 48, 53-54
sexism, 2, 117
sexuality, 24-25, 58-59, 61-62, 76-79, 81-82
Sjöö, Monica and Barbara Mor, 99-100
Smith, Paula M. 134-36

socially powerless, definition of, 5, 168 n. 4
Söelle, Dorothee, 30
Sophia: The Future of Feminist Spirituality (Cady, Ronan, Taussig), 26, 31, 64
spiritualities of women's power, 2, 18, 40-42, 167 n. 1
spirituality, definition of, 10-12, 16
Spretnak, Charlene, 99, 136, 143
Stanton, Elizabeth Cady, 17
Starhawk, 21, 25, 33, 37, 46, 50, 52-55, 59, 61, 75, 79-80, 89-90, 98, 101-02, 133, 143-45, 150, 152, 156-57
Stone, Merlin, 99
symbol, definition of, 28-29

theology, 3-6
Thistlewaite, Susan, 134
Tillich, Paul, 94
Trible, Phyllis, 35
Turner, Kay, 150

Weaver, Mary Jo, 109
When God Was a Woman (Stone), 19
Wiccan tradition, 2, 36-37, 40, 101-102, 156-57, 161, 167 n. 3
Winter, Miriam Therese, 159
Woman and Nature (Griffin), 140
Woman of Power: A Magazine of Feminism, Spirituality and Politics, 3
WomanPrayer, WomanSong (M.T. Winter), 159
Womanspirit: The Irish Journal of Feminist Spirituality, 3
women-church, 3, 32, 50, 54, 162, 168 n. 9
The Women's Bible, 17
women's experience, 18, 20-24, 88-89
women's liberation movement, 16-17
Women's Spirit Bonding (Kalven and Buckley), 79, 151